WHAT OTHERS AR

On the surface, Daisy and Herm might seem like an adventurous account of two free-spirited nomads, who are choosing to live an unconventional life.

Though that may be true, distilling it down and delving deeper, we discover that in essence, this is an account of Terra's (Daisy's) inner journey of spiritual growth, self-discovery and love. Their travels and free-spirited way of living are the fertile curricula in which soul lessons and teachings are revealed.

With her sometimes humorous and uncensored honesty, Terra takes us on a magical and mystical journey. Through the ever-present messages from guardian angels and the "Universe", to nature spirits, foreign lands, vision quests and medicine walks through the desert to name only a few. We are with her through every twist and turn, seeing how she courageously finds her way through the jungles of her shadow self, fear, anger, resistance, change, divorce, finding her way to self-love, compassion, wholeness. Ultimately, claiming her power and birth right, as an "elder woman".

We learn even in our darkest hours we can choose to tap into the highest expressions of ourselves. When we put our trust in that ever-present invisible force, we discover miracle after miracle unfolding. Our own personal light – guiding our every step on this human journey we call life.

— Cara Hope Clark
Award-Winning Author: *Widow's Moon*
A Memoir of Healing, Hope & Self-discovery
Through Grief and Loss

✳   ✳   ✳

Daisy & Herm is a vivid story of love and love lost. Spanning years of adventure across continents, Terra brings to life a relationship and all its complexity in scenes that unfold with intimate proximity. She brings honesty and compelling detail to this unflinching memoir.

— Jarrard Cole

✳   ✳   ✳

Terra Lyn Joy takes the reader on an international journey of mind, spirit and body in a midlife coming-of-age story. She is funny and self-conscious, always willing to laugh at her foibles. Terra is Daisy, and her partner in this narrative is Herm, sometimes known as Robert. While the tale is one of finding love, living love and ultimately marriage, divorce and a new sort of partnership, it is Daisy's trajectory we follow — with pleasure.

In New Zealand, Papua New Guinea, India, Canada, Indonesia and various pockets of the rural United States, the reader participates in Daisy's ongoing search for enlightenment. The "Universe", in quotes, directs the plot. Humor peppers this self-portrait as she charts growth, regression, progress and backslides. "The 'Universe' was on fire that summer!" she writes halfway through the book, pointing toward the couple's encounters with significant others who will shape their path. Later, "I asked the 'Universe' for help with this issue, so with its usual sense of humor it gave me what I asked for!"

— Annie Dawid
author of *PUT OFF MY SACKCLOTH*:
ESSAYS, and other works.

✳   ✳   ✳

Daisy and Herm is the multifaceted, multicultural, multi-continent, multi-lifestyle journey of Terra Lyn Joy, the "Daisy" of the title. It is indeed "an unconventional life". Terra weaves the chronicle of her travels with her husband "Herm" across several Pacific islands, Asia, and the US, a kind of global *Nomadland*. She offers sensitive, self-reflective, and at times fiercely uncompromising portrayals of joys and struggles in an intimate partnership, of her exacting efforts to maintain her footing on a spiritual path, and of the general difficulty of inhabiting a world with Other People.

I am so impressed with her honesty and candor in describing her reactions and inner conflict across such varied territory. Terra is a world adventurer, a spiritual seeker, an intuitive healer who continually challenges her own limits—and the limits of love. The heart that shines through these pages is uniquely the heart of an innocent and a warrior.

— Linda Brigham

Daisy
&
Herm

An Unconventional Life

TERRA LYN JOY

Daisy & Herm
An Unconventional Life

February 2022

Terra Lyn Joy
Paperback: 979-8-9850800-0-1
Kindle: 979-8-9850800-1-8

Editor: CSusanNunn.com
Cover Photograph: Bill Clark - http://www.InkAndAperture.com
Cover Design: Pro_ebookcovers (at Fiverr)
Book Interior and E-book Design by Amit Dey | amitdey2528@gmail.com

TABLE OF CONTENTS

To My Herm –

Without you, my life would have been boring.

APRIL 2016

Herm, my soulmate, best friend and adventure buddy of thirty years turned to me and said, "this just feels unreal, are we really doing this?" We were sitting in the front seat of our Suburban filling out divorce papers and both feeling we were in some kind of an alternate reality. We were about to enter our small-town Colorado County building to begin the process of dissolving a relationship that had seen us through fourteen years of nomadic travel and another fourteen years of off-grid living in the wilds of Colorado. The crazy thing was we still loved each other but it seemed there was something more powerful pushing us apart. As Herm put it, "it is difficult to explain but it feels like there is a much larger force moving me out into the world. I feel like I have to figure me out without you."

I too felt a larger force at work but had been too afraid to admit it. What I didn't realize that day was I was about to drown in a darkness so dense, I didn't know if I would ever see light again.

Herm packed his truck with a few of his belongings the night before. Once we finished our business in town, he planned to drive the two hours to Pagosa Springs to stay with friends to think things through. The only reason we were going through with a divorce at this time, rather than a separation, was it would allow me to get more social security money. That and two other things were keeping me from feeling overly worried about what we were about to do. First, the planet Mercury was in retrograde which meant any contracts signed during this time were subject to reversal. Second, Herm had said, "it's only a piece of paper, it doesn't change how we feel about each other."

I agreed and was convinced it would only be a matter of time before he "saw the light" and returned home. After all, he was "my Herm" and I was "his Daiz", nothing could change that.

Earlier, I had pulled next to the curb in front of the beautiful stone County Building which was set back from the quiet, tree-lined street. Herm had parked behind me and then slid into the passenger seat so we could go over the forms we had printed. He was somber and seemed anxious as we traded papers to make sure there were no mistakes. I just wanted to get this over with and go home but I'm sure it was harder for him as he was actually going out into the world on his own, leaving the sanctuary we had created together. Papers in order, we looked at each other one last time and I said, "are you ready?"

"I guess so," he sighed and opened the door.

As we walked up the cement path together, I pictured the women from the Garden Club tending the gardens, bordering the walk. "The spring bulbs will soon be poking their heads up through the thawing ground," I mused.

It then hit me this was the season of new beginnings, not endings! Oh my God, had I just pulled one of my signature impulsive moves instead of being patient and letting Herm go off and do his thing? Was I trying to control the situation, instead of letting things play out naturally? It was certainly possible but somehow, it felt this needed to be done. It did feel like larger forces were at work and we were just along for the ride.

Herm pulled open the big glass door and instead of going straight down the corridor into the town clerk's office, we took a right to a hidden room behind the court. We approached a window behind which sat two women and slipped our papers into the metal tray which lay beneath the windows. I was feeling a bit self-conscious these people were going to see what our business was, I'm sure they didn't care but wondered how often they had both parties come together to file for divorce. We stood there awkwardly as one of the women took our papers and the filing fee before informing us of the next steps. She gave us financial forms to take with us to fill out and said once they were completed and filed, it would take 2-3 months to receive our final papers.

We didn't speak as we walked out into the bright sunshine and looked around at the quaint town we had discovered so many years before. I was still feeling very removed from it all, like being in some sort of dream state. We reached the bottom of the steps and stood in front of my car not quite knowing what to do. Even though we had only filed some papers, it seemed something had changed. Maybe it wasn't just a piece of paper after all?

Herm said sadly, "well, we did it, I guess that's that!"

I sure hoped it wasn't "that's that"! I was clinging to the story of being apart was only a temporary necessity for both of us.

Herm asked, "can I still hug you?"

"Of course," I replied with a smile, as I gave him a quick, somewhat awkward embrace.

He pulled back, holding onto my arms and gazed deeply into my eyes looking very sad. As he let go, he said quietly, "I'll call you."

I was trying not to get emotional so quickly responded, "OK, great! I'll look forward to it." As he walked slowly back to his truck, I called "safe travels" and swiftly got into my vehicle. I made a U-turn on the wide, empty street and waved as I passed him pulling onto the road going in the opposite direction.

The twelve miles of empty highway through the slowly greening valley passed in a blur. I put on a podcast so I wouldn't have to think too much and reasoned being alone for a while could be a good thing. It wasn't as if I hadn't been by myself before, Herm was often away at rock shows, sometimes for weeks at a time. I always enjoyed those occasions. This would be fine, I told myself.

···•◆•···

WORLD TRAVELERS
1989-1991

···•◆•···

CHAPTER 1

HERM

I saw him look at me out of the corner of his eye as I walked up the hill to join the group that cold December evening in Concord, New Hampshire. He was bent over shoveling snow, bundled in a dark jacket, jeans and black wool hat. It was the night before New Year's Eve, 1988, and my life was about to change.

The divorce from my first husband of 19 years was finalized just over a year before, I had been through a "transitional relationship" and for the first time in many years, I had no man in my life, and I was NOT looking. It felt like I had spent most of my life attached to the male species, preferring their company to that of females. I grew up a tomboy, spending most of my time in the woods with my dog or playing sports with the boys in my 1950s suburban neighborhood. As a teenager, I fell quickly into the one-boyfriend forever mode, having two long-term relationships, spanning my years in high school. The first couple of years of college I experienced a "dry spell" with no boyfriends, which threw me into a depression until I was "rescued" by Jim, my first husband. After getting over the emotional hump of the divorce, I was feeling strong, had a great job, my farm, my animals and was looking forward to casual dating and just having fun!

Lifestyle Network was all about fun. I had found this group on the internet and joined after the divorce. There was a monthly calendar of events such as hikes, game nights, camping trips, cookouts, ski trips, lectures, just about anything one wanted to do. All members had input in setting up the calendar and hosting events and I enjoyed all the positive, upbeat people I had met. I am not usually a group person but the welcoming energy of the young couple who founded Lifestyle permeated each event and made me feel very comfortable.

That December evening, I was feeling tired after work so I called Arlene to tell her I wouldn't make it to Concord that night. I was supposed to help with the snow sculpture Lifestyle was doing for the New Year's Eve "First Night". "Hey Arlene, I'm going to have to beg off tonight, it has been a long day."

Arlene laughed and said, "I think you still need to come; we're here having a great time and when we finish, we're going out for pizza and then a movie! Come on, I know you'll have a blast!"

I should have known she wouldn't take no for an answer. As one half of the bubbly founding couple of Lifestyle, she had a way of making everything sound way too much fun to miss. "Well, I guess I can muster the energy, you never let me get away with not doing something."

We both laughed as she knew me too well.

"I have to feed my dog and then I'll be on my way!"

"Great!" she said, "we'll look forward to seeing you!"

I shook off my tiredness, got my critters settled and drove the 45 minutes to Concord.

The "black hat" man appeared to be in charge of constructing the sculpture but except for telling me where to put the snow, we didn't speak, and I didn't get his name but something about him intrigued me.

Soon we were all headed to the pizza parlor where Arlene pulled me over to where "black hat" was and said, "Terra, I want you to meet Robert, he has also recently been divorced."

We said our hellos and I said, "do you mind if I sit with you, I've been wanting to get a man's view on divorce for quite some time now?"

He said, "sure," and we went to get in line to retrieve our orders.

As I stood behind him at the pick-up window, I noticed we were about the same height and the strangest thing popped into my mind. That's funny, I mused, I was remembering him being so much taller. I had no idea where the thought came from, it just dropped in out of the blue!

We picked up our pizzas and walked over to the long table where the group was seated. We settled ourselves into adjoining chairs and traded divorce-related horror stories as we devoured our food. We discovered each of our ex-spouses had been having affairs and they were the ones to precipitate the breakups but that wasn't the only synchronicity! Our divorces happened around the same time; his ex-wife is a nurse, as I was; he didn't have any children of his own but had helped raise her son and I also had one son; he had lived with horses, dogs and other animals just like me! The shocker came when he told me he used to live on a certain shortcut road I always took when I went to Concord!

"Wait, did you used to have big bushy hair, like an Afro?" I gasped.

He laughed, "sure did, back in my younger days, why?"

"I remember SEEING you one day standing in front of a barn holding a horse while a woman was brushing it!"

"It certainly could be, that's so weird you would remember that!" he said in amazement.

"It sure is," I smiled, "but I can see it as clear as day."

As we chatted, I felt the noise and people around us disappear. I was mesmerized by Robert's soulful, blue/gray eyes, his sweet easy laugh, his animated way of speaking and his focused attention on me when I was talking. The spell was only broken when the group started getting up and asked us if we were coming to the movies?

"Sure," I said, feeling excited to get more time with this intriguing man who had me so enthralled.

"I'm afraid I won't be able to go," Robert said sadly. "I have to get home to take care of my dog, she has been out in her pen all day and I need to get her in."

I smiled ruefully, "I'm sorry you can't come, but I understand about making sure your dog is OK. I hope I'll see you again sometime, I really enjoyed talking with you."

"Yes, me too," he replied with a smile. "Have fun at the movies," he called as he walked away.

On my drive home I couldn't get my mind off of Robert and how I had remembered seeing him standing in his driveway so many years ago. What had made me take note of some random guy that day? It wasn't as if he was doing something to catch my attention, he wasn't even anywhere near the road, he was just standing there with the horse! The picture seemed to be burned into my brain, just like the one of him noticing me this night as I walked towards him. Something was going on; I didn't believe in coincidences. I believe the "Universe" is always communicating with us in one form or another, but we are usually too busy and distracted to notice. I was feeling such a strong connection with this guy, but I REALLY didn't want to get into a relationship, I was only now finally free!

I was doing a good job keeping Robert out of my mind until the following week when I picked up the phone to find him on the other end.

"Hey, I was just calling to see if you were going to the Kinesiology talk on Saturday?"

"Yeah, I am definitely going, are you?" I asked.

"I had planned on it," he replied.

"Oh cool!" We talked for a while about our mutual interest in alternative healing modalities before saying our goodbyes and "looking forward to seeing you". Well, "getting him out of my mind" didn't last too long! This guy was scoring points left and right, not only had he put his dog first the other night, but now I find he is also into natural healing and energy work! My ex-husband had never been interested in anything to do with spiritual matters, alternative healing, or energy work, he thought it was all just a bunch of baloney. The problem was all that "baloney" was important to me! In my 20s, I had studied Kabbalah, Astrology, Tarot and Numerology with a teacher who had taken me under her wing. Faith

Javane was a speaker and author of a number of books on Numerology and I had accompanied her to many of the metaphysical conferences she spoke at. The whole spiritual/metaphysical world had been an interest of mine since my late teens and I had done extensive reading on many different topics related to extrasensory phenomena. To talk with a man who had an interest in those things was something I had never experienced, and I was thrilled!

I was looking forward to the weekend talk and connecting with Robert again, but things didn't turn out quite as I had envisioned. When I walked into our hostess's kitchen, I found Robert chatting with some of the other attendees and went over to join them. Soon it was just the two of us deep in conversation, this time about astrology. I discovered his sun sign was Aries, the same as my son and he asked me what my sign was.

"I'm a Taurus," I said brightly.

His smile instantly disappeared and there was an immediate chill in the air. "My sister-in-law is a Taurus and she drives me crazy, she is sarcastic and when I was at their house last week, I had to restrain myself from slapping her! She has a way of pushing my buttons" he said sourly.

I was taken aback by the change in his demeanor and felt lumped in with someone he didn't like. I didn't know what to say and was relieved the group was getting seated for the presentation in the living room.

We drifted apart to sit on opposite sides of the room and didn't speak for the rest of the evening but as fate would have it, we left about the same time. I had just gotten into my car when I noticed him entering the vehicle in front of me. It was an older model, light-colored Cadillac and it was the clincher for me. For some weird reason, I have always had an aversion to that make of car. So, between the car and the chill he gave me because I was a Taurus, I was over him! Phew! I dodged the bullet and could get back to being my independent self!

Unfortunately, it seemed the spell had been cast and I couldn't shake the thought of him. After a few weeks, I decided to call on the pretense of asking if he would be going to another Lifestyle event and that was that – our fates were sealed. Our long phone conversation led to many more phone conversations and more Lifestyle events together until he asked me out on a date three months after our first encounter.

We met in Concord for dinner but hadn't realized most restaurants were closed on a Sunday night. Disappointed but undeterred, Robert remembered there was a Chinese diner at the edge of town which would definitely be open. We sat across from each other in a side booth, next to a window, in our fancy going out to dinner clothes and talked and laughed for hours! Good thing we weren't paying expensive restaurant prices because I was so totally focused on Robert, I don't remember tasting a thing.

Time flew by as we discovered all the things we had in common and how similar our likes and dislikes were. Alternative healing, personal health, the environment, metaphysics, nature, photography, hiking, food, the surprised and delighted exclamation of "me too"! went on all evening. He told me he was a civil engineer and worked at a superfund site in Nashua and before had worked on engineering projects for the state. It appeared one of the only things we didn't have in common was where we grew up. While he resided in a city apartment, in Chelsea, outside of Boston, I was raised in the suburbs of East Providence, Rhode Island. But even then, we found common ground in the fact my father was born in Chelsea! Now, what were the odds?

We eventually looked up to discover we were the only ones left in the restaurant and were getting meaningful looks from the proprietors.

We laughed and said, "Well, I guess we may have worn out our welcome!"

Robert walked me to my car where I asked, "do you want to come to my house for a visit next weekend?"

"Sure, that sounds great," he replied with a smile. He leaned in, gave me a brief kiss, and said, "I look forward to seeing you next week."

"Me too," I smiled.

Oh dear, I was smitten with this guy. I had never been with anyone who I had so much in common with and when he arrived at my house the following weekend, bearing homemade oatmeal cookies I was blown away....he even cooks!! After showing him around my farm and introducing him to all my animals, we spent the rest of the day talking nonstop about astrology, numerology and other esoteric subjects.

Too soon, the visit was drawing to a close, I didn't want him to leave, and it seemed he was reluctant to go as well. We were standing in the doorway to my living room when he pulled me to him and gave me a long deep kiss which made my heart race, and my knees go weak. I was so turned on by the taste, the smell and feel of him, whoa!

I said quietly, "do you want to go upstairs?"

He looked deeply into my eyes and said reluctantly, "I would love to, but I need to get home. Why don't you come to my house in two weeks for my birthday and stay overnight?"

I smiled and said, "that sounds like a great idea!"

We stood there holding each other for a long time before we parted reluctantly so I could walk him to his car. One last delicious kiss and he was gone.

Those two weeks finally passed, and I was nervously but excitedly getting ready to drive the hour and a half to Robert's apartment. I was feeling pretty wild and crazy hooking up with a guy I barely knew! It wasn't like I had a lot of experience doing that, my husband had been my first sexual partner at age 21, then there was my transitional relationship after my divorce, now Robert. I wasn't exactly a party girl, but I was ready to turn that persona on!!

Robert welcomed me into his living room with a quick hug and kiss before hustling back to the kitchen to attend to the dinner he was cooking. "Make yourself at home while I check on the chicken. Would you like some wine?" he asked.

"Absolutely!" I answered. I was impressed by the decor of Robert's apartment. He definitely had a style; it wasn't anything like I would have thought a bachelor pad would look like! It had a calm, welcoming energy, everything was clean, the furniture was comfortable and neatly arranged, and keepsakes were strategically placed on the tables and bookcase.

"I love your place," I called into the kitchen.

"Thanks," he replied. "Dinner will be right out."

"Can I help?" I asked.

"I've got it, just take a seat."

I pulled out a chair at the perfectly set table with candles and a colorful bouquet in the middle. As I was sipping my wine, Robert came in with a platter of baked chicken, a tossed salad and a warm loaf of French bread. Wow, this guy was full of surprises, I hadn't ever known a man like him!

Dinner was delicious but I think we were both thinking about what came next because as soon as we cleared the table, we were basically rolling around on the floor kissing and getting all hot and bothered.

"Would you like to go upstairs?" he whispered.

"I sure would," I breathed.

He led me up the stairs to his bedroom which had a huge king-sized bed and proceeded to impress me once again by lighting candles and putting on music! Being an incurable romantic, I was blown away, this was another first for me. I was feeling awkward and didn't know how to do the next bit, so when he was in the bathroom, I quickly disrobed and got into bed. The nervousness which had overtaken me as I slipped under the covers was quickly subsumed in the passion of our lovemaking with our bodies fitting together perfectly. It was a wild and very satisfying night.

A shower together in the morning, a quick breakfast, a last kiss and embrace and I was on my way home to take care of the animals, already missing him. I guess my new playgirl persona had a short run for I couldn't deny the feeling I had known Robert for many lifetimes, and we had a deep soul connection.

I felt this was all meant to be, part of a bigger plan and I was excited to see how it would all play out.

In the following weeks, we saw each other every weekend and I found my heart aching when I was away from him. For the first time in my life, I was feeling unconditional love, which was vastly different from the "in love" feeling I had experienced in past relationships.

Interestingly, we discovered we both experienced a discomfort in calling each other by our given names. It was almost like we had known each other with different monikers somewhere in the distant past. Because of that, we decided to come up with new names and I chose Daisy as it is my favorite flower. I found Robert would often retreat inside himself and also had a way of looking out of the corner of his eye which made him seem grouchy, so I called him Hermit the Crab or Herm for short. Thus, the team of Daisy and Herm was born.

Not two months later Herm had given up his apartment, his ex-wife had reclaimed his dog and he had moved in with me, even though it made his commute to work extra long. We made love, worked on the farm together, hiked, biked, talked and laughed. It was the happiest I had ever been. Of course, not everything was perfect, Herm had one quirk which I found very exasperating. I am the type of person who gets really excited about things and loves to share my elation. When I had an idea for something fun to do, for instance, a camping trip, Herm had a habit of immediately saying "no". It always felt like he was stepping on my joy, putting out my fire. I know it shouldn't have bothered me, but it always hurt my feelings and left me deflated. I had never learned how to verbalize my emotions in a constructive way so tended to stuff them only to have them come out as anger at a later time. The frustrating thing was after Herm said his initial "no", he would later come back with a "yes" but with his own take on it after I had already resigned myself to the no! As a Taurus, who doesn't do well with quick changes, this habit of his was aggravating! Little did I know one of his "no's", which later turned into a "yes", would change the direction of our lives.

The "Universe" has a funny way of altering your path just when you least expect it. I certainly wasn't expecting to sell the farm I fought for in my divorce, it was a place I had dreamed into existence from childhood! Growing up in the suburbs wasn't conducive to possessing all the animals I desired, and I spent many a day envisioning the farm I would someday have. There would be fields, woods, a stream, maybe even a pond, a view of the mountains and I would have all the animals I wanted.

To top it off, I would have a like-minded friend who I would meet on the woods trail which connected our two farms and we would ride our horses together. Well, I can attest to the power of imagining things into being as I had just that place, right down to the friend on the other side of the woods road who I rode horses with. There was no way I would have wanted to let it go! …… But I did!

One sunny July day, I was driving up the dusty dirt road to my farm when, out of the blue, a crystal-clear voice said, "it's time to sell the farm." Instead of saying, "no f….ing way!" I immediately agreed! What the hell was going on? How did I just agree to that? Herm had just moved in, things were going great with us, I loved my job, I felt happy, content and strong for the first time in my life, why now? It seemed the "Universe" didn't want me to get too comfortable, and I needed to expand my horizons a bit, and in my soul, I knew it was the right thing to do.

I had some time to think before Herm got home from work and what came to me was I needed to travel. It was so weird how it all just felt so right, I had never entertained the idea of either selling or traveling but here I was all excited about doing both! When Herm walked in, I said enthusiastically, "Guess what? Some internal voice just told me to sell the farm and travel and I'm going to do it!" He stood there in shock as I continued, "You are the love of my life and I really want you to come with me but even if you don't I have to go because there seems to be something bigger than me directing all of this."

"Holy Crap!" he exclaimed. "I can't leave my job!"

"I understand, this is huge and totally out of the blue, just think about it," I told him. For some reason I wasn't at all concerned, it was as if all would be taken care of, all I had to do was sit back and relax.

It was only a few days later when Herm walked in the door after work with a big grin and stated, "I don't need my job, let's go travel! In fact, let's go around the world!"

"Wow, that's awesome! What made you change your mind?" I asked, bursting with excitement.

"I was listening to the radio on the way to work today and they were talking about 'Round the World' tickets. You choose the countries you want to go to, as long as you keep going in one direction, you have a year to use the pass and they aren't all that expensive! I decided I was tired of my job anyway and if we stick to inexpensive countries, it probably won't cost a great deal of money!"

This plan sounded so much more exciting than traveling around the USA that I immediately responded, "yes, let's do it!" I knew there was a reason I hadn't worried when he originally said no, and as he usually did after those "no's", he came up with something even better and this time I wasn't annoyed AT ALL!

The house sold within a month, we had a huge moving sale, gave away what didn't sell, put some stuff in storage, gave notice at our jobs, moved into the "kennel" and started planning our trip! The "kennel" sat on a 3-acre parcel I had subdivided from the farm's 40 acres before selling. Years previously I had a dog and cat boarding and grooming business there but had since converted it into a sweet little house that sat amidst towering pines and oaks just up the road from the farm. Keeping it gave us a place to live after the house sold plus a place to come back to after our trip.

The next few months brought research, research, research. Where to go, in what order, what would be least expensive, what did we need to buy? Passports, photos, vaccinations, visas, anti-malaria pills, health certificates all had to be negotiated. Two of the most important things we had to purchase were backpacks and shoes. Packs had to be big but not too big and both those and shoes had to fit comfortably for the many miles they would be gracing our bodies in the coming year. Many long hours, at multiple camping supply stores, were spent taking packs and shoes on and off, on and off searching for the right fit for each. Once that was accomplished the puzzle of fitting everything in the bags began. When we piled the clothes and other items we intended to bring on the floor beside our packs it was obvious we would have to do some major discarding. Thus, ensued hours of packing, unpacking, re-packing and agonizing over what to leave and what was essential. I mean seriously, how does one live with so few clothes? Even though the preparations for leaving one's life behind for a year were sometimes daunting, I was having so much fun. We were both excited to get going and having this wonderful man at my side felt like a real blessing.

We were prepared and ready to go but now I had to face the part I had been dreading. When I decided to travel, my idea had been to buy a motorhome and go around this country with my 4 cats and 2-year-old Rhodesian Ridgeback coming with me. Of course, now that wasn't going to happen, and I had to give up the animals who had seen me through my divorce and the hard times after. They were my family, and it was killing me to have to place them. Thankfully, Stacy, a woman I worked with, offered to take the cats and my dog's breeder said she would find Zuri a good home, but it still hurt my heart. I was especially attached to sweet, joyful, energetic Zuri who always made me laugh and the day I brought her to Diana's house was really hard on me. While Zuri was busy playing with her siblings I snuck out of the house in tears. I cried for months afterward missing my beautiful girl, but I had been compelled to say "yes" when the "Universe" called.

Goodbye parties over, tickets in hand, backpacks loaded we headed out on our journey, excited but a little sad to be leaving everything and every-one behind. Little did we know this one-year trip would totally change us and end up morphing into a 14-year odyssey of adventure and personal growth.

Dear Diary...

Well, I did it! I have no idea what/who is running this show right now, but it doesn't feel like it is me! I have always been a homebody who would rather just stay with my animals and walk in the woods. Why in the world have I sold my security blanket, cut off my paycheck and abandoned my beloved pets? I sure have been different this past year, I hardly recognize myself, I think my introvert has gone into hiding and this more extroverted version of me has made an appearance. Very strange indeed.

Now I'm on my way to being a world traveler with no plan. It is mind-boggling but feels so right I'm not at all scared and am ready to get out there and see what the world is like. It sure helps that I will be with my long-lost soul mate, I don't think I would have done the around the world thing on my own…but who knows? I'm curious to see which of me will be the most present in the coming months. It better be the new extroverted me as there will be no hiding from people!

CHAPTER 2

HAWAII & NEW ZEALAND

"Watch out!" Herm screamed as he grabbed me by the back of the shirt and yanked me onto the sidewalk. The big red bus sped by with a deafening roar within inches of our shaking bodies blasting us with dirt and grit.

"Don't you ever do that again," yelled Herm wide-eyed as we backed away from the road trying to calm our racing hearts.

I had looked left......we were in New Zealand......where you better look right or end up road pizza! If it hadn't been for Herm, my eagerly anticipated round the world adventure would have ended the first day in Auckland! Look right, look right, look right, was the mantra looping in my head from that day forward.

Not only was crossing the street fraught with tension but attempting to maneuver through the crowds on the sidewalk was like being inside a pinball machine. We were dodging and bouncing off people all the way down the street muttering "excuse me," "sorry," "excuse me." We must have totally annoyed the people moving in the correct "lane" as it appeared we were determined to walk on the wrong side. At least that error would only get us dirty looks instead of getting us killed!

Just that morning we had flown from Hawaii to Auckland, our first foreign country! Since we were new to being backpackers, we decided to be easy on ourselves and not dive right into more difficult Asian countries. We had both traveled outside of the United States before we met but unlike Herm, a hippie wanderer in Europe in the 1970s, I had only been on package tours where everything was all planned and you never had to think. I was so out of touch I never even knew it was possible to travel without consulting an agent or making reservations. This was a whole new world for me and would take some getting used to.

Hawaii had been pretty easy but even our stop there had caused me some anxiety. It started when we were circling Honolulu and I looked down to see all the skyscrapers.

"Oh no," I wailed peering out the window, "it's just a big city!"

For some insane reason I had pictured all of Hawaii as white sand beaches and palm trees, but this looked like any metropolis on the mainland, it was quite a shock.

"I don't want to stay there, do you?" Herm gazed over my shoulder from the middle seat and agreed it didn't look like much fun.

"But what will we do, how do we get to another island?" I asked worriedly.

"I don't know, but I'm sure we will find out."

I thought to myself, see this is what happens when you don't use a travel agent!

Herm was right, as we walked down the exit ramp, we spotted a sign pointing the way to the Inter-Island Terminal. I stopped to hoist my huge pack onto my back, clicked shut all the connections, pulled the straps tight, grabbed my smaller pack in my right hand and hustled after Herm who was halfway down the corridor.

"Herm," I called, "I need help!"

He turned with a look of concern which quickly turned into a puzzled laugh as he saw me crawling on all fours.

"What happened?" he chuckled, as he walked towards me.

"My load shifted when I bent over to pick up the ticket I dropped, and I can't get up. I feel like a turtle, stuck on its back," I laughed.

Herm hauled me upright with some difficulty and declared, "no more bending over."

"That's for sure," I giggled! "This thing may take some getting used to!"

We chose Maui from the intriguing menu of islands and were quickly whisked away from the noisy city into the paradise we had imagined. Finding a place to stay, however, was the next hurdle. All the bed and breakfast places we called from the airport pay phone were full and we didn't want to spend a lot of money on a hotel. Where was my travel agent? I was worried we would have to sleep in our rental car when we spotted a large sign on the second story of a building in Wailuku, that read North Shore Inn! There were a number of young people hanging over the second-floor balcony, so we figured maybe it was a youth hostel. Even though our plan was to stay in traveler's places on our journey, I wasn't sure I was ready to jump in with both feet the first day!

Herm turned to me and asked, "what do you think?"

I looked up at the building, sighed, and said, "well, there doesn't seem to be anything else, and I am really tired, let's just hope there is room at the Inn!"

It seemed the only way to access the Inn was by going through Hazel's Cafe, so we gathered our gear and went in to find a funky, dimly lit restaurant with a few tables scattered about a large room. We asked the waitress how to get to the North Shore Inn and she pointed to a stair-case in the back. We drudged up the steps under the weight of our packs and emerged into a large area arranged with couches, tables and chairs. A symphony of foreign languages and laughter issued forth from the group of young people sitting around playing cards and sharing stories.

A young woman approached us and introduced herself as Katie, the owner.

"Do you have a room?" Herm asked.

"Indeed, I do!" she answered brightly, the rate is $42.00 with an attached bath."

"Great," we said in unison, "we'll take it!" As Katie led us through the sitting room to our place, I noticed the bemused looks of the young travelers as we shuffled tiredly past. I realized with a start we hunched over 42-year-olds were probably the age of their parents! I wondered if, in the coming months, us old folk would be accepted into the "tribe of travelers"?

After a week in Hawaii, acting like tourists, we thought it might be time to take the plunge and move on to our first out-of-country experience. The "Universe" seemed to agree as what were the odds we would end up walking with a man from New Zealand on the lava beds at Volcano National Park? Pretty steep odds I would say, I think our inner guidance was telling us it was time to go for it!

On our flight to Auckland, we sifted through the list of guest houses in our guidebook and chose the one I would call upon arrival. I wanted to make a reservation and not end up going from place to place again as we did in Hawaii. A shuttle bus delivered us to Georgia Backpackers Guest House a large, run-down, older house in a quiet neighborhood. We stood quietly on the sidewalk staring up the paved walkway to our first traveler's place outside our country.

"Hmm," I said, "doesn't look too promising, does it?"

"Not really but at this point, we may as well give it a try."

"Yup," I sighed as I hoisted my pack.

Despite its shabbiness, the place was clean and the managers friendly, but it had one huge problem. No screens on the windows! It was summer in New Zealand and what comes with heat and humidity? Mosquitoes! With no barrier to deter them, they feasted on us at will. It was a really long night and I finally resorted to sleeping on the floor, where it was a bit cooler, so I could put a sheet over me. Needless to say, we were on the streets early the next morning looking for a place that realized screens were a modern invention!

By late afternoon we had transferred ourselves to Parnell Garden Guest House, which was cleaner, friendlier, cooler and had screens! As we were sitting on our bed reading, 9-year-old Megan bounced into the room with a squeal of excitement.

"What are you doing here? I didn't think I would see you again," she asked jumping up and down.

"Oh wow, you moved too, that is SO cool!" I exclaimed. We had met blonde, blue-eyed Megan and her 40ish, dark-haired mom the night before at the previous guesthouse. Megan was bubbling away telling us all about her day and how they moved here because the mosquitoes were so bad.

"I know, right?" I said.

Stephanie, Megan's mom, entered the room and said, "Oh Megan, you shouldn't be bothering them. I'm sorry she barged in on you," she said, sounding stressed out.

"Oh, it's no problem, we don't mind at all." I smiled. "She can visit any time she wants."

"That's really nice of you, thanks," Stephanie replied. "Let's go, Meg, we need to think about where to go for dinner."

"OK, see you later," Megan called merrily as they turned to leave.

When we met them the previous day I said to Herm, "Stephanie is nice, but I feel something is "off" with them, do you get the same vibe?"

"I agree, I can't put my finger on it, but something is definitely a bit strange."

I had worked with many dysfunctional families as a therapist and was pretty good at spotting people in trouble or in pain and wondered what their story was.

I love how the "Universe" puts people in our path at just the right time and place. That evening, Stephanie, Megan, Herm and I ended up at the same restaurant standing in line to place our orders. I overheard Stephanie referring to Megan as Alicia so I turned to ask for clarification.

"Oh, did I get the name wrong, I thought your daughter's name was Megan?" I smiled. I could see my question made them both very uncomfortable, so to ease the tension I laughed and said to Megan, "Guess what, Robert and I have different names just like you do! He calls me Daisy and I call him Herm, isn't it fun to have two names?" They both smiled a bit uneasily, but the tension eased a bit.

"After we get our food, would you like to join us in the park across the street?" I asked.

"Oh, that would be nice," answered Stephanie with a warm smile.

We sat on a tree-shaded bench eating while I casually chatted on about how I had worked as a psychiatric nurse dealing with troubled families.

Stephanie glanced quickly over at Megan who was talking animatedly with Herm and said quietly to me, "I haven't told anyone this, but I feel I can trust you and I really need to talk with someone. Would you mind if I told you something?"

"Of course," I said, "I am happy to listen."

She paused to gather herself, made sure Megan wasn't listening and proceeded to unburden herself. "I kidnapped my daughter a few weeks ago and we have been hiding here in New Zealand. My ex-husband is a bi-sexual pedophile and was abusing my daughter. At our custody hearing his lawyer convinced the judge I was crazy, and he got unsupervised visitation. He's a high-powered, well-respected psychiatrist and he just laughed when I told him I would turn him in. He said no one would believe me. I didn't know what to do but there was no way I was going to let him have her for unsupervised visits, so I left everything behind and ran. I am just hoping the AIDS he has will kill him off so maybe we can go home someday," she added sadly.

"Please don't tell anyone about us or use our real names, I'm afraid he may have hired private investigators to find us."

"I'm so sorry Stephanie, that's horrible! I said. "You did what you had to do to protect your daughter, you are a good mom."

"I hope so," she said with her head down, holding back tears. "I didn't know what else to do, he is very charming and has a way of convincing people that he is perfect, and I'm nuts. I just hope we are far enough away he won't be able to find us."

"You're very brave," I said, giving her a hug.

"Thanks so much for listening," she sighed, "it has been really hard not being able to talk to anyone."

"I'm sure it has, we will be thinking of you two, and don't worry, we won't tell anyone," I said as I got up to leave.

"Thanks," she smiled.

"Bye Megan," I called, we will be leaving tomorrow, you and your mom have a great trip!"

"Okay," she said and hugged Herm as he stood to join me.

When I told Herm the story, he just shook his head dismally, "those poor people, having to pretend to be someone else and always looking over their shoulder, that's tough. I hope they make out all right."

"Yeah, me too," I sighed sadly.

The following morning, we took a bus to the airport to rent a car. We rationalized the expense of a car rental, versus taking busses, as it would give us flexibility and the option to stop any time to take photos. BUT there was no way I was going to drive! I was an anxious driver at home on familiar roads and here you had to drive on the "wrong" side! To make it even more confusing, the operator sat in what is our passenger seat! No freaking way! Poor Herm wasn't feeling very confident either as he gritted his teeth, white-knuckled the steering wheel and promptly pulled out onto the wrong side of the highway!

"Get on the other side, get on the other side," I screamed, wide-eyed as my stomach clenched and I clutched the door handle.

As Herm swerved back into the correct lane I questioned if driving had been the right decision or were we going to get ourselves killed?

Once out of the congestion of the city our breathing returned to normal, and we started to relax. The scenery was mind-bogglingly beautiful and changed around every corner. We must have said, "WOW, look at that" a hundred times and probably stopped as many, attempting to capture the magic with our cameras. Rolling hills of green, dotted with hundreds of white sheep would morph into bare brown slopes topped by lone trees silhouetted against the deep blue sky. The pastoral peacefulness was palpable and made us both smile and sigh with happiness.

The next week passed in a blur of volcanos, hot springs, geysers, bubbling mud and even a hot water beach! It was all fascinating but the stress of traveling in a car on the "wrong side" of the road, with drivers passing us on blind corners, had my stomach in knots and it wouldn't stop burning. I was homesick, depressed and wondered if I was hitting the 2-week "Traveler's Wall" we had read about in the guidebooks. I had to get ahold of myself, emotional turmoil or not, I had committed to this and would just have to work through it. Herm was a rock; he wasn't experiencing any of this and I was grateful for his steadfastness in the face of my moaning and meltdowns. I did wonder though if he was regretting getting into this with me. If I couldn't hack a laidback place like New Zealand, what was I going to be like in the more challenging countries?

The middle-aged man, who operated the geothermal plant we had visited, told us we would love the South Island, that it was "magical". I needed some magic about then so had pumped up my positive attitude balloon for the boat ride to the "enchanted isle". When we arrived at the Wellington ferry terminal, I waited in the car while Herm went to get tickets but when I saw him walking back empty-handed, my balloon threatened to pop!

"The ferry is booked up four days out," he said as he climbed back in the car.

"NO," I cried.

"Wait!" he said calmly, "before you go too crazy, the Ticketmaster said we might be able to get a standby spot. We have to join the line of cars and wait and see."

"But the line is SO long, there is no chance we will get on!" I whined.

"We will get on, I have a good feeling about it," he assured me.

I was too distraught at that point to be optimistic and was convinced we were waiting in vain.

Four hours later, we followed the line of cars creeping slowly towards the ferry. I was sitting in the front seat, totally tense, stomach aching, just praying we would make it on.

Herm kept reassuring me saying, "Don't worry, we will get on," as I saw one car after another disappear into the belly of the boat. He was right once again! We made it with room to spare!

The ship was HUGE! Not only were there hundreds of cars stuffed into two levels but parked to our right was a friggin' train! There was something about the bizarre disconnect of seeing a train on a ship that snapped me out of my doldrums and made me laugh. I spent the 3-hour journey smiling for the first time in days and feeling I had turned a corner. We hadn't even reached the magical isle yet, but it seemed it was already casting its spell on me.

The weather was sunny and warm, the deep blue water was calm, and the scenery was magnificent! The last leg of the journey into Picton Harbor was like a dream. The monstrous ship wove its way amongst the green hills and mountains which grew directly out of the sea. We passed hundreds of tiny, picturesque coves with white sandy beaches, some decorated with one or two anchored sailboats, but most empty and peaceful. As soon as we entered this enchanted area, most of the passengers came to the rail and a hush descended which didn't dissipate until we docked. It was apparent we all felt the special energy of the South Island as its shores embraced us.

The next day I was excited to get on the road to explore this land that had already worked its magic on me. We set a slow pace in order to enjoy the surrounding nature and stopped often to take photos. When we arrived in Motueka, late in the day, all the inexpensive lodgings were full, so we had to settle for a Bed and Breakfast. We had been staying mostly at inexpensive Motor Camps so paying $55 just to sleep was a little overwhelming. "Oh well," we shrugged, "at least we would get a nice big breakfast!" We had been living on dry cereal for weeks and were looking forward to the eggs, hash browns and pastries we had ordered when we checked in.

Early the next morning, I was lying in bed, lazily browsing the menu anticipating a yummy breakfast, when I noticed the fine print at the bottom of the page, "Breakfast - $6.50"

"Oh my God, Herm, we have to pay extra for breakfast, it isn't included!"

"What, that can't be right!" he said grabbing the menu.

We both figured that "bed AND breakfast" meant you paid one fee for both, like most places in the States! Neither of us wanted to pay so much for a meal we could get cheaper elsewhere. We looked at each other and asked, "what should we do now?" We sat on the bed, heads together, whispering as the clock clicked closer and closer to serving time. With five minutes to go, we decided to make a break for it. Giggling nervously, we threw everything in our packs, crept by the kitchen, while the cook's back was turned, and snuck quietly out the door. We jumped in the car, backed over the lawn to get around the car parked behind us, and sped away like a couple of thieves, laughing all the way. We were Bonnie and Clyde after a bank heist, expecting to be pursued through the streets of Motueka. I must admit we carried a tiny bit of guilt with us, but the adrenaline rush was enough to overcome our slight indiscretion.

Driving on the South Island was easier in some respects but the steep, coiled roads with precipitous drop-offs and no guardrails still made my stomach clench. What was even more worrying were the one-lane bridges where oncoming cars were blocked from view! Do you go or don't you go, was always our question? Most of the time, we took a deep breath, sped across and prayed but one day, we found ourselves in quite the conundrum. Speeding was not an option on THIS single-lane bridge because we were on railroad tracks!

"What the hell?" I cried. "Where did the road go, did we take a wrong turn somewhere?" I questioned incredulously.

"Crap, I don't know, the road just went this way I think!" Herm answered nervously, clutching the wheel trying not to get stuck in the tracks.

My mind grasped for an explanation. How does a road turn into tracks? It felt like a bad movie where the heroes were suddenly faced with an oncoming train! My stomach was on fire again as Herm finally maneuvered the vehicle off the bridge and onto a real road again. Phew!!! That was NOT fun!

We loved meeting all the local people we had interacted with but hadn't met any other "travelers" until we visited Westland National Park.

A hike through the rain forest over swaying suspension bridges, up steep ladders and over plank walkways, suspended on the side of cliffs, brought us to a viewpoint overlooking the mighty Franz Josef Glacier. There we found hikers from Europe, New Zealand, Canada and the U.S.A all gazing in awe at the beauty and immensity of the crevassed ice field. As we rested together, a spirited conversation ensued covering topics such as the environment, greed and other world problems. This was our first time meeting people from other lands and we felt an instant acceptance and camaraderie which left me looking forward to many more such exchanges. I realized seeing the sights was great but more importantly was the connection with people.

The next day, we had the opportunity for more interaction with travelers when we stopped to help an Irish family whose motor home had run out of gas. When we gave the parents and two kids a ride to the nearest station, I wanted to wait and give them a lift back, but Herm wanted to keep going. I was surprised and annoyed he wouldn't wait for them, but the "Universe" has a way of making things right. A few miles down the road, I smiled to myself as I discovered the little girl had left her coat in the car.

"Hey Herm, look what I found," I smiled as I held up the jacket.

"Oh no," he groaned.

"It's always interesting how the "Universe" works to teach us lessons, isn't it," I grinned.

"Yup," he sighed as he turned the car around to go back to the station.

We had so much kindness extended to us in the past few weeks I was happy we could give a little back.

The largest three-dimensional maze in the world was a large, square, wooden structure with dividers throughout which formed the labyrinth. It was constructed to confuse and confound and just like the pencil and paper mazes, you had to find your way from beginning to end through dead ends and twisting passages. An added challenge, if one chose to accept it, was to find the four corners. For more than an hour we laughed and staggered into dead ends, sometimes retracing our steps over and over. We would often bump into the same people where we would stop to exchange hints and encouragement before returning to the challenge of the puzzle. Groans, curses, giggles and the occasional whoop of celebration could be heard from our fellow questers from the other side of the partitions. What an incredible gift this was, inexpensive, fun, the freedom to be childlike, and a good brain workout. The best was saved for last, however, when the exit opened into an enchanting coffee shop set in a peaceful, flower-filled garden where we savored Boysenberry scones with whipped cream. The perfect ending to a most delightful afternoon.

We finally got our feet in the ocean near the town of Kaikoura. Even though the tide was coming in, we took the shoreline route, so we could wade in the warm water. To our delight, we found the beach decorated with strands of pearl-like seaweed beads in a rainbow of colors, along with brown leathery sea plants and iridescent shells. Decomposing seal carcasses were the other interesting decorations on the sand perfuming the air with the scent of decay. I know, most people would find this disgusting but this weird couple loves finding animal parts.

When Herm called excitedly, "Look what I found!"

I hustled over to take a look. With a big smile, he held up a white, pointed seal's tooth. "Oh wow," I exclaimed, "that is SO cool!"

He quickly pocketed his find, and we began searching for more treasures.

It wasn't just dead seals on the beach. Surrounding us were close to hundred live ones! Most barely moved as we passed within a few feet of them, some air scented us, and the really worried ones slid into the water and watched from a safe distance. We soon ran out of beach, however, and in order to continue, without joining the seals in the ocean, we had to negotiate a cave-like tunnel guarded by two huge bull seals.

"Hmm," I muttered, "do you think they will let us through?"

"Well, I don't want to turn back, do you?" Herm asked.

"Nope, let's send them good energy, not make eye contact and just keep walking."

"Sounds like a plan," Herm replied.

Good vibes sent, breath held, no eye contact, check…. off we went. Out of the corner of my eye, I saw them watching us and one let out a bark but thankfully let us pass unharmed. Phew! They were BIG!

The gem of the South Island is Milford Sound. It is accessed by a one-lane, mile-long tunnel, both dark and wet. The long downhill slide in the pitch black, births you into a deep canyon whose walls course with streams of water sparkling like stars on a moonless night. Before you lies the still, azure waters of the Sound mirroring Mitre Peak and its lesser-known neighbors. Waterfalls splash over every rock face providing nourishment to the plethora of vivid green plants which cling to the steep slopes. We were in awe, there were no words to describe the beauty and the peace that permeated our souls. This was most certainly the crown jewel among all the jewels that made up the breathtaking beauty of New Zealand.

After almost four weeks in this incredible country, it felt like home, and it was hard to say goodbye. Herm was now driving like a native and when we returned to places we had stayed previously we were greeted like long-lost relatives which warmed our hearts. I would always cherish Kiwiland for its qualities of friendliness, peace and indescribable beauty.

Change is always hard for me. I like things to stay the same. Sometimes the adventurous woman within gets hidden by the one who doesn't want to let go. Herm, on the other hand, is all about change so I can't stay hidden for long with him along for the journey. What I had learned from our first foreign country was the following: It took time to adjust to traveling and to new customs; the two-week travel "wall" was real; driving on the opposite side of the road was really stressful; AND….most importantly, I had learned to look RIGHT!

Dear Diary...

Phew, I made it through the first foreign country! Of course, it was an easy one, but it wasn't as undemanding and romantic as I imagined it to be. I miss my home, critters, my normal food and especially my own bed! It's difficult to be in a new place every night with the various comfort levels of the accommodation. Also, sleeping in single beds all the time isn't very conducive to snuggle time with Herm!

I do love New Zealand though and would live here in a heartbeat. Besides the incredible natural beauty, I also feel transported back in time to my 1950s childhood. The people seem friendlier, more trustworthy and happier than Americans are these days. It almost doesn't feel real! Maybe we are so far south we entered a time warp LOL!

Well, Australia is next, we will see what we find there. At least it will be another English-speaking country. I sure hope I stop missing home soon!

CHAPTER 3

AUSTRALIA

It is mind-boggling to realize time is so fluid, or, in all actuality, there is no such thing as time! Since Australia was three hours behind New Zealand, our three-hour flight took no time at all! We arrived in Sydney at 10 a.m., the same time we left Auckland! Crossing all those time zones made my head spin!

We were starting to get more comfortable with the arrival routine. Customs, change money, call a cheap hostel listed in the guidebook, and find public transportation. We each had our assignment and were starting to function smoothly as a team.

A busy guest house, adjacent to Sydney's red light district, became our home for the next week as we explored this vibrant city. During that time, we realized there was no way we would be able to see this huge country by car, so we bought the around Australia flight pass. Following a brief stop in the seaside city of Adelaide, we hopped to Alice Springs where we rented a car so Herm could keep practicing his driving skills. The wide-open spaces of the red desert brought only one stressor, "Road Trains". Huge 18-wheelers pulling two or three cargo trailers traveling at breakneck speeds, on a one-lane road, isn't something you wanted to argue with. The only thing you could do was get off the road, roll up your windows and hang on tight as they blew by like a tornado rocking and sandblasting the car. It was my job to keep watch as we didn't want to end up like all the flattened cattle and kangaroos we passed on the road!

It was late afternoon when we arrived at Ross Homestead, one of the smallest "stations" (ranches) in the region, encompassing an area of only 888 square miles of desert bush. The owners, who no longer counted on raising livestock for their income, had turned the spread into a rustic tourist resort. Twenty-two log cabins were neatly arranged around a large swimming pool to the left of the main lodge, where the bar and restaurant were located. I was delighted to find that our high-ceilinged cabin was spotlessly clean, had an attached bath, and was stocked with towels, soap, and cups. It was nice to feel pampered and comfortable for a change!

We were starving after our long drive so went in search of food. The house, which was the original homestead, had a cozy feeling with its dark wooden beams and a blazing fireplace. We soon discovered, however, we wouldn't be eating too much that night, as the minimum dining room charge was $29.50 each! Whoa, that certainly was out of our price range! A group of people on a tour were enjoying the expensive fare, while we were the only ones searching the bar menu for something cheaper.

While waiting for our soup and nachos, we chatted with an Aboriginal man who introduced himself as Alec. He was a rugged, friendly, soft-spoken guy, probably in his early 60's, who was quick to smile. He invited us to attend a lecture he was giving to the tour group at 8:30 PM and we quickly accepted his invitation.

Alec related the history of the area, demonstrated how to play Aboriginal musical instruments, and explained the use of some everyday tools, such as a hunting boomerang, a spear chucker and a baby carrier. Before leaving, Alec suggested we come for Damper and Billy Tea in the morning and said if we arrived early he would show us how to throw a boomerang and crack a whip. What a wonderful and unexpected surprise to be included in the activities the tour group was paying big bucks for!

As we walked back to our cabin in the dark, we drank in the warm air and the nighttime stillness of the desert. It was so pleasant to be back in nature and I looked forward to a peaceful rest in a nice big bed!

"Eew, what the hell was that?" I cried as I jumped up from a sound sleep and threw the light on.

"What's the matter?" Herm asked sleepily.

"Something big and wriggly just bounced off my face!" I answered as I searched the bed. "Oh yuck!" I said in disgust, it's one of those humongous cockroaches we saw by the pool."

Herm was wide awake and out of bed in a flash! "Where?" he asked anxiously.

I pointed as the creature launched itself out of the bed and scurried across the floor. Since neither of us likes to kill living things, however gross they may be, Herm opened the door and eventually was able to herd it out.

"Oh my God, I said with a shudder, that thing could have fallen in my mouth!"

When we went to climb back in bed, there on my pillow was a pincer assed earwig! "OK, I'm done," I said in exasperation, "let's put up the mosquito net."

It was easier said than done as we had yet to use it and hadn't a clue how to erect it. After an hour of fiddling and giggling, it was finally ready and we crawled underneath and lay down. I glanced over at Robert and cracked up as there he lay on his back with the net draped over his face.

"What a shit show," I laughed, "you can't sleep like that!"

"Nope," he chuckled. "I think it might work if I sleep with my head at the foot of the bed."

And that is what he did as we attempted to keep our feet out of each other's faces all night.

We rose early to join Alec for the promised boomerang and whip lessons. The whip was mastered in short order but the boomerang had a mind of its own. It had no intention of returning to me and much preferred resting in the fire pit while Herm's seemed to prefer nesting in the trees. As we were failing boomerang school, the tea had been brewing and the bread baking.

A billy is a metal bucket used to heat water on a campfire, thus the name Billy Tea. I'm not much of a tea lover but a touch of Eucalyptus leaf added to the brew was a game-changer. It was the best tea I ever tasted. Damper is a traditional Australian soda bread and much like the beer bread I used to make, and Spotted Dog was Damper with raisins. Both were cooked in an iron pot sunk into a pit, lined with red hot coals. Stuey, the pet kangaroo, was "helping" with the preparations and allowed me a brief pat after handing him a piece of bread. I was fascinated to discover kangaroo fur feels just like rabbit.

As we ate, I asked Alec about his life. He told us he was a "half-caste", half-Aboriginal, half white, and had been taken from his family when he was very small and placed in a boarding school. The Australian government, like the Americans with our Natives, didn't feel the Aboriginal people could properly raise or educate half-white children. It was so sad that most of those kids never saw their families again but were left to fend for themselves in a society where they didn't fit into any group. Once grown, Alec spent most of his life working as a cowboy on bush stations such as the Ross Homestead and had recently retired and taken up his present position as guide and historian. I loved Alec's quiet, humble demeanor, he had a special energy and despite a difficult life appeared to be at peace with himself and the world. As the tour people began to dribble in for their breakfast, we said our goodbyes and thanked Alec for being so kind in making our stay memorable. As we walked to our car, we could hear him teaching the newly arrived group how to crack the whip and throw the boomerang just as he had done with us.

A day of driving and sightseeing brought us to an overnight stay in Alice Springs. In the late afternoon, we were resting in our motel when I noticed movement on our closed door. "Herm, what is that crawling on the door?"

Herm got up to see what it was and called, "Daize, you've got to come see this!" As I got closer, I could see thousands of tiny caterpillars coming in all around the loose frame. We were being invaded!

"Lovely! Now what?"

We opened the door to see where they were coming from, but it appeared they were only at our room! There didn't seem to be much we could do but pick them up by the handful and toss them out which we did over and over until bedtime. I wondered what the attraction was. As we got ready for sleep, we joked about being devoured by the caterpillar hordes during the night with only our bones remaining. But of course, caterpillars are vegetarian....... right? In any case, I was happy I was on the bottom bunk so at least they wouldn't be dropping from the ceiling into my mouth like the cockroach the previous night!

We survived the night and made our way to a campground in Yulara, the desert oasis adjacent to Ayers Rock. When we arrived, we realized it was the one-year anniversary of our first date the previous April!

"Isn't it weird how a year ago we were walking around Concord looking for a place to eat dinner and now we're in Australia about to climb Ayers Rock?" I said incredulously.

"Totally weird," Herm agreed.

"Life sure is strange! I wonder where we will be next year at this time?" I mused.

"All I know is I won't be back working in Nashua," he laughed.

A short drive took us to the base of the sacred rock, Uluru. As I stood there looking up I exclaimed, "You've GOT to be kidding! Pictures lie!"

I was referring to the cover photo on our Australia guidebook which showed people walking across Ayers Rock on a gentle slope. Sure, it might have started at a 45-degree angle but quickly got much steeper. Chain was run between poles anchored in the stone to assist the climb but as we got higher, we literally had to haul our bodies along hand over hand.

"No freaking way!" I exclaimed as the chain came to an end just as the slope went close to vertical! "How are we supposed to get up there now?" I huffed in exasperation.

"Do you want to turn back?" Herm queried.

"No way, I'm not a quitter," I said with determination.

We searched for handholds in the smooth red stone and pulled ourselves upward like rock climbers. Those who were descending gave encouragement and we all agreed we were crazy to be climbing this thing.

Our upward struggle was rewarded when, on wobbly legs, we reached the top of the sacred monolith of the Aboriginal people. The undulating summit of smooth red sandstone felt sensuous and alive, but it was difficult to fully appreciate in the howling wind! We held our hats, leaned into the gale and pushed our way toward the small stand which contained the visitor's log. We sat huddled out of the wind, writing our names in the book, when two young Aussie guys approached us.

"G'day," they shouted against the wind. "Would one of you guys videotape us as we roller-skate around the top?"

"What! Roller-skate up here in this wind?" I laughed incredulously.

"Yup, we bet our mates we could do it and we just drove all night from Adelaide," they replied a bit drunkenly.

"Oh my god, you guys are crazy!" I said as I shook my head and laughed.

"Sure, I'll do it," Herm said,

"Great!" Their voices exuded youthful excitement, as they handed Herm the camera.

They strapped on their skates and wobbled across the surface of the rock doing a pretty admirable job of staying upright and not rolling over the sloping edge. We just shook our heads in amusement and muttered "crazy Aussies".

We left the dry desert heat and flew to the dense tropical humidity of Darwin, "the beer-drinking capital of Australia". I lay sprawled on the bed, not moving, sweat running off me. The slowly moving, battered ceiling fan doing little to mitigate the oppressive heat of the oven-like room. It was nighttime and as I lay there listening to the drunks yelling and cursing outside the open window, I was overcome with a feeling of unreality. Had I been dropped into an old movie set deep in the tropics? Was Humphrey Bogart about to walk in the door? I was glad we would be leaving the next day, as this place was really weird!

Little did we know what we were getting ourselves into when we rented a car complete with camping supplies and made our way to Kakadu National Park, not far from Darwin. I was looking forward to our first camping trip together, being out in nature and sleeping under the stars. As we drove into the park, we stopped to look at the huge termite mounds, some over 10 feet high.

"Oh my God," I said as I got out of the car, "I think it is hotter here than it was in Darwin!"

"Yeah, it is pretty hot," said my heat-loving partner. "Do you want to go back?" he asked.

"No, we paid for the car for three days, we may as well stay. I don't know where else we would go?" I replied resignedly.

We pressed on, set up camp, and went for a hike to view some of the ancient Aboriginal rock art the park was known for. I walked very slowly, starting to adapt a bit to the heat, and enjoyed seeing all the wildlife. There were SO many different birds, lizards, unusual insects and the usual kangaroos and wallabies. We also heard there were saltwater crocodiles and water buffalo, but thankfully we didn't come across any of those!

We figured when the sun went down we would get some relief from the heat, but by some terrible practical joke of nature, it felt even hotter!! We were sitting at our picnic table finishing dinner amongst the mosquito swarms, our bodies slathered in DEET with mosquito coils smoking.

"Well, even though it is friggin' hot, at least the mosquitoes seem tolerable."

"Yeah, not too bad as long as we stay near the coils." Herm agreed tentatively. THEN.......... darkness fell.

Huge clouds of blood-sucking attack mosquitoes dropped from the sky breathing in the coil smoke with a grin and lapping up the DEET on our skin.

"Holy shit!" we cried as we flailed our arms helplessly, totally covered with the attackers.

We dove into our tiny pup tent, bringing hundreds of those voracious vampires with us. We were being sucked dry inside our tiny sweatbox and Herm, who hates mosquitoes, was frantically murdering all he could see by the light I was holding. Finally, the last monster was slain, and we lay down to catch our breath only to find the walls of the tent had sagged so much it was inches from my face. I was suffocating from the heat of our exertion and with the tent collapsing, claustrophobia was closing in fast.

Calm down Daisy, just breathe, pretend you are somewhere in the wide-open spaces, I said to myself.

"How are you doing?" Herm asked concerned.

"Not great," I said as he took my hand.

Okay, breathing back to normal, no mosquitoes in the tent, resigned to having a tent in my face.

"I have to pee!" I groaned.

"Me too," Herm lamented. "I have been trying to put it out of my mind but......".

"Yeah, me too but I don't think I can hold it," I sighed.

"Okay, I guess we have to do it."

"Let's go on three and watch out for the crocodiles! One, two, three." Grab a flashlight, unzip the tent, I get out and run, Herm re-zips and follows, hot on my heels.

In the bathroom, I was startled when my flashlight caught large-eyed, ghostly lizards and frogs hanging stationary on the walls. It was pretty creepy knowing I was surrounded by creatures in the darkness but not as disturbing as knowing that re-entering the tent was going to start the whole mosquito scenario all over again…sigh!

We survived the night and were able to enjoy a relaxing, bug-free river cruise the next morning. After viewing some additional Aboriginal rock art, we discovered a small park in town with a crocodile-free lake, safe for swimming. Even though Herm almost never likes to swim he was all into going for a dip. I was disappointed to discover it wasn't the least bit refreshing but was more like swimming in a hot tub full of slimy weeds. The relief came when we got out and the slight breeze touching our wet bodies left us feeling cooler than we had been in weeks! We stayed right there in the shade of the trees for the rest of the afternoon before going in search of a new campsite.

We were determined to be better prepared for the mosquito war that night, so we set up camp next to the marsh, got our cookstove out, lit mosquito coils and went for a walk on the nature trail. The wetland was covered with beautiful pink Lotus Lilies, and we came across the tracks of water-buffalo, horse and pig but didn't catch sight of any of them in the head-high grass. We were feeling relaxed, not too hot after our walk and proud of ourselves for being prepared for the night. BUT…nature had different plans.

Ants! Big... black... ants along with all their relatives, eggs and children had moved into our stove in the short time we were gone. Why would they do that, I wondered. The sun was setting so we labored to get them out, but they didn't want to leave! Herm lit the stove figuring the heat would drive them off. Nope, they seemed happy to sit around a fire. Water proved to be their nemesis but, of course, now we couldn't use the stove, so we opened two cans of beans and ate them cold.

With the mosquito coils burning and our bodies soaked in bug dope, we managed to stay outside longer than the night before but couldn't endure another minute of it by the time the clock hit 7:20. We made sure to empty our bladders, made an unhurried entry into the tent, and Herm calmly killed the interlopers without bringing the tent down on top of us. Even without the drama of the night before, it still took us hours to get to sleep. There was something about the steady drone of an army of bloodsuckers sticking their "noses" through the tent screen next to your head that was a bit unsettling.

"Okay, let's have a plan," Herm said as we prepared to leave the tent and break camp the following morning. "We will unzip, get out, you take the tent down. I will grab the stove and our things; we will throw it all in the car and be out of here. Plan?"

"Plan," I laughed. "One, two, three, go!" Unzip, dive out, tent down, everything in the car and off we went in under seven minutes! We gave each other a high five as we headed back to the lake to clean up and eat breakfast.

The "Universe" is very funny. We were so proud of ourselves for outsmarting the mosquitoes, but it looked like the ants got the last laugh. I opened the back door of the car to get the stove to cook breakfast and....

"Oh my god! Herm, come look!"

Those big black ants were all over the back seat and our belongings, not appearing at all happy we had taken them for a ride!

"Oh no!" he exclaimed "They must have moved back into the stove overnight!"

I was grateful they weren't an aggressive variety of ant or we would have sustained far more bites than we did as we evicted them once again from the stove and swept them out of our belongings and car.

We had planned for one more day in the park, but the crushing heat and the hordes of mosquitoes had pretty much taken the fun out of it. I was trying to be brave but was almost in tears with the thought of enduring another long night lying uncomfortably in the hot tent with the mosquitoes at my head.

I said to Herm, "I don't think I can take another night; do you want to get out of here?"

"Oh my God yes," he said relieved.

We laughed as we packed up and got the hell out of there as fast as we could, got back to Darwin and on a plane to Cairns the same day. Good riddance!

The laid-back, seaside city of Cairns was such a relief after Darwin. It was also our departure point for our trip to Papua New Guinea, a place I had wanted to visit since looking through National Geographic magazines as a child. I wanted to see those fierce-looking muscular men in loincloths with painted faces, bones through their noses, carrying spears, bows and arrows. So many of the cultures I had been fascinated with in my youth were either dead or dying in the 1990s. I was hoping there was still something left of the wildness of the Papua New Guinea culture I had felt from those photographs.

Herm had no idea where Papua New Guinea (PNG) was, or what was drawing me there, so before we left home, I picked up a book by "Fred" who had recently traveled to PNG and wrote about his many exciting adventures. By the time he finished reading Fred's story, Herm was as excited to go as I was. Even though the guidebook talked about the crime problem, and the need to be somewhat cautious, we weren't overly concerned, as every country had its issues. We did start to wonder, however, after we met an American man at Tongariro National Park in New Zealand, who told us he had been part of an Earthwatch group in PNG. They had been researching volcanoes when their Jeeps were stopped by a group of young men wielding semi-automatic weapons. They were robbed of everything, including the Jeeps. That was disturbing news for us to hear, but we wouldn't be driving around in Jeeps and were planning on being very cautious.

We had applied for our visas to PNG as soon as we had gotten to Sydney but when the Papuan man who took our applications looked at us with eyebrows raised and said, "Boy, you're brave," we were a bit taken aback!

What did that mean? Was it another warning? Were we making a mistake by going there? Our minds began to create fearful images of being robbed, murdered and eaten by cannibals.

The Sepik River region was one of the places we wanted to visit but read it was one of the deadliest malarial areas in the world. We had brought anti-malaria pills with us but learned they wouldn't protect us from the strain prevalent there. Thus, we paid a visit to the Traveler's Medical office, in Sydney, an organization that gave medical advice to travelers. While reading the bulletin board, where disease outbreaks around the world were posted, we discovered there were other dangerous sicknesses and parasites we would have to watch out for in PNG as well. Was that another warning?

Because we were encountering so many negative messages, we began getting a bit concerned. Maybe it wasn't safe enough to travel on our own, or maybe the messages just meant we should be well prepared and fully aware? Herm and I have tried to live our lives on what feels right for us. Since we have a long way to go in sorting out what are reasonable fears versus unreasonable fears, at times of confusion we would ask for "signs" to give us answers. We had found the system worked well for us if we asked clearly for what we wanted, and then kept our minds and hearts open to the answer. With this in mind, we asked for either a positive or negative sign as to whether or not we should travel to Papua New Guinea.

It wasn't long before we got our first signal when we spotted a place called Niugini Tours, near the PNG consulate in Sydney. We stopped to see what they had to offer and as might be expected, they were very enthusiastic about Papua New Guinea and the many exciting things to see there. They explained it was quite safe to go out and about during the day, just not at night. They offered us a tour and even though it sounded great, it was way above our budget. It was well worth the visit though, just to hear someone speak enthusiastically about the country and it helped restore our confidence and enthusiasm. Sign number two came at a nearby camping store where we discovered "Fred's" book. That was a real surprise as we had never seen it in any other store, even in America. We re-read Fred's upbeat section on PNG and felt we had gotten our answer.

Just in case we were still in doubt, that evening the "Universe" sent to our door a warm, outrageously funny British travel agent who was staying across the hall at our guest house. She was responding to the notice we had posted on the bulletin board asking to talk to someone who had been to PNG. She had recently returned from a one-month adventure and entertained us with stories for over two hours. Traveling by herself, she had found the "Nationals" to be friendly, helpful and even protective of her. They were well aware of the danger from "Rascals," (what the criminals were called), and made sure she never had to walk anywhere alone. By the time she left that evening, we felt we had gotten our answer loud and clear. The "Universe" seemed to be saying, go, use common sense, plan well, and keep a look over your shoulder.

By the time we reached Cairns, we were starting to obsess again about the dangers. Herm was also concerned about the challenging astrological transits he was supposed to be experiencing, and the fact numerologically speaking we would both be in a 9 or ending year. Because our fears were once again getting the better of us, we stopped at "Papua New Guinea Adventure Travels," two days before we were due to leave. Suzanne, the young, energetic owner, was upbeat and positive and told us she could set up a tour for us. We didn't want to spend the extra money and agonized for over an hour before deciding to have Suzanne arrange the first part of our trip to the Sepik River, and after that, we would go it alone. We were really going to do this!

A few days later, we waited at the airport in Cairns with a number of well-dressed Papuan Nationals and three other white passengers. With only 7000 tourists visiting PNG each year I guess it was to be expected. This would be our first visit to a non-western country and leave it to me to pick an adventurous one!

Dear Diary....

I finally stopped missing home, I guess I am turning into a traveler! Woohoo! Except for the bugs, Australia was really fun and easy just like the people. We do need to stop spending so much money though. It is so hard to give up the old ways of doing things, like car rentals and taking plane trips. It might be a gradual evolution, I guess I will find out!

One thing I discovered that I didn't know, is Herm is very competitive and not a good loser. Unfortunately, another thing we have in common. We played miniature golf when we were in Adelaide, and I beat him which didn't go over too well. I must admit, I felt kind of guilty. It even briefly crossed my mind I shouldn't have been so good at it, but it was brief as I really enjoy winning LOL! Isn't it awful how women carry around that smidgen of guilt if they do something better than a man? I sure wish I could get rid of that!

I am SO excited to finally be going to PNG! A lifelong dream comes true! I can still see myself as a little girl thumbing through those National Geographics dreaming of seeing those strange people in person. Who would have guessed I would actually get to go there?

CHAPTER 4

PAPUA NEW GUINEA

I was full of anticipation as the coastline of Papua New Guinea came into view. The plane circled the wild, rugged land where 14,000-foot peaks floated above the clouds like islands in a sky ocean. It was easy to see why so few roads had been built through those impenetrable mountains.

We were met by a very pleasant Papuan man from the hotel where Suzanne had reserved us a room. A short ride through crowded streets brought us to the Civic Guest House, which was entirely surrounded by a tall wooden fence topped by three strands of barbed wire. It appeared most people in Port Moresby lived behind walls and wire, in order to protect themselves from intrusion by "Rascals".

We felt somewhat comforted by the peaceful grounds of the hotel, where a tropical garden, full of colorful flowers, surrounded the clear water of the pool. Under the breezy shade of the trees, were tables and chairs where one could sit and sip a cool drink while listening to the raucous cries of the resident hornbill, cockatoo and parrot.

After settling in, we gathered the courage to step outside the secure walls of our compound and walk to the nearby outdoor market. The dusty streets were crowded with friendly, smiling faces, all dressed in

Western clothes. Many people, however, still bore the scars, tattoos and holes in their noses as evidence of their tribal identities. There were a number of "Bible pushers" around, and one Jehovah's Witness was orating loudly in the park about the evils of the world. One shop-keeper, who wasn't taking any chances as to who was going to save him, was selling pictures of both the Pope and Rambo!

As we walked through the crowds, we kept our hands firmly attached to our bags, especially after spotting some young men surveying the scene for easy targets. Thankfully, there were a large number of security police present keeping an eye on them as well.

Having survived our first excursion into "Rascalville", we spent the afternoon sitting in the shade by the pool eavesdropping on the conversation of a group of Americans at the next table. The two Peace Corps volunteers were telling their friends from California, about the rape of one of their compatriots and how being attacked was the main threat women faced working in this country.

Yikes! I had read about that danger in the guidebook, but it was more frightening to hear about it from real live people! It made me even more determined to be watchful and keep my eyes open.

The next day, at the airport, we got to experience the concept of time as experienced by native cultures. Schedules were in place, but they were only loosely adhered to. Planes arrived when they got there and left when they took off. Sitting and waiting was not something to get anxious about, it just was. The only ones uptight were those visitors who were stuck in a Western mindset. Thankfully, sitting and waiting has never been an issue for me, but Herm was a bit restless. His Aries isn't much of a sitter.

The dark, low-ceilinged, waiting room, was packed with people, and was quite warm, even with the whirling, clanking ceiling fans turned to high speed. Papuan families of all sizes filled the chairs and spilled onto the available floor space. The women, who wore colorful lap laps (wrap-around cloths), bilums (string bags) and tops, sat and nursed their babies and small children. The men wore western t-shirts and trousers and gathered in groups to smoke and talk. My smiles to the women and young ones brought big, white-toothed grins in return and a 10-year-old girl told me about her family and her school.

We finally heard something on the loudspeaker about Wewak and my young friend told me that was our flight.

As we approached the tiny runway in Wewak, we were congratulating ourselves on prearranging the first part of the trip. Since this was our first non-western country, we were a bit unsure of ourselves and were comforted to know lodging, transportation, food and safety were all being taken care of by our guide who would greet us when we landed. Little did we know how relevant the Papuan motto, "The Land of the Unexpected" was going to be.

We entered the hanger-like terminal building scanning the area searching for a man who looked like he was expecting us. Since we were the only white folk among the 30 people on our flight, we wouldn't be difficult to spot.

"I don't see anyone that might be Joe, do you?" I asked a bit concerned.

"I don't either, why don't you sit with the bags, and I'll ask the guy at the ticket counter if he knows him." When Herm returned, he said, "he does know him but hasn't seen him, so will give him a call."

A few minutes later the Ticketmaster beckoned Herm over and told him he had reached Joe and he would be sending a car for us. Phew! THAT was a relief!!

Three hours later we were still sitting there with no car and no call from Joe. We were getting very anxious as the last flight of the day was processed, the janitor was cleaning up and we were about to be put out the door. The admonitions of "don't be out at night" and "don't be standing around with your bags alone anywhere", echoed in our heads.

"What are we going to do?" I asked nervously.

"I don't know, I'll see what the ticket guy recommends," Herm answered.

A few minutes later Herm returned and told me, "He called this guy Ralf who has a guest house and Ralf said he would pick us up in about 30 minutes. The ticket guy said he would stay with us until Ralf got here."

"Oh, thank God!" I said with relief. "That is so sweet of him to do that for us. I think I remember seeing this Ralf's name in the guidebook, I guess we should have thought of calling him ourselves…duh!"

Soon, a battered, open-backed truck with a ripped canvas cover pulled up to the building. A tall, thin, balding man with a red beard and glasses called gruffly from the driver's seat, "Get in, why didn't you call me first?"

"Uh, thanks," I waved lamely as we climbed in the back squeezing our bags and ourselves onto the bench seat among the other transport-ees. A cloud of choking, eye-burning exhaust enveloped us as Ralf pulled onto the road leading to town.

"Oh dear, what are we getting ourselves into?" I asked Herm, concerned.

"Who knows but it was our only choice," he shrugged.

In the middle of the dusty, run-down village, everyone got off and Herm climbed into the cab leaving me to choke to death amidst the fumes as the truck headed up a steep grade.

Ralf's simple home, built on short stilts, was situated in the cool, breezy hills with an expansive view of the sparkling blue bay below. Several rusted, moss-covered cars with their guts half removed littered the yard. Even though the outside of the house looked shabby and rundown, the inside was homey. The "guest room" was small, with a narrow aisle between four sets of wooden bunk beds, on which lay woven grass mats posing as mattresses. A spotless privy and small shower house, plumbed to a rain barrel on the roof, were located close to the front door. Little did we know this would end up being our home for the next four days while trying to figure out what to do next!

We quickly learned Ralf's gruff demeanor hid a heart of gold. He told us he had come to PNG 20 years ago as a Catholic missionary from Germany but had fallen in love and married a local woman. They had several children together but during the delivery of their last child, five years before, his wife died from a botched C section.

Besides Ralf and his daughter, another four or five Nationals boarded there as well. It was like living in a village and was great fun meeting and conversing with all the people coming in and out. It was especially interesting and actually quite intimidating having discussions with Ralf. He was highly intelligent, well-read and could converse on almost any subject. Conversations with him could range from the mundane to the esoteric and we found it hard to keep up!

In the room next to ours resided a mystery man. Through the walls, we could hear him mumbling and sometimes yelling angrily amidst a hacking cough. The outside of his door was painted with a skull and crossbones and a paper affixed there read: "Anyone who enters, dies!" Food was quickly handed off to the "thing" through a partially opened door as if the delivery person was feeding a wild animal that would bite!

A couple of days after arriving we were alone in the house when the door to the mystery room slowly cracked open. OMG! Our imaginations had run wild in the intervening days and we were a bit nervous to discover what might emerge. We were stunned when out waddled a substantially built, very friendly, middle-aged dwarf! In almost perfect English he introduced himself and apologized for all the noise the last few days! He told us he had been suffering from malaria but was now on the mend. We had a delightful visit with our imaginary "monster" who was actually quite urbane! He was named Little Man and had been a cook on a tourist class riverboat that used to ply the Sepik. He had interacted with many famous people in his years on the boat and while we would have loved to hear more stories, we knew he needed his rest.

Even though Ralf had put the word out in town that Joe Kinney could find us at his house he never showed up. We found this whole scenario kind of interesting since we hadn't REALLY wanted to do the whole package tour thing in the first place but had given in to our fears. It seemed the "Universe" was giving us another chance to go it alone. So, when Joe Kone called Ralf's looking for customers, we decided to go for it. We had read good things about him in the traveler journals Ralf kept and he seemed on the up and up when we spoke on the phone. As much as we loved staying with Ralf, we were ready to move on so made plans to meet Joe at the Ambunti Lodge, the following day.

Our 10-seater plane taxied onto the short grass landing strip at Ambunti, a tiny, roadless village on the banks of the mighty Sepik River. A small group of locals met the plane and when we asked the location of the Ambunti Lodge were directed down a dirt track. Plodding slowly through the palm trees a voice from behind called to us. We turned to see an old man approaching, carrying a string bag and spitting red betel juice. He introduced himself as Joseph and offered to help us to our lodging. Herm immediately assumed this was Joseph Kone but something felt "off" and I couldn't get Herm's attention as he and Joseph were ahead of me. I heard Joseph agreeing he was the one Herm had talked with, so I tried to suppress my suspicions.

At the lodge, we sat down with Joseph and discussed the details of the trip. We gave him a down payment to get supplies and gas for the canoe and agreed to meet him back at the lodge at 6 p.m. In the meantime, we decided to go for a walk and explore the area. A boy on a bicycle approached us and said Joseph was looking for us which we found strange as he said he would be gone for several hours. When we neared the church mission, a nice-looking young National came towards us, hand extended, saying, "Hi, I'm Joe Kone." Oh crap, my fears had been confirmed, THIS was the real Joseph, the old guy was an imposter just as I had feared! Herm was in shock and felt pretty foolish for being taken in. Joe Kone was none too happy either when he found out Joseph was stealing his clients and he went to see if he could catch Old Joe before he went down river.

We could only go back to the lodge and wait to see what would happen. We were the only ones staying at the 10-room facility which was set up motel-style. A large green lawn stretched to the river where children played, and dugout canoes were moored. The rooms were small and dingy with two tiny windows, two beds, and a chair. Toilets and showers were located down the patio toward the main lodge. The inn had a kitchen, bar, and sitting area decorated with local art and the cooking facilities were made available to the guests to make meals as there were no restaurants in town.

As we waited, we tried not to obsess but Herm lamented,

"I feel bad about not realizing the old guy wasn't Joe Kone, I am usually not fooled so easily."

"I know you aren't. You usually spot them before I do. I had a bad feeling right away and should have spoken up." I said regretfully.

Since we had prepaid the original trip, we hadn't brought a lot of cash with us, and it certainly wasn't enough to get us through the following weeks. When neither of the Josephs showed up that night, we figured we had kissed that money goodbye too!

The next day, Old Joseph came with a tall tale about the motor falling off his canoe and spending all the money to fix it. When we told him we were going with Joe Kone and wanted our money back, he said he would give us the petrol he bought but that was it. We were upset but chalked it up to experience and needing to pay attention to the "little voice"! Thinking all the hassle was finally behind us, we were relaxing by the river when young Joe came to tell us old Joe was bragging to everyone that he still had our money, and we should go to the police. We didn't feel comfortable doing that, but Joe insisted, so we reluctantly agreed. By that time, the whole village knew about our little drama and crowded around as the constable asked old Joe about our money. He just repeated what he had said to us, so we told the constable to let it go. There wasn't much we could do at that point.

With the plethora of Joe's sorted out and the new Joe paid, we were finally off on our Sepik adventure. That is if I didn't capsize the canoe first! I struggled with my pack to get to the middle of the rocking sixteen-foot dugout where I was directed to sit by John, our driver. With Herm and Joe settled behind me, John motored upriver against the swift current then turned off to follow a small passage through a grassy tributary toward a large lake. It was a wild place with a profusion of water birds peering at us through the tall reeds and grasses. Around the lake were a few villages where we stopped to visit. At most, we were warmly received but at others, the energy was decidedly cool, and we were happy to make a quick getaway.

At the end of the first day, John pulled the canoe into Joe's home village of Pruknawi where we were welcomed by his father, Adam. He was a short, heavily muscled, healthy-looking man of indeterminate age. His nose and ears sported holes, where bone ornaments could be inserted, and around his waist, he wore a plain cloth which hung almost to his knees. He showed us to his two-room bush material home where we would be staying. There was a small room on the first floor for cooking and hanging out, with sleeping quarters on the second story. The second floor was reached by an outside stairway made from large round logs which the natives negotiated with no problem. Herm and I felt foolish, as, despite all of our efforts, we couldn't keep our balance and had to literally crawl up and down the logs. The floor of the room was made from woven reeds laid over poles which we were amazed to find could actually hold all our weight!

John cooked up delicious smoked fish and gluelike sago which made me want to gag but I choked it down with a smile as the men watched for my reaction. There was no way I would let them see that tasteless starch made me want to puke. After a much-needed swim in the river, we relaxed on the second-floor veranda watching the dinner fires across the river being lit. It was so peaceful and I felt right at home with these people who lived so simply and close to nature.

Once the multi-colored sky darkened, we went inside and set up our mosquito nets next to Adam's. We rolled out the reed sleeping mats we had been given and fell asleep to the drone of voices downstairs talking about the Americans, old Joe, and the money we had lost.

Early the next morning, John motored down a series of "side roads" which kept branching to smaller and smaller tributaries thick with tall grass. He finally had to cut the motor and Joe poled us through the weed-choked water. Where were they taking us and how would they find their way out of that maze? I wondered.

We beached our craft at a small clearing and stepped onto mud which threatened to suck our shoes off. John stayed with the canoe while Joe led us into the thick forest onto a narrow, well-worn path. The air was warm and heavy, and the only sounds were the jungle birds and the bubbling stream that ran along beside us. The trail soon crossed the creek and I welcomed splashing through the cool water with flecks of gold glittering at our feet. I was giddy with the adventure of it all and must have had a big silly grin on my face. When I spotted a mass of bare-footed prints in the sand, I imagined being peered at by natives hidden in the thick undergrowth. Sunlight filtered through the trees, birds screeched, and the air was crowded with iridescent-winged hornets, multi-colored butterflies and moths. Slimy green lizards skittered into the bushes and large, long-legged spiders waited for their prey. It was magical, and I felt wild and free, an explorer, not knowing what I might encounter around the next bend. Where were we being taken and what was at the end of this journey through the jungle?

Steep steps were carved into the slippery slope, and we climbed and climbed and climbed, our breathing becoming labored, our sweat washing away our protective mosquito repellent. The sound of voices could be heard up ahead and soon the first palm leafed huts of the village came into view. Without warning, we burst through the leafy canopy into a brightly lit clearing where the whole village was gathered for Sunday service. Men, women, children of all ages came running as the word spread quickly that strangers were in their midst. I was overwhelmed as the mass of people approached us wanting to shake our hands. I don't know who Joe told them we were, but they acted as if Jesus Christ and his disciples had just arrived at their church service. We felt embarrassed by all the attention and adulation which was being heaped on us. We were told to take a seat on a huge log carved into the shape of a crocodile. It was hollowed out to serve as a drum for ceremonies and for communicating messages across long distances.

All eyes were upon us, and I didn't know if we were going to be roasted or toasted as we heard whispers of "Amerika", rippling through the crowd. As we sat in the shade of the longhouse, young men with strips of dry sago leaves bound to their feet for traction, scaled tall Coconut Palms to cut refreshments for us. Herm and I were each presented with a large green coconut with a small hole cut neatly into the top so we could gulp down the most delicious, refreshing drink I had ever tasted. As we sat cooling off from the trek, people continued to come forward to shake our hands. Young folks with delicate blue designs tattooed on their faces, runny-nosed children, men with the scarred marks of initiation covering their torsos and babies suckling half-hidden breasts and crying in fright at the white strangers.

Too soon we had to leave and as we walked away, the villagers waved and cried "apo", goodbye and "come back" until we were out of sight. I was practically in tears over the incredibly warm, enthusiastic reception we had received from those friendly people. I had never experienced anything like that in my life. Maybe that is how celebrities feel when greeted by their adoring fans. If so, I could understand why they continued to want more.

After our last day of visiting villages, we returned to Pruknawi to pick up our gear and found Adam dressed in full ceremonial costume. He wore a feathered headdress; his ankles were encircled with ornaments, and in his armband, he carried a carved dagger made from the leg bone of the huge ostrich-like Cassowary. Around his neck hung pig tooth, dog tooth and Kina shell necklaces. His outfit was complete, right down to the bone through his nose and various articles dangling from his ears. It was as if he had walked out of one of those magazines from my childhood. It was a dream come true for me to see those pictures from long ago come to life. He then presented me with a dog and pig's tooth necklace and Herm with a very old stone carving of a face. We were touched and honored by those gifts, and the warm hospitality Adam and the rest of the village had shown us. As we left the peaceful place by the water the entire village, dogs and all, lined the bank waving good-bye.

It was time to head back to Wewak but due to our money situation, we couldn't afford for both of us to fly. Herm's back was bothering him, and he didn't think he could handle the jarring trip on the PMV (public motor vehicle, ie. open-backed truck). After much discussion, we decided he would fly, and I would go via road with Joe accompanying me. I was a little nervous but trusted Joe to keep me safe and I was always up for an adventure. Joe and I headed out at 8 a.m. for the two-hour canoe ride downriver where the nearest road was located. As luck would have it, the PMV was full, so we had to wait five hours for the next one. When three o'clock came and went with no truck, Joe went to find out what was going on and was told a PMV had left Wewak that morning, but the road was really muddy from the recent rain, so there was a good chance it wouldn't get through.

Night fell and still, we waited, and I was getting anxious about the dark and who might be lurking there. I could tell Joe was worried as well and we moved our sitting spot from the river to the porch floor of a closed store. Ralf's warnings about being out after dark, and about Rascals and rape kept echoing in my head. Everyone in town had seen me sitting there all day, so I would be an easy target, especially if Joe left my side.

We were getting PMV news left and right. One had arrived but the driver wouldn't travel at night due to the danger. Another was parked outside of town because of the muddy roads but had already left. I was trying to hold it together, looking pretty cool on the outside, but I was really uptight. The other travelers we had met during the day had gone with the second PMV, so it was just me and the natives. Poor Joe was running around doing his best to find us a way out of there and trying to protect me at the same time. Suddenly, an empty truck appeared on the street in front of us, and some men started loading it with empty petrol drums. "Let me go see what's going on," Joe said as I waited alone in the dark, trying not to move, and making myself as small as possible. I kept picturing a protective aura around me at the same time I was wishing for some charcoal to blacken my white face.

"We have a ride!" Joe reported as he came back to get me. "The truck which brought the petrol barrels is heading back to Wewak tonight with the empties and they agreed to take us, but we have to walk to the edge of town to get it."

"Thank goodness," I thought as Joe rounded up some boys to carry our bags. The scene was surreal. By the light of the truck and a few flash-lights, the shadowy figures of a couple of dozen men, lurched towards us balancing 55-gallon drums on their shoulders. They were cursing and laughing as they slid through a sea of deep mud. It was unnerving being the only woman, in the darkness, surrounded by all that testosterone. I couldn't wait to get on the truck and out of there!

A small space in the back of the cab had been reserved for us to squeeze into with the rest of the back full of empty barrels stacked on their sides. As I began to climb up the side of the stake-bodied truck, I felt hands going up my long skirt "helping" me. Laughing and jok-ing, I could hear the young men daring each other to grab my crotch. Even after I had gained the relative safety of the truck, hands still came through the sides like hungry buzzards. I was so pissed, I grabbed one of the hands and bent the fingers back trying to break them until he pulled away laughing. Joe was busy trying to find a place for our gear so didn't see what was going on. When I told him, the truck was already pulling away so there was nothing he could do. He was beside himself with fury, he had promised Herm to keep me safe and I know he felt responsible for what had happened.

It was almost 10 p.m. when the truck lurched down the muddy track and for an hour more careened from one mud hole to another throwing us from side to side on the hard steel ridged floor. We were holding our breath praying the truck wouldn't get stuck again. I didn't want to think of what would happen if it did and feeling Joe's tension didn't help my nerves any. When we finally reached the tar road, bruised and sore, we thought we could finally lie down and get some sleep, but the tension only grew as the truck driver kept stopping. Each time, Joe nervously got up and looked around and we were both thinking this was it, the Rascals had blocked the road and that would be that! It was nerve-wracking!

The night air became cooler as we left the flood plain and began to climb into the surrounding hills. The starry sky we had been star-ing at while lying on our backs, began to share its space with feathered palm fronds, and the gnarled branches of trees. The truck labored up steep hillsides then careened downhill and around corners. Joe and I were again thrown from one side to the other but were now in danger of having our faces smashed in by those loose barrels! When the truck descended a hill or hit one of the many potholes, some of the barrels moved ominously towards us and we had to hold them back with our feet. We took turns staying awake in order to be in one piece at the journey's end. It was exhausting!

At 3 a.m., safe, sore, tired and filthy I was deposited at the bottom of Ralf's driveway, and I bid a hasty thank you and goodbye to my guardian angel. When the driver tooted, the door to the house flew open and Herm came running down the driveway.

"Oh my God, are you okay? I was so worried when Mike and Solomon got here and told me you were probably stuck in Pagwi for the night!"

"It was an adventure," I laughed tiredly. Everyone in the house, was awake and dear Ralf, our mother hen, wanted to make me some food but all I wanted was a shower and a bed that was safe and not moving.

Only two hours later we were in the air, leaving our adventurous time in Wewak and the Sepik behind, and flying down the coast to begin the next leg of our journey. Having come through our Sepik adventure alive and well, we agreed we should have planned on staying the whole two months the Visa had granted us. Our fears had limited our perspective and we were regretting our short-sighted decision to stay only three weeks. There were just so many places to see, and we were not going to have time to do it all.

After a brief visit to the seaside, we were in the air again headed to the mountain village of Kegasugl to climb 14,000-foot Mt Wilhelm. The road from the airport in Kundiawa to Kegasugl "had to be seen to be believed", Tony Wheeler had written in his guidebook. It was a one-lane dirt track winding its way up the sides of mountains. In many places, it was no more than a "donkey trail" etched into the side of the cliff, with a rock wall on one side and a sheer drop-off on the other. It was as much of a thrill riding along that road as it had been landing at the Kundiawa airport where the pilot dove out of the sky, pulled up at the last minute and came to rest in front of a cliff!

At one of the stops up the mountain, a young Peace Corps volunteer, named Lawrence, got on. He was also going to Kegasugl where he had been teaching English for the past five months. As we talked, we discovered, to our surprise, we were all from New England! The world was a very small place indeed! Lawrence volunteered to find us a guide for the mountain ascent and would also lend us blankets and some warm clothes. Wow, meeting him was a real gift!

Three hours into the trip, we said good-bye to Lawrence when we spotted a hand-painted sign by a fenced yard proclaiming, "Herman's Guest House." Herman, another German ex-pat showed us the bush hut across the dirt lane from his dwelling, then left us to take care of ourselves. The "guest house" contained two large sleeping rooms with plank platforms lining one wall, as beds. The rooms were arranged on either side of a central kitchen, which contained a sink, cooking utensils and a smoky wood stove. Just out the back door and up a short incline was another small hut that contained a flush toilet on one side and a hot water shower on the other! Wow! We certainly hadn't expected luxuries like that!

Two days later we were packed and ready for our ascent of Mt. Wilhelm when Michael, our guide, arrived barefoot and with far fewer clothes hanging on his thin body than we had on ours. He easily shouldered our big pack and silently led us up a wide muddy road toward the trailhead. The rain of the night before had turned the red earth into a slippery track, and although the rain had stopped, the sky was heavily overcast, and the weather didn't look promising. With Lawrence's warning about keeping our feet dry, ringing in our ears, we jumped over puddles and tried to stay out of the mud, but it was all but impossible. Soon the road ended, and we started climbing the steep, narrow jungle path thickly lined with fern trees and multicolored flowering bushes. Our breathing became labored as we scrambled over logs laid across the trail to help with footing on the slick earth. As if it wasn't muddy enough, it began to drizzle, then rain lightly, as thick, grey clouds and fog kept rolling in and out of the valleys and mountainsides.

After two and a half hours of trudging uphill, we reached the halfway mark where Michael signaled us to stop for a much-needed rest. Just as our breathing was returning to some sort of normalcy the fog and clouds rolled towards us bringing the heaviest showers of the day. Our efforts to keep our feet dry became impossible. I climbed into my raincoat and pants thinking I would at least keep my body dry, but soon found the exertion of climbing with the resultant sweat, wet me from the inside out. The next two and a half hours of climbing were absolute hell as we slogged up and down the hills through the muck that was over our ankles. Our shoes became so caked it was difficult to gain any purchase in the mire. My feet were soaked, my body was soaked, my legs had become leaden, and I was getting more and more light-headed.

Just as I felt on the verge of passing out, the forest service hut came into view. I was never so happy to see a building in my life! The three-roomed hut sat beside a lake which was surrounded by sheer cliffs. Herm and I stumbled into the cold empty hut and collapsed on a bed in one of the rooms. As soon as I stopped moving, I started shaking with chills as I was soaked to the bone from head to toe. My fingers were white and numb, and I was becoming disoriented. Hypothermia was upon me. I stripped off my wet garments and put on every piece of dry clothing I had brought. I found enough for seven layers on top and wrapped a blanket around my waist. Herm covered me with four more and also lay on top of me, but I still couldn't stop shivering. Meanwhile, Michael started the kerosene stove, whose fumes gave everyone an instant headache, and heated some water. After two cups of tea, I finally stopped shaking and the feeling came back into my fingers. I had never experienced hypothermia before and never want to again, it was scary.

We hung our soaked clothes next to the kerosene heater after Michael was unable to get a fire going because the wood was too wet. All afternoon the clouds unleashed their water and we huddled near the stove and under the blankets. Michael didn't seem to be in the least affected by the rain or the cold, he still wore no shoes and very few clothes. He just kept boiling water for our tea and noodle soup and attempting to get a wood fire going. He was very patient and helpful, trying hard to make us comfortable.

Not only were we freezing but Herm was suffering from a severe headache and nausea from the 11,500-foot elevation. When 2 a.m. arrived, Herm said he had no intention of getting up in the cold to climb a slippery mountain in the dark, especially when he was suffering from altitude sickness. It had stopped raining and I was agonizing about whether I should go by myself or not. I was feeling I could do it physically, but I just didn't want to get up in the dark and cold and put on wet clothes and shoes. I was afraid of getting hypothermia again. My inertia finally won out and I huddled back under the blankets for some more sleep.

When I got up at first light, Michael rose from his bed on the floor to start the stove for breakfast. The day had dawned bright and clear with the sun sparkling on the lake and the only sound was the water cascading from the rock faces surrounding us. We climbed into our wet gear and got down the mountain so Herm would feel better, then spent the rest of the day washing out our mud-caked clothes and sitting on our front stoop soaking up the warm sun.

It was early morning when I opened the curtains to discover the old man from next door was lining up bows and arrows against the fence across the lane. As soon as we opened the door and said "mornin", people appeared from both directions as if a loudspeaker had announced, "they're up!" It was flea market time! The men brought guy stuff like bows, arrows, pig's tusks, stone axes, bone daggers, and bone carvings. The women's section had multi-colored bilums (string bags), jewelry made from shells, seeds, and teeth, Cassowary headdresses, and fiber belts decorated with shells. One young man was telling Herm about the uses of the different kinds of arrows. One for bird hunting, one for animal hunting and with a grin on his face, he gently stuck an arrow into

Herms's mid-section and said, "this one is used for hunting humans." I sure was glad he had a smile on his face!!

While Herm bargained with the men, the women were having a grand time dressing me in their various wares. A Cassowary feather headdress was tied to my head, several pieces of jewelry were draped around my neck, and a belt was tied around my waist. An old woman then attached a second headdress to herself, grabbed my hand and engaged me in an impromptu dance much to the enjoyment of the remaining women. It was so much fun interacting with these women, they felt like kindred spirits and seemed more free-spirited than ones I had met previously.

We reluctantly said goodbye to our new friends in Kegasugl and made our way to Mendi in relative comfort inside a van instead of the back of a truck! During the five-hour journey, we were befriended by a schoolteacher who offered to escort us to the Mendili Lodge once we reached Mendi. He said it was about a 20-minute walk from town and we needn't worry, as he would be happy to guide us there. This was a big relief as we had no idea how to get there and didn't relish wandering the streets of Mendi alone carrying all our belongings on our backs.

The town was jam-packed with people and Peter told us to wait by the bank for him as he had to deliver a package to someone, but he would be right back. We weren't exactly convinced of our safety in the middle of that crowd, so we leaned our backs to the wall of the bank and just stood there waiting. We must have seemed a bizarre sight to the hundreds of people milling about the area. Here we were, the only white faces in sight, somewhat bedraggled, large backpacks strapped to our backs, just standing there leaning against the side of the bank. Who knows what they were thinking, but all eyes were upon us, and especially on me, as there were very few white women backpackers who traveled to PNG.

Eventually, the people attached to those eyes began to file past us staring as if we were an art exhibit or a freak show or something. When we said "apinoon" to each person who passed we got the same in return with big smiles. The old people came up to us with their shining eyes, big toothless grins and warm handshakes, while the young women smiled shyly. The adolescent and young men looked grim and serious and began to circle us like sharks coming in for a kill. Ninety-nine percent of the people were open, friendly and wonderful as they were all over the country, but the look of those young men made me really nervous.

A number of folks asked if they could help us, but we told them no, we were waiting for our friend. We waited and waited and waited, the minutes dragged by, with the sharks circling closer. Not long after we took up our stations at the bank, a young man, about 13 years old, came to stand next to me as if assigning himself as my bodyguard. I must admit I felt somewhat comforted by his presence.

After more than thirty minutes had passed and Peter hadn't returned, we decided we had had enough and would take matters into our own hands. Just as I turned to ask our "bodyguard" where we might find a telephone to call the guest house, another young man materialized out of the crowd to tell us he would take us to one. He guided us to an office down the street, our young protector in tow. Not surprisingly the phone didn't work, and when we told the man in the office, that we wanted to go to the Menduli Guest House, he asked our "bodyguard" if he would take us. That made our young friend beam from ear to ear and as we set off, we were joined by an older boy who also wanted to be our guide. They led us through the crowds, then down a steep muddy hill, where I kept slipping and losing my balance because of the heavy pack. I was so grateful when several kind, wizened old men stepped in to grab my arm or hands to keep me from falling. Once through the slippy-slidey area, it was a long haul up a very steep hill to the guest house where I arrived panting and dripping with sweat. We gave each of our guides a Kina for helping us and they went off smiling from ear to ear. Standing in that crowd, with all the scowling young men sizing up their opportunity to rip us off had been pretty unnerving but we had been rescued again, just as we had been for our entire journey.

That evening, at the family-style dinner served by our hostess, we were telling the other guests how we had felt in town with the young guys gathering around us like predators. They said one of the reasons things had seemed tense was the police had recently burned down 100 houses suspected of harboring Rascals and the church had to step in to keep them from burning their crops as well! The townspeople were up in arms as they said the wrong houses had been targeted.

Note: A few days after leaving Mendi we heard the town had been virtually burned to the ground during rioting which occurred the day after we left. I was thankful we had gotten out of there when we did!

Before dinner, we had been perusing the bulletin board and noticed a handwritten advertisement for a guest house in Tari which is where we were headed the next day. The guidebook had only listed an expensive tourist hotel for that town, so we were very excited to have discovered this notice. Once again, in the nick of time, we are given guidance along our journey.

The all-day PMV trip to Tari turned out to be an expedition straight out of an adventure movie. It began with me joining the women on the plank bench at the back of the truck as Herm engaged in conversation with four friendly young men seated on the side. No sooner had we started when the foursome asked the driver to stop. They ran up the hill to a store and quickly returned with a couple of six-packs of beer. We weren't the only ones on the PMV rolling our eyes at that troubling development. It was obvious they hadn't purchased the brew to enjoy the taste for they gulped it down as quickly as possible, throwing the empties out the back of the truck. At our next stop, they got off and got two more six-packs which they downed just as fast.

Thankfully, they were happy drunks, laughing and singing native songs but trouble came at the next stop when they yelled something to a crowd of men standing nearby. I guess they weren't shouting compliments, as once the words were uttered the whole group of men surged angrily toward the truck. All of us women started banging frantically on the cab and yelling to the driver to get going fast. He did just that as the mob chased us down the road until we were out of sight, with the young men laughing hysterically. Papuans anger easily and it wasn't uncommon for their rage to escalate to murder. I was very thankful the driver was quick to respond!

We made stops at a couple of large villages where crowds were gathered for the Saturday markets. The sight of our white faces caused people to stop what they were doing and just stare. The children would come up to the truck to peer at us with open-mouthed curiosity. As soon as we smiled, they returned the action with giggles attached. It was comical to watch everything stop in mid-motion when people spotted us.

As we approached the village of Margarina, crowds covered the roadway making it almost impossible for the PMV to pass. The atmosphere was tense as the people gathered around two women who appeared to be trying to kill each other! They were both screaming, and one was brandishing a machete, while the other was throwing rocks. The crowd ran and parted and screamed as the women chased one another through the streets. A man, who also appeared to be involved, kept trying to break up the fight but wasn't having much success.

"What's going on?" we asked one of our friends on the PMV.

"I would guess the man is probably the husband of both. The women are most likely fighting because of some jealousy thing. It happens quite often."

Wow! These people are certainly intense, I thought!

Not long after that incident, we passed groups of warriors walking along the road, dressed in native attire, carrying bows with human-killing arrows. Some of the men wore elaborate headdresses and their bodies and faces were painted in some sort of design. Nearby, a village of bush material huts was in flames. It was so unreal, it looked like a set from a movie! Again, we asked our PMV friends what was happening.

"A man from one of the villages was murdered, so this fighting is "payback" for his death. Once a person from the other village has been killed the score will be evened and the hostility will stop, but not before then," he told us matter-of-factly. That was how life had been lived for thousands of years in those parts, and even though the missionaries and the outside world had invaded, the tradition of "payback" continued.

Later in the afternoon, we were nearing our destination but no matter how many times we told our driver we were NOT going to Ambua Lodge, he insisted upon taking us there.

"No, we are going to Koli Guest House," we insisted as we sat in the parking lot of the fancy tourist hotel. It took some prodding for him to move along but finally did so with a shake of his head. He obviously thought we were totally crazy.

Of course, no one knew where Koli Guest House was, so our friends on the PMV suggested we get off at the Catholic Mission and ask there. Our knock at the mission door brought us face to face with a very unfriendly American priest who acted as if Satan was standing before him.

"Hi!" I said brightly, "do you know where the Koli Guest House is?"

"I have no idea what you are talking about," he said gruffly and slammed the door in our faces.

"Whoa!" Herm exclaimed in surprise, "so much for Christian values!"

"Now what?" I asked a bit concerned as we walked back toward the road.

"We know where you want to go," said one of two young boys who approached us. "Follow us."

"What do you know about that!" I grinned to Herm, "I guess our angels are still watching out for us."

We followed the boys down a dirt track that headed into the jungle where they pointed and said, "follow that road."

Just as they turned to leave, we were tag-teamed by another young boy, named Homer, who took over as guide. He was pointing out the sites when we were joined by a group of women wearing traditional grass skirts and tattooed designs on their faces and legs. None of them spoke English but they were all smiles and I hung back with them as Homer and Herm went on ahead. The women shared the nuts they were snacking on and had me repeat some very complicated Huli words. Their laughter at my butchering of their language was infectious and I felt a real connection with those beautiful souls.

As we walked along with our new friends, a van full of tourists from the Ambua Lodge passed us. The faces of the people inside showed their shock at seeing two white folks carrying backpacks walking down the road into the jungle with the natives. Their mouths were literally hanging open. I'm sure they had been told how unsafe it was to walk around and they couldn't believe we were doing it. As the vehicle passed, we noticed a guy about our age, turn in his seat, give us a big smile, and a hearty thumbs up. It looked like he wanted to be with us, instead of being chauffeured around and shown only what the lodge wanted him to see. I felt truly blessed to be out here instead of in some stuffy van.

Our two-mile walk ended when Homer stopped in front of a large bamboo gate and announced we had arrived. We pushed through the opening and followed a narrow path towards a small house where we were met by John, an ex-pat Australian, his Huli wife and their two blue-eyed children. They were shocked to see us, as they hadn't had guests in over two months! They got busy cleaning the bush material guest house as we wandered through the beautiful gardens. Colorful flowers, a multitude of vegetables, a plethora of herbs and fruits were set along winding paths, creating a peaceful Eden.

The guest house was made of woven palm leaf walls, with a dirt floor. It had two sleeping rooms and a primitive kitchen with a one-burner kerosene stove, a table, chairs and some shelves with food supplies. We were shown to a room with two small cots and were told we would be sharing the house with John's 17-year-old brother-in-law, Paul, and his friend Peter-John. Not too far out the back door was the outhouse and another small building containing a shower. A river bordered the back of the property, where women were washing clothes.

The peaceful day turned into a horror movie night with bloodcurdling yells and screams echoing from the direction of the river. It made the heart race and eyes pop open wide, and I was certain I wouldn't want to be caught outside of our walled compound after dark!

Peter-John had appointed himself our caretaker, and had breakfast ready for us when we got up. He had cooked the most nauseating tasting porridge we ever had, but we choked it down with smiles as we didn't want to hurt his feelings. He was a sweet man in his 30s, short and walked with a limp from a motorcycle accident.

Paul, the teenager, tall and good looking, had a real knack for storytelling and regaled us with tales of the Huli people each night. He explained going to war was the Huli man's profession. Murder, theft, rape, were all reasons for revenge and since there is always something to avenge, there never seemed to be any resolution. They would do a raid in the morning, go home in the afternoon and were back at it the next day. He told us gruesome stories of people being shot with arrows and hacked to pieces with axes and machetes. On the other hand, when we saw those same warriors in the village, they would call a friendly, "mornin'" to us as they went to "war work" for the day. It was crazy.

It all seemed so meaningless, but I guess if you are a warrior, you need to go to war! What a crazy system but not all that different from what we still experience in our times in the West. How sad to keep wanting revenge instead of having forgiveness and being able to talk with each other instead of fighting.

We were thrilled when Peter-John said he and Paul wanted to show us around the village. We followed them along narrow dirt paths, through sweet potato gardens and to a place where children were collecting Pie nuts which fell from oak-like trees. I discovered they were what the women had been feeding me the day before. Pigs roamed everywhere and were a traditional form of currency with the mountain people. The more you had the more status and wealth you possessed.

The Huli people, despite being part of large clans, didn't live in a village but built their houses and gardens in isolation, surrounded by huge walls and ditches with only one way in and out. That entrance was guarded by a spiked gate on the other side of a trench, making their houses easier to defend. They are a culture of warriors and don't trust people outside of their clan. Anyone who intruded was believed to be up to no good and could easily be killed. Their speech and language are volatile and forceful, and they always looked and sounded angry. They didn't smile easily and didn't appear to be very friendly. The young men looked fearsome, but the elders were very sweet, smiled a lot and wanted to shake our hands. I wondered about the difference and if it was just a factor of age and experience or of the changing culture and how the younger people were caught between the worlds.

Men lived communally and women stayed in separate houses with their children. At the age of three the young ones were weaned. The boys were sent to live with the men while the girls stayed with their mothers. The couple would then live together again until the woman became pregnant. Thus, married couples were only together every three years which is why men were allowed to have multiple wives. I wondered how the women felt about having the guys move in to get them pregnant and, also how it was for them to give up their little boys at such a young age. Also, how those boys managed without their mothers. Was this why the men were all so war-like and seemed so angry? It certainly didn't seem like a very happy culture, at least not in this day and age.

Each night Herm and I looked forward to story time. The four of us would gather around the candles in the dark and our roommates would have us laughing our asses off or shaking in our boots with the tales they told. The following are a few of the best ones:

This is a story about how new technology was perceived by some of the old people. One day, a boy brought a radio home and left it by the fire where his father sat cooking. Since the radio was "talking", the father asked it if it was hungry but got no response. When he finished cooking the sweet potato, he put one by the radio, but it didn't eat so the father said," do you want some water"? He got no answer, so he put some water by the radio, but it didn't drink. The father said, "oh, you must want some smoke" so he put some smoke by the radio, but it didn't smoke. The father didn't understand why the radio wasn't eating or drinking or smoking. Then he said to himself, "oh, I didn't cut the potato", so he cut the potato, "I didn't open the water", so he opened the water, "I didn't light the smoke", so he lit the smoke. The radio still didn't eat or drink or smoke, but it kept on talking. The father was getting so annoyed with the radio for not responding to his friendly overtures, he smashed the potato into the speaker, poured in the water and stuffed in the smoke but the radio talked on. Now really angry, he got out his knife and chopped up the radio into little pieces and threw it out the door. When the boy came home, he saw his radio in pieces and was very upset. He asked his father what happened and was told "I tried to feed it, I offered it water and a smoke, but it wouldn't take any of my offerings, but just kept on talking, so I took my knife and killed it and threw it away."

I laughed so hard just envisioning that scene, it is kind of like talking to Siri these days when you can't get her to listen!

This next one was about a cousin of Peter-John's, an old man living in the bush, who had never experienced white man's ways. One day, this old man's son brought some rice, tinned fish, a pair of trousers and a warm shirt. They ate the food; the son helped his father into the new clothes and then he left. The problem was the father had never worn clothes and didn't know how to get out of the trousers to go to the bathroom. For a week he urinated and defecated with the pants on until his son returned. The lad, horrified to find what had happened, got his father out of the slacks and told him, "go in the river and swim and swim and swim and never wear those pants again but keep wearing the shirt to keep you warm."

The story of the "Magic men" who resided in every village was pretty creepy. They have the power to do good or evil and Paul told us many send malevolent spirits to others to make them sick and die. Some of these "Magic men" have entities which accompany them through life and when they pass, they ask their sons to take them. If the son refuses, he will die. Paul said when his grandfather passed his father refused to take on the spirits. Three of Paul's brothers then died as did his father. Paul was saved when his uncle took him to another village to live, or he would have died too.

That story reminded me of a recent event we heard about in the Chumbu area. A well-respected, young man, dropped dead of an apparent heart attack. The community was greatly saddened and went to the "Magic man" to find out who had killed him, as they believed someone in the community had taken his spirit. The "Magic man" took a stick which guided him to the culprit, but the person ran away and had himself put in jail for protection. The stick then pointed to the man's wife, so the village people took her away and stoned her to death.

Once again, it was the woman who took the blame.

After a few days with our friends, it was time to fly back to Port Moresby, but they told us it wasn't safe for us to go ourselves, so we had an entourage accompanying us to the airport. Peter-John, dressed in his best clothes and led the way with Herm and some other men, while I hung back with my new friend Elizabeth and some other women who wanted to see us off. As we walked, Elizabeth told me about what it was like to be a woman in that area, how dangerous it was since women were routinely raped, beaten and even murdered. The people of the Highlands were much more warrior-like than the ones we had met on the Sepik and the coast. Such different cultures isolated from each other by the impenetrable mountains of the beautiful country.

When we approached the main road, the tension in our little group rose as we entered the crowd going to market. Two mean looking dudes began joking with the girls and eyeing our packs, so Peter-John began to slow his pace saying he was getting tired. As we dropped back with him, he said quietly, "they are Rascals, we should let them walk ahead."

As we encountered more and more groups of hungry sharks, Peter said, "I think it's safer if we walk behind the runway instead of going through town."

We were relieved as we were feeling very uncomfortable.

The folks at the Jalair office kindly provided us with chairs and a shady, safe place to sit, within a fenced area, while we waited for our flight. I sat gawking at all the traditionally dressed, almost naked men with their colorful, crescent shaped Huli headdresses, arm and leg bands, necklaces made of teeth, Kina shell, hornbill and bone.

A huge crowd had gathered on the hillside for the big once a week event. Hundreds of men in native dress looked like a war party waiting for their cue to descend on the arriving passengers. Off to the side a group of guys were fighting, yelling and throwing rocks. It was wild! Was this what the Old West was like?

When our plane landed, the crowd surged toward the fence and our friends encircled us to keep the little pickpockets away. Even with that I caught one young boy trying to sneak his hand into Herm's pants. When I grabbed him and said, "Don't you dare!" He just smiled and shrugged. Rascal in training!

In the midst of all the chaos, we were dumbstruck as a blonde woman stepped off the arriving flight, blouse opened to her breasts and festooned with gold jewelry. Oh my God, talk about dangling a morsel of meat in front of a hungry lion! What was she thinking? As soon as she reached the gate, the staff from Ambua Lodge surrounded her and quickly whisked her away as the Rascals were closing in.

We bid our friends and guardian angels good-bye and with relief, boarded the plane to Port Moresby. As much as we loved living in National Geographic for three weeks, we were looking forward to stuffing ourselves with pizza, spaghetti and garlic bread. We never wanted to see another bowl of porridge ever again! Civilization, here we come!

Dear Diary....

WOW! WOW! WOW! What an adventure THAT was! It isn't every day you get to have your childhood dreams come true. I am SO grateful! A bit scary at times but really fun!

What made it so special was hanging out with the locals and learning about the culture. Such dear, dear people, who always watched out for us. Also being in nature most of the time was a real plus.

Herm has been great this whole trip but spending ALL our time together exclusively can get a bit wearing. I had "asked" to meet other people and we did! I realize more and more that we get what we ask for, we just need to have patience and trust.

Certainly, the trust thing was big in this visit as well, I think I have finally gotten it through my head that all will be taken care of, and we are always watched over. You just have to have an open heart and be in a positive vibration and that is what will come back. It certainly did here and in spades.

The only thing that bugged me a bit was Herm flying back to Wewak after our Sepik adventure and not going on the PMV with me. I know his back was hurting but I would have gone with him if our positions were reversed. I don't think enduring some discomfort is a big deal but that's me. Maybe him taking care of himself is more important? Not sure.

Now we are off to the city and our first REAL Asian country. I wonder how this will go? I'm not sure I am ready?

CHAPTER 5

CHINA

Alittle too much civilization too fast! The frenzy and sensory overload of Kowloon and Hong Kong were totally overwhelming after the natural world and primitive culture of PNG. It was our first Asian country, and we were finding the cultural differences hard to adjust to. The sense of personal space was so different. It felt like people were always in our faces, which was totally annoying. Then there was the lack of what we consider manners. Pushing and shoving, not standing politely in a line, spitting food out and leaving it on the table, blowing noses on the street, my mother would have been appalled! We definitely weren't in Kansas anymore!

Visas in hand, we planned on spending a month exploring China, but two weeks was all we could take. Even though we met some wonderful people, I found myself angry most of the time. I didn't know if it was due to the abrupt change of culture or if it had something to do with an unpleasant past life in China a psychic once told me about.

The trip actually started off well when a Chinese man kindly intervened to help us change money. We had been trying every which way and backward to get the woman at the hotel to understand what we wanted. Our frustration level was rising quickly as we were getting absolutely nowhere!

"Here, let me help," the older Chinese man said, "I have been assisted by many Americans when I have traveled in the US, and I love to return the favor when I can."

"Thanks so much!" we replied gratefully.

"Where are you headed?" he asked.

"We are planning on taking the overnight boat trip down the Pearl River."

"That's great," he said. "Why don't you let me set that up for you?"

"Awesome!" we said in surprise!

Once the money situation was resolved, we stood aside as our friend asked the woman to call and reserve our spaces. "All set," he said as he joined us.

He handed us a piece of paper saying, "this is a note for your taxi driver to get you to the right place. Just check in with the office when you get there."

"We can't thank you enough," we both enthused.

We said our goodbyes and as he walked away, I said to Herm, "Wow, we are really being looked after today, what are the odds we would be next to the one man who was willing to help. Definitely our angel!"

"Totally agree, I am grateful," Herm said as we shouldered our packs to go find a taxi.

We got to the dock thinking we would be leaving at 4 p.m. but when we bought our tickets, we were pointed toward our boat which was leaving in 10 minutes! We had no time to think, just move, following pointing fingers to the dock, then across four bobbing boats tied side by side. With my big pack behind and a small one in front, it was all about balance navigating the moving boats and I was afraid I would plunge into the dirty water at any moment.

Once onboard we followed more pointing fingers, to our cabin below decks and were delighted we were the only ones there! The door opened to a small room with two bunk beds on either side, each with a foam cushion covered by a bamboo mat, a blanket and a pillow. We followed the urine smell to the bathrooms down the alleyway and discovered our first squat toilets. A porcelain bowl sunk into the floor with ridges on either side to put your feet. Not growing up Asian was a distinct disadvantage as my squatting muscles definitely weren't in shape. Holding onto the wall to keep from falling over I mused this would certainly take some getting used to! There were three decks, two of which had cabins like ours but the third had what can only be described as concentration camp beds. They were two-story slabs running the length of the boat divided by 4-inch petitions. I was happy our angel friend had reserved the cabin bunks as I didn't think I was quite ready for the prison beds yet!

Standing on deck we watched the sampans, ferries, barges, and others cruise the busy Pearl River where everyone threw their garbage and human waste. The buildings along the shore looked dirty and decrepit, black smoke poured from stacks, the air was hazy with smog, the water brown. I was appalled people actually fished, bathed and washed clothes in that filth.

"Hello," I said with a smile to the old man standing near me.

He replied in Chinese, so I held up my finger to signal "wait" as I dug out my tiny language book. He took the book and pointed out a phrase which read, "what is your name?"

I said, "my name is Terra," as I pointed to my chest and smiled. A group of young men quickly gathered around us, all wanting to get involved. They tried saying the English words in the book while we attempted the Chinese. Much fun was had by all and after the old man had read the entire book, he handed it back and we said good night.

I had spoken too soon about having a private room. When the boat made a stop at 9:30 p.m. we were joined by two men, one of whom was very friendly and tried to talk with us. When the language book didn't work, we all smiled, turned off the light and went to sleep. At 3 a.m. I was startled awake by the wriggling of a large cockroach crawling on me. I flipped it off in disgust, but it hit Herm who was in the other upper bunk. That woke him and he flipped it to the wall where it eventually either made it out the door or onto the guys below us. I wasn't as freaked out as I had been in Australia, I guess I was starting to become a real adventurer!

At 6 a.m. the boat docked in Wuzchuo where we were directed to the bus station. We played charades for twenty minutes, with three women, while trying to communicate our wishes for a bus to Yangshuo. They gestured back trying to tell us when, where, how long and how much. They were sweet and we all had a good laugh before we finally got it straightened out.

Yangshuo and the surrounding region are known for their karst mountains. The scenery was like something out of a fairy tale. Hundreds of limestone pinnacles sprouted sharply skyward from the vibrant green farmland which hugged the sinuous Li River. Lush vegetation embraced the steep rock faces speaking to the excessive moisture experienced in this area. It was totally magical, and we were looking forward to exploring.

Rain was falling lightly as we rode our rented bicycles out of busy Yangshuo into the mysterious, mist-covered countryside. As we peddled along the quiet road, we saw people working the rice fields or tending gardens and animals. Women washed clothes in the streams, children played in the muck and mire and yelled hellos and goodbyes as we rode past. This was more like it, peaceful farmland and friendly people, I guess it is true in all countries that rural folk are more relaxed and welcoming than city folks.

A sign by the side of the road read: "Black Cave, Best Cave, Come In, Welcome, 200m." We both went, "Oh cool, a cave, let's go!" We wondered if it would be like the one we had toured in New Zealand? We walked our bikes up a path that ended at a wooden door set into the hillside.

"Um, I wonder what we do now?" I asked.

As we looked around, we noticed a man in the rice paddy below yelling and waving his hat while simultaneously calling in the direction of a stone house. The waving man soon arrived and through sign language, explained his son was on the way. The boy, who came running up the hill, looked about 14 years old and was carrying four flashlights. He handed one each to Herm, me and his father. The old man stationed himself by the entrance of the cave as the boy beckoned us to follow him inside.

As we stepped into the cool darkness, I felt the vastness of the expanse around us. It was almost like falling into deep space and was quite dizzying. With only the beam from our feeble lights in that cavernous blackness, it brought up all the old childhood fears of something lurking in the shadows. Not knowing what lay to either side of the path, I concentrated on placing one foot in front of the other imagining being swallowed in a deep black pit if I strayed an inch to either side. I was very aware that if our lights went out, we were screwed. I was thankful papa was standing at the door but wondered how he would know if something happened? Would our screams even reach his ears? Squeezing through narrow passageways we were spat out into immense chambers which made me feel very small and insignificant. I was thankful our young guide seemed very familiar with the layout of the cave and was ever mindful of shining his light on the path for us. Even though he spoke little English he was able to convey how some of the stalactites and stalagmites had formed into the shape of animals and how each formation held a different note when "played".

We eventually emerged from a second door where papa stood looking relieved we had made it. We thanked the boy and his dad; paid our fee and walked our bikes back toward the road.

"Oh man, that was awesome," I enthused.

"Totally! It's the best cave tour we have had yet!" Herm grinned.

"It felt like we were in the womb of the earth," I said. "No electric lights, no other tourists or loud tour guides, just us small humans being held by the mountain in total silence and complete darkness. I felt a presence, did you? Nothing negative, maybe the presence of the mountain?"

"Yes," Herm replied, "it was very strong. I definitely felt we were only visitors."

Touring the countryside had been wonderful but even though the people in Yangshuo were laid back and friendly, the culture was making us grouchy. In addition to that, we were starting to get sick from all the rain and mold in our room. Our pillows, bedding, clothes, were all damp and mildewy, nothing ever dried out. The floor and chairs were all a nice shade of gray/brown mold and even Herms's shoes were growing gray patches. We figured we'd be next if we didn't get out of there. We considered pushing on to a different city but we both decided we had had enough; China just wasn't our place. We needed to make our way back to Kowloon and see what our next country would bring.

The short flight to Guangzhou was totally bizarre. The Chinese passengers pushed their way onto the plane, yelled to each other the whole trip and never stopped taking pictures. The flight attendants were stone-faced; peanuts and a watery sugar drink in a carton were tossed to us; no trash was collected; there were no safety instructions; no one bothered to check if seat belts were fastened or tray tables up. On our approach for landing, I thought the plane would surely tip over as most of the passengers got up and crowded to one side of the plane. They jabbered loudly, craning their necks to see out the windows. As soon as we landed, they scrambled to their feet and rushed for the door as we sat and waited for the mob to pass.

The "drama" continued at the railroad station. Before we could even get out of the cab we were accosted by an old woman and two kids begging for money. I was in no mood for this and told them to "fuck off". When one of the kids kept pulling on my sleeve, I threatened to hit him with my pack. I had turned into an ugly American monster! It was all way too much for me.

We couldn't find the ticket counter, couldn't find anyone who spoke English, went to the CITS office only to find they were closed for another hour. I was soaked with sweat, disgusted, angry and sick. Just then a man in the crowd who must have seen our distress asked, "can I help you?"

"Yes!" Herm said with relief, "we are trying to get tickets to Senshen but have no idea where to get them!"

"Come with me," the kind man said, "I am also going there."

The line was long and just as we reached the window, they ran out of tickets! ARGH!!!.

"Oh no," I wailed in despair.

Charles, the nice man, said "don't worry, if you want, we can split a taxi fare for almost the same price as the train."

"Yes," I said in frustration, anything to get out of here."

Finally, the three of us settled into an air-conditioned cab and we were on our way! I was so grateful the "Universe" took pity on us and sent another good Samaritan. It was interesting that when we arrived at this station, we had our first angel and when leaving the same place, we were sent another. I knew we were being looked after and I was very grateful.

My last frustrating encounter with Chinese bureaucracy came when I tried to cash my traveler's checks in Hong Kong. Because they had gotten wet from my sweat, they wouldn't take them! Seriously?? They sent me to the American Express office, and they said they wouldn't cash them because I had already signed them at the other bank!! ARGH! On top of that, they told me I hadn't bought them where I said I had. That was the last straw, I was SO fucking done with the stupid Chinese system! Onward to Singapore where I hoped everything would be better, including my sour mood.

Dear Diary.....

OMG!!! What is wrong with me? I totally lost my shit in China. I was SO frustrated all the time with all the bureau-crazy! There were two kinds of money and it seemed you never had the right kind, so it was always an argument. Everything had to be just so, even trying to mail a package was a total shit-show! Contents had to be examined, things had to be packed just so, then wrapped just so, then addressed just so! ARGH!

I wonder why I got so triggered with all of that? Must be the old "I don't like to be told what to do thing?" LOL. I guess I wouldn't make a very good communist, I like thinking for myself too much.

As usual, everything bothered me more than it did Herm. He seems much better at rolling with the punches than I am but even he wanted out of there! I am still SO tense!

Well, I just have to calm down and hope Singapore isn't as bad and then we'll go for a beach vacation in Malaysia. I am looking forward to that. We REALLY need some easy traveling to recharge after China!

CHAPTER 6

SINGAPORE & MALAYSIA

Let me tell you a little story about our introduction to the super clean, modern Singapore the government prides itself on.

Once upon a time, there were two weary world travelers who had been on the road for four months. During that time, they had experienced cold, heat, humidity, smoke, dust, noise, roaches and mosquitoes. Some of the rooms they had rented were dirty, had stained sheets, holes in the walls and broken plumbing. They had gotten pretty cool about everything and had come to accept most situations. On June 6th they arrived in Singapore, tired and stinky, and checked into a small Chinese "crash pad" which appeared pretty clean. A balcony overlooked the street, a fan spun lazily, there was a broken toilet down the hall and a slimy shower. After perusing the city, eating and reading, they settled down for a restful night's sleep under the whirring fan.

Tossing and turning began almost immediately as they felt as if something was tickling the hairs on their legs, taking little bites out of them. Feeling restless, Daisy got up in the dark and went to the balcony for some air. She tried settling again only to be awakened by tickling feelings whenever she was dropping off to sleep. Up again, she found Herm in the same state, so they decided to turn on the light to see what was going on. EEEEEEEEEEK, AAAAAAhhh, their beds, clothes, walls and packs were crawling with bugs! Quarter-inch, shield-shaped, gray-brown bugs and "spider-mite" sized red-brown ones were everywhere!

Bug flicking and bug squashing commenced amidst grimaced faces and high-pitched disgusted squeals from Daisy. The sheets were cleared but the intrepid travelers were surrounded by the creatures crawling on the walls, packs and clothes. They sat in the middle of their beds frantically looking around them, horrified to see more appear on the bedding as if by magic, seemingly materializing out of thin air. They did the unthinkable and bravely lifted the mattress to discover thousands of creatures scurrying for cover. Totally grossed out they looked at each other with pained expressions and said plaintively "what are we going to do?"

Daisy, being of semi-sound mind said, "Well Herm, we have three options: 1) sleep with the bugs 2) sit up with the bugs all night and watch, squash and flick 3) find a new hotel at 1 a.m." #3 was considered and eliminated as impractical, #1 was out of the question, so #2 was acted upon.

Daisy sat cross-legged and vigilant in the middle of her bed reading of peaceful, bug-free beaches in Malaysia, but between paragraphs would glance around to flick off the latest invasion. Meanwhile, Herm was getting sicker from his recent cholera shot and more desperate to sleep. Something more drastic had to be done. An abandoned mosquito coil holder was discovered under the bed and thoughts of previous bed-bug victims killing armies with poisonous gas came to mind. Packs were quickly opened to find coils and matches and just as quickly closed to keep the enemies out. The fire was lit with angst over the possibility of alighting the bedclothes. Herm and Daisy waited, the bugs continued to advance, oblivious to the fumes, as the travelers coughed and sputtered from the gas. The flame was quickly extinguished to save their lungs. The bug army had won that round.

The squishing and flicking continued to stave off the hordes, but Daisy and Herm tried frantically to think of what to do next.

"The Rid!" Herm cried, "get the Rid mosquito repellent."

"Oh, that won't work," Daisy scoffed, but Herm insisted.

She quickly zipped open and closed her pack, flipping and squishing as she went to prevent bug invasion of the inner sanctum. Herm doused himself with Rid and lay down again to try to sleep while Daisy kept watch.

Out of nowhere, Daisy seized upon the idea of smearing Rid on the sheets as a barrier to the invaders. She experimented with a small dab, nudging the troops close to see what they would do. They retreated, woohoo!! Daisy encircled herself with a line of repellent and Herm did the same.

It looked like our travelers had finally won but they were cautious and skeptical. Herm slept while Daisy kept watch. When she was convinced no soldiers would cross the boundary, she carefully curled herself into the middle of the bed and dozed fitfully. The light was left on so every few minutes either Herm or Daisy could examine the battle line to be sure no creatures were getting through. During one such check, Daisy raised the alarm, "the line is breached, the line is breached!" More Rid was applied to bulk up the defenses, but alas, the ammunition was depleted, and the fortification work could not be completed in toto. The pair curled within their fortresses as the enemies massed at the borders waiting for an errant toe or finger to cross the line to provide a bridge to the interior. The pair hoped they could hold off until dawn and could do nothing but doze and wait.

Morning light appeared just as the barriers were crashed but Herm and Daisy were up and out, shaking their clothes free of the clinging enemies and beating a hasty retreat to the streets below and a new and clean hotel. BUT...........Dum di dum dum, EEEEEEEEEEKKK! The invaders had hidden in Herm and Daisy's clothes, there was no escape, the attackers were with them still!

The bedbugs did indeed hitch a ride with us from Bencoolen House to the Southeast Asia Hotel. They appeared on the walls at night, and we also found some in our packs! We felt terrible we had contaminated that super clean lodging! We did a lot of squishing and just hoped we got all of them.

That wasn't to be our only bug incident in Singapore, however. Always on the lookout for inexpensive places to eat, we were excited to find an open-air restaurant serving stir-fried veggies. We sat at an outside table chowing down our pile of noodles and veg when .....

"Hmmm, there is something crunchy in here," I said to Herm, as I searched through the noodles. "Well, what do you know, it seems the cook didn't understand when I ordered the vegetarian," I mused, as I held up the body of a cockroach.

"Oh yuck," he choked as he pawed through his own food. It appeared I was the only one who had received the non-veg meal. Never one to waste food, I picked out the rest of the bodies and wings and continued eating. No worries, they WERE deep fried!

Between stir-fried cockroach and bed bugs, we were looking forward to moving to Malaysia and its dazzling beaches. We were SO in need of a vacation.

It was now the middle of June and instead of weeding my burgeoning vegetable garden in New Hampshire, I was walking across the border from Singapore into our first Moslem country, Malaysia. We were tired and looking forward to some lazy beach time where we didn't have to make big decisions every day!

Tioman Island was our destination as we putt-putted four hours in a decrepit, open fishing boat which belched diesel fumes and rolled in the waves. Even though I don't get seasick easily, I was on the verge of hurling after riding in that contraption for hours! Just as I was about to get a second taste of my lunch, we pulled up to the longest dock I had ever seen. It ended on the sands of a deserted beach lined with swaying coconut palms. A tropical island paradise that immediately calmed my roiling stomach. Before us was a post covered with crude wooden signs advertising lodging with arrows pointing in both directions. Not knowing whether to go right or left, we flipped a coin and "right" won.

Not far down that right-hand path, we stopped at a small cafe to fill our stomachs and ponder what to do next. Wanting to keep things simple we decided to stay right where we were, the Nordin's Guest House and Cafe. Our beach house was a tiny A-frame with the entire interior taken up by a raised platform covered by a mattress. We dropped our bags, changed into our swimsuits and melted into the warm sea. It was hard to believe we were floating in the tropical waters, off the coast of Malaysia, with this stretch of beach in front of our guest house, all to ourselves. No city noises, no Rascals, no bedbugs, no uptight Chinese, no decisions except what to eat and how long to sleep. This was heaven!

A thunderstorm had been booming its way towards us from the mainland all day and just as we finished showering and washing clothes the storm hit with a fury. Herm and I sat on the porch of the proprietor's house and marveled at the downpour. Storm tossed dinghies fought their way through the waves offshore, coconuts plummeted to the beach, palm fronds crashed onto the aluminum roof, and the thunder was deafening. It was our first experience of a tropical thunderstorm, and we were quite impressed!

Neither of us liked sitting around for too long so we were off on a hike. Our destination was a small village further up the island which we thought was reached by walking along the beach. Much to our surprise, the path led into the thick jungle and over several mountains, not what we were expecting at all! The forest was lush and full of wildlife. Monkeys and lemurs peered at us from above hooting as we passed, some sort of squirrel and chipmunk lookalikes scurried in the undergrowth and lizards were everywhere. I love reptiles so I was thrilled when we surprised a four-foot Monitor Lizard which scurried away on our approach.

Fist-sized vines were utilized to haul ourselves up the steep stretches of the trail and also to grasp to keep us from slipping down the inclines. All the while, we had to be cognizant of the nasty plants, covered with thorns, which tried to grab us unexpectedly and painfully. Every now and then the path would end suddenly at a secluded, white sand beach where we would stop to rest and cool off in the water. Upon leaving one of those beaches, we became disoriented and couldn't find the trail we had emerged from. I am usually great at finding my way in nature, but I was stumped. We searched and searched but it was as if it had just disappeared. We were getting a little nervous so asked for "help" from our "guides" and a few minutes later, the only human we had seen all day appeared and set us back in the right direction. We smiled at each other and said, "Thank You 'Universe'!"

Four hours after leaving our guest house, we arrived at the small village of Salang to collapse in the first restaurant we came to. We guzzled bottles of water, then hit the waves to cool off and do some snorkeling. Feeling rejuvenated, we headed back over the mountains, but this time encountered rain which turned the dirt into a mudslide, and once again the trail suddenly disappeared! Since it had worked last time, we asked for "help" and this time it wasn't a human but a squirrel who came to our rescue. He was on a log in front of us and kept coming towards us and going away as if he was beckoning us to follow. Follow we did and were led directly to the lost path! Phew! Twice in one day, we had been rescued.

Four relaxing days lying in hammocks beneath the palm trees, roaming the beach, swimming and snorkeling, had refreshed us both physically and emotionally. It was also the first time we had the opportunity to connect with fellow travelers. Some had been "on the road" for many months and it was fun to exchange stories and get travel tips. With all that under our belts, we were ready to plunge back in and get moving. This time, however, we said no more fishing boats and treated ourselves to a tourist craft back to the mainland!

The climate in Kota Baru, on the northeast coast of Malaysia, was as torrid as Darwin, Australia but the cuisine was amazing! Just across from our guesthouse, we discovered a night market with dozens of food stalls. Everything looked and smelled incredible but with no idea what anything was we had a hard time choosing. Luckily, a kind young man saw our confusion and walked us from stall to stall explaining the contents of each dish. We took our selections to the eating area and sat at a picnic table with several other people. There were no utensils in sight but come to find out we come equipped with our own – fingers! We copied our fellow table mates and dug in. This was our first experience with "finger" eating, it was like being a little kid with no one telling you not to touch your food! Even though we had been ugly Americans in China, we were determined to mend our ways and fit in with cultures for the rest of the trip.

It was so humid I was pouring sweat sitting still. We were both feeling so disoriented and kept saying "where ARE we?" I like Pico Iyer's quote about traveling, "the exotic becomes familiar, and the familiar becomes the exotic." It was very true and made me feel weirded out at times. This way of living was becoming the familiar and the Western ways were slowly becoming the exotic.

Were we listening to a pornographic movie? Day and night loud moans, groans and screams echoed off the tall ceiling. A huge room in the guest house was divided into tiny cubicles just big enough for a bed. With the walls only three-quarters of the way to the high ceiling every sound above a whisper echoed. Some of us guests were lounging in the adjoining sitting room listening to the sexual athletes, sneaking looks at each other, rolling our eyes and giggling. Did anyone know who these people were, we asked? "Nope!" Shortly after the screams of ecstasy stopped, we heard the couple walking down the corridor toward us and all eyes were surreptitiously watching the doorway to see who would emerge. I had to stifle a laugh as the major noise maker turned out to be a petite young Indian woman swathed head to toe in drapes of cloth. The sight of her and the animal sounds which had emanated from the room were quite incompatible.

A ferry ride from the west coast city of Butterworth brought us to Georgetown, the capital of the state of Penang, Malaysia. The Chinese hotel we had chosen from the guidebook was owned by a wizened proprietor who was all business, no smiles and very particular. It felt like we were writing our life stories just to register, not once but twice! The place had an air of mystery that was very intriguing. A large lobby with ornately carved wooden chairs lined the walls, an old desk was topped with a bulky black telephone, an abacus and a "No Spitting" sign. The back of the hotel was open to a courtyard with two wings. Outside staircases climbed to the second floor which had a metal railed walkway in front of the rooms. One small tree huddled in a corner near a kitchen area strewn with woks and utensils.

Throughout our stay, I sometimes felt we were living in a John Irving novel with all the strange characters who resided there. A skinny, ancient Chinese man with thick glasses sat curled in a chair in the lobby for most of the day squinting at a newspaper. Every evening, American country and western tunes were strummed on a guitar by a friendly, middle-aged, Oriental man but the most curious of all were the two humans who were so strange in appearance we were unable to decide if they were male or female or even oriental or occidental! One was petite and slim with long dark hair and a deep voice. He/she walked around with a towel wrapped around the body as a woman would. Another was a very tall, beefy person with a voice like a woman. A third, who we never saw, sang haunting tunes, in a high voice from behind one of the doors upstairs. Except for the two elderly Chinese men, the rest of the hotel gang were very friendly and welcoming. I loved this crew; they were right up my alley as I am always drawn to people who are a bit different. Same reason I like John Irving novels!

Tioman had been a great respite, but Malaysia wasn't our place and we were excited to get to Indonesia. With 25,000 islands to choose from, it was difficult to know where to start but since Sumatra was just an overnight boat trip away, we decided to start there.

Dear Diary....

Well, I guess I'm a real traveler now that I have passed the bed bug initiation. I know from now on I will look under mattresses before paying for a room! LOL

I never would have guessed travelers need vacations from traveling but we sure do! Making decisions on a day in and day out basis is exhausting! Where to go next, where to stay, where to eat, how to get to the next place and the list goes on.....and on...and on!

The Tioman Island stay was the BEST beach vacation I had ever experienced! I had been on a number of Caribbean Island trips with my first husband's company but never felt comfortable with the tourist hotel scene. I had to look and act a certain way to fit in and it was difficult not being myself. It was also wearing being with our group who I had nothing in common with. On Tioman, I could be the down and dirty me and look any way I wanted. There was no dressing up to go have cocktails at the bar and hang around with a bunch of drunks. Here it was flip flops or bare feet, shorts and a t-shirt. Even that was a treat as I had been mindful to always wear long skirts out of respect for the Muslim culture. Here it didn't matter, I could wear what I wanted.

It was also totally awesome to hang out with so many other travelers. It was actually the first time we had gotten that opportunity for days in a row. Sitting in cafes swapping stories and travel info, playing cards or lying on the sand watching the stars while talking about our families was something I treasured. It didn't matter that we were so much older than everyone else, we were all just travelers experiencing new cultures far away from what was familiar.

I hope to have many more opportunities to hang out with other wanderers in the months to come. Maybe we will find some in Indonesia!!!

CHAPTER 7

INDONESIA

The overnight ferry ride from Malaysia to Sumatra was a hoot! It was filled with travelers, and they were all in a party mood. We hung out with Jenny, who was about our age and were soon joined by Jock, a tall, good-looking, recent college graduate from the Netherlands and Sue and Peter, an outgoing couple from Australia. We became our own little pack and did our best to get some sleep curled up on the floor with the rest of the adventurers.

Upon arriving in Sumatra, we parted ways with our new friends as they were going to visit the Orangutans before joining us in Brastagi. A brightly painted minibus packed with people, luggage and produce stacked on top, was our ride to the mountains. We stuffed ourselves into the only remaining seat which was in the back of the bus, and I thanked God I had a window. I am a bit claustrophobic at the best of times but when you add cigarette smoke to the mix, I was in danger of having a panic attack. I grew up with parents who were heavy smokers and it always felt like I was pushing through a blue fog whenever I went into the kitchen. I so hated those fumes and it made me cough and feel like I couldn't breathe. The smoke in the bus hung from the low ceiling and was so thick I could barely see the front where the bursar was literally pushing people in to get the tightest fit possible. The folks who couldn't be shoehorned in hung from the roof and out the doors. I kept my face glued to the window imagining I was outside, so I wouldn't lose it!

We careened through the busy streets of Medan, horn blaring, dodging people and other motor vehicles. The fun began when we barely missed hitting a car and another bus, but I guess our driver thought the car had hit him. He screeched to a halt, jumped out, pulled the car's driver onto the road and started throwing punches. The Chinese man was backing up when his son vaulted from the car, yelling, fists up, ready to dive in. The wife then flew out of the vehicle, screaming, pocketbook swinging to protect both her men. If that wasn't enough, a second man interposed himself in the melee and began pulling the wife's hair!

All this action drew a large crowd as riders jumped off our bus. Cars and trucks stopped, and their occupants spilled out to gawk at the scene. The whole brouhaha took place directly outside of our window, so our fellow passengers were literally hanging all over us, hands on our shoulders, to get a good view of the fight. Finally, a couple of levelheaded bystanders got things calmed down and our still fuming driver jumped back into the bus and raced off.

Welcome to Indonesia, the land of peaceful people!

We left the craziness of the city behind and started to gain elevation. Mountains, valleys, gardens, clean, neat, modern-looking homes, sat next to older palm roofed dwellings. In many ways, the scenery reminded us of the Papua New Guinea Highlands. The air became cooler, drier and very refreshing. I felt as if I could breathe again as we came to the small city of Brastagi deep in the mountains.

Our guidebook recommended Wisma Sibayak, a guest house run by a family who catered to travelers. The bulletin board in the common room was pinned full of information about local treks, proposed trips, and village events. There was a restaurant, a garden, tables on the lawn, and a place to wash clothes. The rooms were simple but clean.

There were no showers or hot water to be found, instead, we had our first introduction to a "Mandi," the traditional Indonesian way of washing oneself. A large concrete pool sat in the middle of a cement floored room with a drain in the middle. The first time I went in there, I had no idea what I was supposed to do. Was I supposed to get in the pool? I found out the deal was the following: disrobe; hang your clothes and towel on pegs; take the large cup sitting on the edge of the pool; fill it full of the cold water; take a deep breath and dump it over your head, trying not to scream; soap up; repeat the cold-water torture to rinse. To make this at all tolerable, we learned to wash when we were hot and sweaty and never at night when it was cold.

The pace in Brastagi was slow and the people were open and friendly. There was plenty to do and when we weren't hanging around playing cards and socializing with our friends, we climbed our first volcano and walked the village lanes. We even attended a wedding and a reburial ceremony which our guesthouse owners arranged. On the ride back from the wedding, we were squashed in with some local women who asked if we would like to see some dancing at their village and we said "sure". We arrived when the final dance was about to start and were invited to participate. I was the first to volunteer with many in our group following. There was a line of women on one side and a line of men on the other. The dance started off slowly, we dipped our bodies, moving our outstretched hands with palms down then up to correspond with our body movements. This was done slowly and rhythmically by the locals and spasmodically by us. The music sped up and our movements became even more erratic. The dance ended with the women, smiling sexily, beckoning to the men. Once the guys came closer, however, the women laughed and pushed them away. The crowd was roaring at the round eyes stumbling through the moves. What a great time was had by all, connecting with fellow humans on the other side of the world.

Our little group of friends, Jenny, Jock, Sue and Peter, shared a bumpy taxi ride with us to Lake Toba which fills a humongous, ancient volcanic crater. A decrepit ferry chugged us to Samosair Island where we found comfortable duplex cabins situated on the shore of the lake.

The village of Tomok, not far from our cabin, was densely packed with tourist shops carrying a colorful collage of hand-woven cloths, wooden carvings, walking sticks, antiques, and much more. The selling style of the shop owners was assertive but not as overbearing as the Chinese vendors we had encountered earlier. Herm looked at a few old knives, but the opening prices were too high. He picked up one with a bone handle and asked "barapa"(how much) and the smiling old woman answered 200,000 rupiahs.

Herm smiled, "that's way too high" and walked away.

"What is your price?" she called in a sweet but pleading tone.

Herm answered, "if I give a price, you will get angry."

"No angry," she said teasingly.

On a lark, I chimed in, "20,000 rupiahs."

The old woman didn't flinch and said, "too low, 80,000 rupiahs."

I started moving away shaking my head saying, "too much".

She then said, "50,000 rupiahs."

And Herm got sucked back into the bidding. He smiled and said, "25,000 rupiahs."

She shook her head and sighed, "my grandmother gave me this knife and would be angry if I sold it too cheaply."

Herm laughed and said, "don't make your grandmother angry," and turned away.

"30,000 rupiahs" she called, Herm answered back, "27,000 rupiahs, as we drifted further down the road with the shop owner and a crowd following us.

"3000 rupiahs more for my children." she pleaded.

Herm knew he was in trouble when she dragged her kids and grandmother into it.

He came back with, "I already gave you 2000 rupiahs for your kids."

She smiled. We were halfway back to our cabin when she yelled, "29,000 rupiahs."

Herm and I looked at each other and laughed, the crowd around us waiting expectantly.

"Oh, okay, 29,000 rupiahs it is!"

The sale was made, the crowd cheered and slapped Herm on the back. Now, that was fun, I may finally get the hang of this bargaining stuff.

On a small hill overlooking the shops, we explored an old cemetery. A tall, good-looking, young Batak man politely introduced himself and asked if he could tell us about the graveyard in order to practice his English. We were delighted and happily agreed. Lucas stood nervously at attention in front of us relating the Batak legends of the stones. He explained the huge Egyptian-looking image carved into the stone sarcophagus was the resting place of the Batak King. According to legend, it had originally resided at the top of the mountain but was moved, by magic, to its present position. The king's slave and lover were in the smaller sarcophagi beside him. Lucas proudly related this dead king was a distant relative of his.

After the history lesson and a tour of the local museum, we invited Lucas to join us for lunch. While we ate, he said he was disappointed he couldn't take us to visit his village and family. Unfortunately, this was his only day off and his village was many miles away. Before we parted company he stated, "I want to give you a gift so you will always remember Samosair Island. Would it be all right if I bring it to your Losman this evening?"

"Of course," we said. "That would be wonderful!"

That evening, we entered the dining room at our lodging to find Lucas waiting nervously in a chair. When he spotted us, he jumped up, face alight with a big smile.

"I am so glad to see you again," he grinned shyly. I was so happy to meet you and tell you about my special island. I want to give you this so you will happily remember me and my home forever."

He held out a package wrapped in newspaper secured with elastics and said, "please do not open now, wait until later."

"Thank you so much, Lucas, this is really sweet of you," we said as we hugged.

"It was great to meet you as well and we will always remember our time on this wonderful island."

"I hope you will visit here again," he said. "Now I must be getting back to my village, may God bless you."

Inside the newspaper, we found a sweet note, addressed to "Mother and Father," which is what he had called us all day. Under the note lay a beautiful red and gold Batak marriage shawl, similar to the one he had shown us that day in the museum. We were both deeply moved and felt truly blessed by our encounter with that sweet soul.

The next day, the African Queen cruised north in slow motion giving us a chance to view life on the shore of the lake. The open, rolling countryside was dotted with a few trees and we could see elaborate gravesites in the shape of churches with tall spires, and boat-shaped metal roofs perched on the hillsides. It was a leisurely day of boating, stopping at markets, hot springs and lunch but as we started back in the early evening, the sky turned black, lightning flashed, and the wind drove the rain under the tarpaulin covering the upper deck. As the boat pitched and rolled in the large waves, most passengers dashed below for warmth and dryness but Herm, Sue, Jenny and I stayed bundled up topside to avoid the suffocating diesel fumes below. Sue was close to panic, afraid the boat was going to sink, so we huddled together under umbrellas, talking and joking to keep her from going off the deep end.

Except for the lightning it was now totally dark, and the boat had only one small handheld spotlight. The crew had been taking "magic mushrooms" all day, so they were in la-la land and weren't worried about much of anything. We noticed the boat kept zig-zagging slowly around the island not making much headway. It was pretty obvious the crew had no idea where the dock was. It wasn't until 8 p.m. that the drugged-out "sailors" finally found the right landing.

It was our second week in Sumatra and between our new-found travel friends, peaceful, interesting surroundings and relaxed, friendly natives, we were having a blast. We parted ways with our pals again for the 13-hour bus trip to Bukittingi, with the promise they would join us in a few days. We gradually transitioned from the predominantly Christian Batak region of the north to the Muslim area in the west. The dress of the people changed from western clothes to that of more conservative Muslim attire. Women's heads and faces were covered, and men wore sarongs and black caps. The ever-present spires of churches morphed into the minarets connected to mosques.

We knew the best way to get a feel for a place and meet the locals, was on foot. The village to village "Singalang" walk, suggested in our guidebook, seemed like the perfect way to do that. It was a gorgeous, cool day in the Minangkabau Highlands just outside of Bukittingi. Gently sloping pathways ran adjacent to rice and vegetable fields broken into well-defined, perfectly arranged plots. In the distance, Mt. Singalang belched clouds of steam and ash into the deep blue sky. Traditional multi-peaked, Minangkabau houses with their saddle-shaped roofs, were scattered among modern concrete structures. In front of each home, cement ponds containing large carp and paddling ducks were sunk into the earth.

We had only a rough map, but we soon found our concerns about getting lost were unfounded. The locals we encountered would ask where we were going and kindly point out the route. There was no way to go unnoticed with the children around. They loved shouting hello, whether it was from the roadside, a far-off field or from behind a bush. One kid would start, and it was like a rolling ball of hellos following us down the path.

About mid-morning, I was wondering how I was going to relieve my bulging bladder when we came across a village "bathroom". I assumed it was for girls as there were a number of other women using it. Waist-high cubicles with no doors were aligned in a row with squat toilets inside. As I hesitantly approached, the women's stares turned to giggles as I pondered the protocol of using a toilet with no privacy. I finally shrugged, dropped my pants and joined the other squatters. The women all seemed to get a kick out of this crazy westerner using their facilities.

The final event of the day was the "bull fights" in Kota Baru. We followed the crowds of men to a large village field, paid our entrance fee, and took a seat on an earthen ledge above the "arena". Staked around the perimeter of the acreage were four huge, water buffalo. When the fight was set to begin, two of the bulls were pulled off the field and the remaining two were brought head-to-head. The crowd surrounded the beasts as the bulls locked horns and pushed each other around. As they moved, the people shifted, trying to stay out of the way but continued to encircle them. At times, the group had to scatter and even vault the fence to keep from being run over. At last, one bull ran into the woods with the other one chasing him, then both bulls chased the people, then the people chased the bulls. It was hysterical, like watching a Laurel and Hardy movie. It was a fun ending to a super perfect day.

The road to Lake Maninjou was poorly paved and under construction by an army of workers doing everything by hand. The forty-four hairpin turns descending the steep mountain wall to the volcanic crater lake had us all thrown from one side of the bus to the other. It was like an amusement park ride, and the smell of vomit permeated the vehicle causing even more eruptions. I was counting the minutes until we reached the bottom so I wouldn't be adding to the retched aroma.

A lakeside room, good friends, a relaxing daily routine had us feeling more rested than we had been since Tioman Island. With time to write and meld with my surroundings, I was inspired to record the following about the dawn of each new day:

> Silence, the prayer of night,
> broken by tentative cock crows,
> in the pre-dawn darkness.
> Chanting,
> echoing across the lake.
> A long, drawn-out note,
> from deep within the muezzin,
> saturates the darkness
> as it grows in strength,

climbing the tonal scale.
A musical alarm clock,
it half arouses, half soothes,
bringing a peaceful smile to awakening.

Life stirs.
The cock's crows grow stronger.
A veritable chorus of cock a doodle doos
awakens those trapped in dreamland.
Strains of music fill the air,
dogs bark, dishes clank, motorbikes roar.
The squeals of children
pierce the gray light.
The sweet smell of smoke fills the nostrils,
watering the mouth with anticipation,
of the nourishment
to start the new day.

And this:

Mountains ringing the placid lake,
lay shrunken under low-hanging clouds.
Men paddle dugout canoes to fishing grounds,
women wash clothes at the shore.
The mountains grow,
as clouds rise with the sun.
Fish jump for breakfast,
on the rippling pink surface of the water.
The perfect mirrored world

distorts and disappears,

as dawn brings rippling

to the expanse of the lake.

The mystery and magic of the new day

disappears in the drudgery and routine of life.

Time, we were always worried about time and that darned one-year return ticket. We had just used up a month of our 4-month Indonesian visa, so needed to move on once again as we had so much more to see. It was a delightful month of fun adventures, spent with good friends. I had especially enjoyed hanging out with Jenny, who was a strong, adventurous, upbeat woman. I was in a really good place, finally relaxed and calm and enjoying traveling. I was looking forward to taking on Java.

Our rattle trap prop plane from Medan had ripped seats, taxied down the runway sideways but surprisingly delivered us to Jakarta in one piece! The next trick was finding the right bus station to get us out of the city. We were fighting off cabbies and touts all yelling at us to get in their cab or bus. It was late in the day; I was dead tired and in no mood for this chaotic scene.

When we arrived in Bandung, it wasn't any better and I just wanted to scream at them to leave me the fuck alone!! My peacefulness of a few days prior had disappeared and I was back to ugly American mode. I just wanted a shower and a bed and hoped that would restore my good mood.

Java had a totally different feel than Sumatra. Except for the common language it was like being in a new country. The roads were smooth, there were lots of cars, streetlights, motels, hotels, bungalows, restaurants, amusement parks, and tourist spots. The Javanese people were more refined, sophisticated and lighter-skinned than the Sumatrans and their way of dress was more Westernized. It was almost like going to the city from the country.

We were getting used to grubby, rooms so the one in Garut wasn't so bad, especially when the sweet grandmother of the house brought us tea and goodies. She sat down and chatted in Bahasa Indonesian, not seeming to care that we didn't understand a word she was saying. Her grandson, looking embarrassed, told her we couldn't speak Indonesian but she just shooed him away and kept talking to us. Way to go girl!!!

We wanted to visit a waterfall in a neighboring town but sometimes things just don't go according to plan. We asked at the bus station if they were going to the village of Tarongong to the Air Turjin (waterfall) and they said yes. After driving around and around, they stopped and the driver pointed down a street and said something about a hotel. We were confused and thought we were still in Garut so asked the driver again, "Tarongong?" and he said yes. We shrugged our shoulders, got off and walked the length of the street to the next corner. We turned to each other and started laughing, we weren't crazy when we thought this all looked familiar. After almost 2 hours of wandering around, we were right back to where we started. So much for communication!

Gluttons for punishment, we decided to try once again and stopped at a Notary's office hoping someone there would speak English. The woman at the desk asked where we wanted to go and when we told her Tarangong she understood and drew us a map. Not wanting to trust a bus again, we got a bemo, (motor tricycle) which delivered us to the correct place.

Volcanoes backed the small village where houses were positioned along winding dirt lanes that were more like mazes than streets. Water was everywhere, housing fish, supporting rice growth and in mineral baths heated by the volcanos.

We wandered the lanes asking the way to Citicus, getting the usual hand signals and words we didn't understand. A young boy noticed our predicament and beckoned for us to follow him. We didn't want to pay a guide price, but it was apparent we would never find the way on our own, so follow we did. It wasn't long before an older boy got in on the action and took the lead. It seemed he had a better plan so led the way while the younger boy followed.

The winding paths of the village led us to tiptoeing through the cultivated rows of young tobacco, soybeans, rice, and tapioca. The land rose sharply from the fields and we found ourselves clambering over walls of lava rock and sliding across bare stretches of old magma flow. The soil was so rich from the volcanic ash the grass beside the trail was at least 7 feet high! We kept climbing through bamboo and pine forest and by the time we reached the river, I was drenched in sweat and breathing hard, my legs shaking. Herm wasn't in much better shape. The younger boy, seeing our distress, yelled at the older one to slow down, so we could take a breather.

The kids said only one more kilometer, so we gathered ourselves and hopped onto rocks to cross the water. The trail got steeper, my legs grew heavier, and I ceased jumping rocks, just sloshed, exhausted, through the streams in my sneakers. This was like climbing to the hut on Mt. Wilhelm but this time I was in danger of heatstroke instead of hypothermia. Herm had gotten a burst of energy and was up ahead with "speedy" but the sweet young boy stayed with me. I dragged myself up one more steep section, grunting and groaning and had to be steadied to make the final leap to the cascade.

A booming torrent poured over the cliff into a large pool at its base. I sloshed immediately into the water, clothes and all and splashed heavenly cool liquid all over my broiling body. If I hadn't been wearing my money belt under my clothes, I would have been standing under those falls with "speedy". Herm, not being a fan of cold water, stood at the edge with the young boy as "speedy" and I hooted and hollered in the refreshing coolness.

Cooled down and soaked, we headed back. The boys stopped a couple of times, supposedly to rest and admire the view, but we could tell they were trying to figure out how to ask us for a guide fee. Meanwhile, Herm and I had been talking "in code" as we walked, discussing what to give them and when. At the next stop, we handed them each 500 rph, which was a very generous tip. Oh boy, did that ever bring big grins to their faces! They fairly skipped the rest of the way down the mountain.

Near the end of the trail, they directed us to the road where we hopped on a bus. I certainly got a lot of strange looks as I sat there in my wet clothes and hair, but I just smiled as I was still nice and cool.

The next adventure we undertook was to the volcano, Papandayan. The owner of our guest house warned us we would probably have to walk the 14 km road to get there. He said public transportation only went as far as the base, but you needed a private car to reach the top. Despite that news, we decided to go for it and see what would happen.

We got an oplet (like a taxi) outside the Terminal Bis and from there we were sardined into a minibus to Cisarupan. The other passengers kept staring at us curiously until one young man asked, "Kemana" (where are you going?) When we told him Papandayan, the word spread through the bus like flowing water as everyone nodded their heads and muttered Papandayan. The mystery of where the "honkies" were going had been solved.

When we reached Cisarupan everyone on the bus was trying to help us with directions and then a crowd gathered to see what was going on. Two English speakers emerged to offer their services as guides and transportation. They were willing to take each of us up the mountain road on their motorcycles for 5000 rph so we accepted.

Much like other craters we had visited, sulfur dioxide smoke rose from holes surrounded by yellow sulfur crystals. Water and mud boiled, and steam roared out of the earth in blinding clouds. We were once again the object of everyone's attention and a group of school kids descended upon us to ask questions, practice their English and have the obligatory picture taken with us. We enjoyed these encounters as we both love young people's energy and it was always fun to sit with them, chat and laugh.

We had walked maybe three km down the road when we were rescued again by a van full of middle-aged Chinese Indonesians. We gratefully accepted their offer of a ride, and they were even so kind as to take us all the way to our Losman. What a wonderful gift today. I am glad we were open to just going for it with no idea how we would get up the mountain, it all worked out beautifully. That trust thing can really work!

It was another travel day and to keep us fed on our long trip to Solo, "our grandmother" provided us with a doggy bag full of goodies. She waited with us by the road and even flagged down a minibus for us. As we rode away, we could see her standing in the street waving until we were out of sight. We were so touched by the care and kindness that sweet woman had shown us throughout our stay.

One of the main reasons we went to Solo was to attend meditation classes. The guidebook mentioned a man named Pak Suyono who was a theosophist and meditation teacher. I was intrigued to find out more about him as I had done a lot of reading on Theosophy. We followed the directions in our book to Shanti Lokar, a walled compound within walking distance of our guest house. A roomful of European travelers, along with some locals, sat in a half-circle of straight-backed chairs in front of floor to ceiling bookcases. Pak Suyono rested in an upholstered seat against the wall, facing the westerners, with his young Indonesian protegé by his side. Pak Suyono was a small, thin man with gray hair, possibly in his sixties, quiet and reserved.

He welcomed us with a nod as we took our seats. After a short talk and introduction, we were led through a body awareness meditation which was followed by a question-and-answer period. This type of meditation wasn't new to either of us, but we found it relaxing and it was fun to be with the other travelers.

After two weeks of regular attendance, we were both intrigued by how Pak Suyono would secretly "send" ideas, pictures or words to people during the meditation. He wouldn't tell people what he was doing but, afterward, would ask if anyone "got" anything interesting during the session.

When I learned he sometimes accepted individual students, I decided to approach him to see if he would take me on.

"What are your intentions?" he asked as he stared at me intently.

It felt like he was looking right through me, and I was caught off guard by his question. Truth be told, I had no clear intention, I just wanted to see what I could learn from him. I stumbled nervously over my words mumbling something about always being interested in metaphysical things and wanting to learn more, etc. I held my breath waiting for his reply, sure that I had not passed the "test".

He continued to study me and finally said, "I think you can advance if you stay awhile. You and Robert can move into your room tomorrow."

"Thank you so much!" I replied as I let out my breath. Phew, that was pretty scary!

There were five, tiny, one-room cabins placed against a wall of the compound, two of which were occupied by long-term locals and the other two by women, one from Denmark and the other from England. Each of our rooms had a covered porch overlooking the beautiful jungle-like gardens. Inside, were some shelves and cubbies for supplies and two mattresses on the floor. Pak Suyono's house was located near the large, gated entrance, directly across the garden from us. A separate structure housed the kitchen, and another held the toilets and mandi. In addition, a small building to the right of our cabins accommodated the full-time caretakers and their young children. Stone paths, surrounded by dense vegetation, connected all the structures. With the tall trees draped in vines, a plethora of flowers, bushes, birds, lizards and rats, we felt like we were in the jungle despite having busy streets just on the other side of the wall.

We learned Pak Suyono had traveled and studied in many Asian countries, spending a great deal of time in India. His library was full of metaphysical, religious and history books, all of which I was sure he had read. Even though he billed himself as a Buddhist, it became clear he was actually a shaman, and many locals came to him for clearings and exorcisms. In fact, one of the local men, who came regularly to meditation, had "sold his soul to the devil" to get the money to attend medical school. He came often for cleansing and soul retrieval.

I was excited when Pak Suyono invited me to sit in on a past life regression he was doing for his protege. It was evening when the three of us sat quietly in the private garden by the house. As I centered myself, breathing quietly, I noticed hundreds of tiny points of light scattered throughout the vegetation on the ground. I blinked, thinking I was imagining it but couldn't ask Pak Suyono about it as he was getting ready for the session. I just sat there, closed my eyes and listened to the two men speaking in Indonesian. Behind my eyes, I saw primitive-looking, sparsely dressed, dark-skinned people with tall, pointed hats gathered around grass huts. I then started seeing scenes I somehow knew were from Atlantis. It was all pretty strange, and I figured my imagination must be in high gear. Later, I told Pak Suyono what I had experienced and was blown away when he told me he had seen the same thing during the reading. When I asked about the lights in the garden, he told me I wasn't crazy, that they were nature spirits and he saw them all the time. WOW, WOW, WOW!!!

The four of us students staying at Shanti Lokar all had our "issues" with Pak Suyono. He wasn't a warm fuzzy teacher and being able to "read" our energy, there was no "hiding" from him. If our words didn't match our intentions, he would call us on it. He would push us constantly and knew all of our weak spots and triggers. We would often sit around our cabins complaining about how he drove us crazy. Invariably, the following day during meditation class, he would weave what we had been complaining about into the session. Oh My God!!! We couldn't get away with ANYTHING! We joked our cabins were bugged or he was hiding in the bushes while we talked. No bugs, no hiding, he just always knew what we were up to.

Two meditation sessions a day left plenty of free time and there was so much to do in Solo! We loved it there, it was like living "inside of art". Everything was art, it was ingrained in the people's DNA. If we complimented someone on playing an instrument well or being a good artist, they just looked at us confused because it just came so naturally to them. Dance, theatre, gamelan, painting, wood carving, masks, puppets, the list of the forms of art being engaged in was endless. We wanted to learn some of it ourselves, so Herm found an artist who taught him traditional Javanese painting and I took gamelan flute lessons. Between that, Tai Chi, and swimming at a local pool every day, we kept ourselves quite busy.

In addition to becoming friends with our "art" teacher, we made a number of local friends. One of these was Fanie, a bubbly young woman who was an English tutor for the children of some of the wealthy Solo families. She wanted to improve her English and we wanted to improve our Bahasa Indonesian, so we traded lessons. As we got to know each other, she asked if I would be willing to accompany her to her classes so the kids could have exposure to a native English speaker. I was thrilled to accept but the first class didn't go so well. Only three children showed up as most were too afraid to come and the ones whose parents pushed to be there were too shy to speak.

The next time was better, I guess the word had gotten out I wasn't a monster, and 18 students came. This class was held in the function room of a restaurant owned by one of the parents and some of the mothers came to watch. In addition to practicing their English, one of the boys, who had studied dance for many years and performed on TV, did a traditional Javanese dance for us. After class, the restaurant owners served us all a delicious meal!

A lot of things were happening with Herm and me on an energetic level. Pak Suyono was doing some mini cleansings on me to get the energy flowing and also did a "laser" treatment on my pineal gland to stimulate clairvoyance. All this clearing got my Kundalini in workout mode and even though Herm wasn't getting all the extra treatments, he was also experiencing clairvoyance and Kundalini energy. At the same time, my left arm started jumping at random and my right hand seemed to want to write. I asked Pak Suyono about it and he said to just go with the flow and allow the energies to come.

I began to draw, letting my hand move as it wished, and it created some interesting scribbles. When I showed them to Pak Suyono, he told me Devas were coming through and manifesting in the artwork. Another time I had a vision of a long path lit by a strong golden light and heard "Path of the Golden Sun." The energy was so strong I felt I wanted to get up and walk down that path, it was almost literally pulling me. When I asked Pak Suyono about it, he said the Path of the Golden Sun was the Atlantean religion! Holy Crap!! Now I was having Atlantis flashbacks?

We became good friends with the owners of the nearby restaurant we frequented and many of the young men who hung out there. "Our boys" were always telling us about their woes with girlfriends, jobs and life and asking our advice. We had such fun with them and learned so much about what life was like in Solo. Wahu was one of the young guys we became particularly close to and one day he told us his boss had invited us to the wedding of his niece.

This was one of the wealthier families in town and I had nothing to wear, so asked Fanie for help. Always ready to shop, Fanie helped me pick out some new clothes and coached me on what would go on and how to act. The family's chauffeur picked us up and took us to a huge house where we were treated like royalty. We sat with the other guests viewing the many ceremonies and rituals. We had no idea what was going on but truly enjoyed the show.

After the final ceremony, a man dressed in traditional brown patterned batik and sporting the ceremonial dagger began to dance a Wayang Orang story. This is a type of classical Javanese theatrical performance with themes taken from episodes of the Ramayana or Mahabharata. I was standing in the doorway taking pictures as he danced gracefully towards me and when he approached, he looked at me with a mischievous glint in his eye and said, "do you want to dance with me?"

"Sure," I said, putting my camera down and taking his hand.

I was about as graceful as a bull in a China shop but did my best to follow his lead. The crowd had a good laugh to end a long day of celebration.

Magic, both white and black was practiced by many within the population. In the museum, food and water offerings were left for the ceremonial dagger called the Kris so it wouldn't become possessed and cause trouble. Supposedly, black magicians were able to put a spell on the knife and direct it to a target. Pak Suyono told us during the War of Independence the Indonesian fighters would put a protective energetic shield around them to keep any projectiles from hurting them. He had been one of those fighters and could attest to the effectiveness of those spells.

One morning after meditation, I don't know if he used one of those spells on Herm and I or what? We were sitting across from him watching as he talked quietly with his protege. We stared in astonishment as his head slowly morphed into what can only be described as something alien-looking.

Wide-eyed I turned to Herm, "do you see something weird?" I whispered.

"Uh-huh," he nodded, staring across the room. As we continued to gawk, Pak Suyono's head slowly went back to normal.

He turned to face us with a little smile and said in all innocence, "did you see something?"

We just nodded our heads. Wow! We knew he was powerful but ... wow!

Our visas were due to expire, and we had to wrap things up in our beloved Solo. On the last day of teaching our students, we were picked up in a plush van and driven to the Orient Restaurant. There we were greeted by all of our kids and their parents plus served a feast in our honor. We were treated like celebrities, speeches were given, pictures taken, and we were presented with a gift of 100,000 rupiahs, which all the households had contributed to. We were humbled by the outpouring of kindness and grateful for the opportunity to have helped the kids in a small way.

The goodbye celebrations didn't end there. Yanti, the owner of "our" restaurant and "our" boys gave us a going away cake and presents to remember them by and Fani, who was always bringing me presents and food brought more. All of us were in tears. These people had become good friends over the last months, and we would miss them dearly.

The last person to say goodbye to was Pak Suyono. I hate goodbyes and just wanted it over with quickly. Here is your gift, thanks and good-bye sort of thing but Pak Suyono wouldn't let me get away with that. Yanti and her husband had offered to drive us to the airport, so while we waited for them, Pak Suyono had us sit down. I was so uncomfortable not knowing what to say as he sat there in his quiet inimitable way, probably reading my mind!

I thanked him for all he had taught me and as enigmatic as ever he said, "there is no need for you to come back."

Now what the hell did that mean? Had I succeeded in learning something or was I just totally hopeless? I laughed to myself, thinking, yup, pushing my buttons right to the end.

Dear Diary....

What can I say, I am totally in love with Indonesia and the people and the FOOD! OMG, the food is to die for! I could easily live here even though it is freaking hot if you aren't in the mountains. I'm so sad we didn't have more time to visit other islands, I would have especially loved visiting Bali.

I already miss our friends and our life in Solo. I felt so at home there and was entirely at peace in the culture of "art" and how it permeates every facet of life. I feel in my soul that is how our world is meant to be...a celebration of life through every form of art .... which is creation itself. Sigh!

Staying with Pak Suyono was definitely challenging in more ways than one, but I am so grateful for every one of them. Having to deal with one of the boarders, who came to stay not long after we moved in, was interesting. She was definitely "out there" and pushed my buttons big time as did some of the other meditators who came. Never mind the old man triggering me all over the place. LOL, I leave with every button and trigger point being fully exercised! LOL. I have learned a lot and mostly learned I have a lot more to learn and a lot more work to do on myself! Whoopee-do!

CHAPTER 8

INDIA & NEPAL

I ndia, the place we had been both dreading and looking forward to. With all the negative stories we had heard from other travelers we didn't know what to expect. They told us India would push all of our buttons. That we would find ourselves angry and yelling at people and we had to be careful not to get ripped off by everyone. In addition to that, we read there was political unrest in many places which could impact our travel! Despite all the warnings, here we were, ready to discover the truth about India.

So far, so good. We had successfully negotiated our airport arrival and found our way around Bombay/Mumbai without incident and were about to embark on our first overnight train trip. The humongous Victoria station was packed with people and totally overwhelming. It was so huge, whole trains drove right inside the building! We clutched our small bags close to our chests as we kept watch on each other's back, aware a thief could covertly unzip the packs in the crowds.

We walked from train car to train car examining the list of names posted on the outside of each one searching for our nighttime home. "Here we are," called Herm as I joined him at the entrance to our car.

"This ought to be interesting," I said as we passed the reeking bathrooms at the top of the filthy stairs. I was determined I would not have to pee all night. A narrow corridor ran down the center of the car. To the left, were three-sided compartments with six bunks each. On the right, were two-tiered bunks running horizontally which left the middle with very little room to move. Our compartment was already occupied by two Indian families and their children who were eating their meal. The middle bunks, on each side, folded down so one could sit on the bottom seat without hitting one's head. We heaved our bags onto the top bunk, almost beheading a couple of people in the process, and sat down on the lower bench with the family.

I felt like I was coming down with a cold and I just wanted to go to bed. I wondered how long we would have to wait for it to be bunk time. Thankfully, as soon as the train started to move, everyone began fixing their "slab". I climbed into the middle one using my pack as a pillow and scrunched the rest of my body into the small space that was left. With my head pounding, sinuses aching, nose stuffed up, coughing, wary of anyone trying to steal my pack or somebody groping me, I attempted to sleep. Unable to dull the pain in my head, I broke down and took a Sinutab and quickly dropped off into a restless, uncomfortable slumber. It was almost impossible to stay asleep as each time the train stopped, the buskers came aboard yelling for people to buy their food and drinks.

Awakening at a stop around 5 a.m., Herm and I became more and more concerned we wouldn't know when to get off. As the train began to slow down again at 5:30, a nice young man told us this was the stop for Jalgoan. How he knew we wanted to get off there is beyond me, but I was so thankful for his help.

Jalgoan was the town closest to the famous Ajanta and Allora caves we had come to visit. In order to get to the site, however, we had to endure our first Indian bus ride. Nothing had prepared us for the scene that ensued when it was time to board. Everyone pushed and shoved and massed against the doorway to the bus not even letting anyone off! Herm and I just stared at each other, eyebrows raised.

"Okay then," I said to Herm, taking a deep breath, "I guess we just dive in!"

"Yup," he responded as we moved into the crush, pushing with our packs and bodies. We squeezed ourselves in, with Herm securing a seat in the back while I found one near the front. Once on the bus, everyone was quite civilized but getting on they were like animals! Not angry or mean, just super determined! We later found the trick was to climb up the side of the bus and put something on a seat inside so when you got through the mob you would have a seat saved. People seemed to respect that… go figure!

The twenty-nine massive caves were totally awe-inspiring. They were arranged in a horseshoe shape around a steep-walled canyon with a waterfall at the open end dropping into a deep blue pool. Three of the caves were two stories high and some were ornately carved with designs, pillars and statues on the outside as well as in. Some were temples, others were monasteries with small monk cells with the beds carved in the stone. It was mind-blowing! How was it possible an ancient culture was able to do that?

When we finished our tour of the caves one of the young shopkeepers met us as we waded across the river. As an enticement to visit his establishment, he gave us each a small geode containing quartz crystals. Little did he know Herm was an avid rockhound and giving him that geode was like dangling a piece of steak in front of a dog! While I guzzled a few cold drinks, Herm bargained hard for a few mineral specimens. By that time, we had several of the other shopkeepers bringing us their rocks to peruse.

The bus back to town never showed up but our shop friends, Rafik and Edward, came to our rescue. They said they lived near our hotel, and we could all walk to town together. We were always up for an adventure so off we trod. They knew all the shortcuts through the fields, by rivers, over hills, through gardens and over back roads. Instead of walking five km via the road we only had to walk two or three. The scenery was beautiful, peaceful, and quiet.

When we got to town, the guys invited us to their village. It was just like out of the movies. Mud and stick houses, a maze of small winding lanes with rivulets of sewage water running down the middle. Small shops offered fruits or vegetables for sale and a "fish market" sold minnows displayed in metal bowls. Goats, cows, pigs and dogs wandered with the snotty-nosed kids who were either naked or wearing old, stained clothes. Grim-faced men, sari-clad women, young girls with black braids and nose rings all stared as we paraded past. Many of the kids fell in line with us, smiling and practicing their hellos. I unwittingly committed a huge faux pas by patting one of the boys on his head, with my left hand! Both are huge no-nos. He was horrified and shrank away from me in terror. Left hands are only used for toilet purposes and you never touch a person or food with that appendage. AND, the head is considered sacred and not to be messed with. I felt terrible I had breached customs and traumatized the child. Another cultural lesson learned.

We left Edward, who would meet us later, and followed Rafik to his home to meet his family and have tea. It was a simple, clean house with a goat and water buffalo calf tied just inside the front overhang, munching hay. Momma buffalo grunted from the other side of the wall, stretching her head over the top to see her baby.

We were seated on a bed which was against the outer wall of the house under this overhang. The critters were in front of us and Rafik's family was preparing dinner in the open alcove to our left. His young mother, sisters, aunts and various sets of children, all watched us as we sat there. While we waited for the buffalo to be milked and our tea to brew, Rafik showed us the photo album of "foreign tourists" he had met and brought home. I laughed to think our mugs would soon make their way into his trophy collection for the next set of strangers to gawk at. After drinking the rich, sweet buffalo milk tea we took photos of Rafik and his family for our album of "native people". It was odd to think about how we collected each other's images as if we were exotic creatures.

Oh my God, what an awesome day! Connecting with people, especially of other cultures is one of my favorite things to do! I was energized and flying high! The Indian people we had encountered so far had been so friendly, much different than we had expected, not quite as open and warm as the Indonesians but still really nice.

We had been traveling and sightseeing for two weeks and were feeling in need of a break. We chose one of the many hill stations where the British used to have their summer homes and take their vacations back in the day. It was hard to believe we were in India as the vibe there was much more relaxed. The remnants of rundown mansions from the British occupation could be glimpsed behind crumbling moss-covered walls, while the town was fairly modern with interesting shops, restaurants and grocery stores.

We were waiting for take-out food at the Imperial market, when we noticed a crowd of people pressing their faces against the large plate glass window. Now, we were getting used to being stared at but in that town, we weren't all that interesting, so what was the attraction? I glanced around and noticed a bald man in the store with another well-dressed curly haired guy. It seemed whenever he walked from one end of the store to the other the crowd would drift as well. We asked the store owner who the man was and were told he was a famous Hindi movie star called the "Great Chameleon". I was watching the crowd trying to storm the door the owner was guarding, when I spotted a young man we had met earlier in the day. He was waving a piece of paper and a pen trying to get my attention. He asked if I would get the actor's autograph for him. I said, "sure" and took the pen and paper.

I approached the bald guy and asked, "who are you anyway?" He said he was a film actor.

"Do you always draw such a crowd?"

He answered tiredly, "Yes, I'm afraid so."

I felt sorry for the poor guy, who couldn't even go food shopping in peace!

We hadn't realized how cold it was at the hill stations in November, so we didn't stay long. We were freezing, so headed to the warm southeast states of Goa, Karnataka and Kerala. What a different feel they had from the other areas we had traveled through. They appeared to be more westernized, the atmosphere more relaxed and Christians composed more of the population than other parts of India.

Goa was a Portuguese state until 1961 and still had a European feel. Everything about Panjim, the capital, was fun and upbeat with many smiling, friendly people. There was one funny incident though. One night we treated ourselves to a fancy restaurant, which we hardly ever did. As I was served my meal I was surprised and amused to find a dead cockroach lying atop my rice, legs in the air, as if it had been placed there as a garnish. There is no way the waiter wouldn't have noticed…. I was definitely being played. I nonchalantly picked it off, put it on the table and commenced to eat. The staff got no western hysterics from me!

We both loved food and had been in food heaven in Indonesia and now in India. We had gotten used to the super spicy food in Asia, but the South Indian food took heat to a whole new level, leaving us gasping for breath and sweating like pigs. We especially loved the restaurants where you ate off a banana leaf "plate". The cost of the meal was under a dollar and there were unlimited refills! They were informal affairs where you were seated at long tables with bench seats. A server dropped a blob of rice on the "plate", another waiter spooned on the dahl and still others came with condiments and chapatis. You squished everything together into a pile with your right hand, never the left, then attempted to tear the chapati into pieces with one hand, which wasn't an easy trick. The piece of bread was your "utensil" to grab some of the pile in order to get it to your mouth. It was sooooo good!

The highlight of our trip to Mysore came about 45 minutes from our destination. As the bus was in the midst of one of its heaves, rolls and thumps, the woman standing in the aisle next to us dropped the large can of Lassi she was holding. It was flung under our seat disgorging its sour-smelling contents in a flood over our feet and packs. At the same time, the woman's young son disgorged the contents of his stomach onto the floor in a brown soupy puddle. The mingling of the two smells set people to flinging open the windows and pressing their faces to the breeze to blow away the gagging odor. When the lady and son got off, the next group of aisle passengers innocently dragged their long saris through the goo while their bare feet squished it all together.

When we finally reached our destination, we had to yank our packs out from the small space under the seats, which meant sliding them through the goo. Sour-smelling, coagulated milk dripped off the bags and was seeping into the zippers. We stood on the street, disgusting packs at our feet, trying to summon the fortitude to hoist them onto our backs.

"Oh man, this is so gross!" I grimaced, as I put the bag on and felt the wetness soak into my shirt.

Holding his breath, Herm did the same and we made our way through the city streets in search of a hotel to get everything cleaned up.

I needed to get out of the city and back into nature. Unfortunately, my pissy mood had reared its ugly head once again. I was exhausted from dealing with beggars, touts, taxi drivers and all the other people who shouted for our business. Nothing worked to make them stop! Not being nice, not even yelling or swearing. They were like flies on shit…relentless! Herm was faring a bit better than I was in the patience department. He didn't like it either, but he didn't get as strung out as I did when I was tired. Ahh!! India, everyone told us it would be a challenge!

Even though I felt I was being tested over and over again, I can't tell you the number of times the "Universe" provided "miracles" to brighten my day. There were situations at bus stations when two empty places miraculously appeared after we were told there were no seats; there was the day we arrived at a national park with no reservations and someone had just canceled their cabin; other times random people somehow seemed to know where we were going and helped us get the right bus without us ever asking. The mother of all gifts came the day we were standing on the side of the road trying to figure out how we could possibly stuff ourselves into the packed local bus in front of us. Out of nowhere, a fancy tourist chariot pulled up, the angel driver leaned out and said, "Would you like to come with us?"

"Hell yes!" We had no idea what it would cost but said to hell with it, we will pay whatever it is not to have to ride in a sardine can for once! Ah, luxury! Reclining seats, no crowds, a fan, big, clean window and …a tour! Our driver narrated us through the national park, stopped at the botanical gardens in Ooty, took us to a restaurant for lunch and dropped us at the doorstep of our homestay, all for less than we would have paid for the sardine can! Wow! Sometimes I felt guilty for being so grouchy after so much kindness was extended to us. I found every day was a practice in attempting to stay in balance.

I got a reprieve from the chaos when we went to Ernakulam for Christmas! The shops were ablaze with multicolored decorations, and I couldn't resist buying a string of brightly-hued stars to hang in our room. The state of Kerala has a large population of Christians, so Christmas was a big deal. Everyone was in the holiday spirit with shopkeepers and people on the street all smiles and Christmas greetings. What a delightful change from some of the other stone-faced places we had been. My mood was happy and relaxed for the first time in a long while. I am so affected by the energy of those around me that it was sometimes almost painful being in crowds of frantic people.

In Kerala, the women had their hair loose and uncovered and wore more skirts than saris. The men were dressed in the usual drab button-down shirts and dhoti (sarong) which they seemed to be constantly fiddling with. When left alone the cloth wrapped around the waist and hung to their feet but it was rarely left to dangle. This is what I observed: first they would hold the dhoti up by the edges, flap it about like wings, then tie it up double so it looked like they were wearing shorts with their boxers hanging down. But it didn't stop there! They would then untie the cloth to let it drape and repeat… all day long! This wasn't just the occasional man; it was all of them! I didn't get it!

The women further north did the same type of thing with their saris. The piece of cloth that draped over the shoulder was used to cover their head. Because it was silk, it would soon slide off, so they would put it on again. Slide off, on again, slide off, on again, just like the men playing with their "skirts". What would everyone do with their hands if they didn't have their clothes to play with, I wondered?

We had been looking forward to a beach vacation so headed to the popular traveler's hangout at Kovalam Beach on the Kerala coast. It was easy to see why Kovalam was a refuge from the stresses of constantly dealing with an alien culture. Finally, some peace and quiet with no speakers blasting Hindi music at ear-splitting decibels! Noise has always stressed me out. During this trip, I had to work hard to stay sane when we were in the noisy cities. Even worse, was when we got to a quiet country place and suddenly Hindi music came blasting through huge speakers hung on poles. Even with earplugs it was painful. Many times, I thought I would go stark raving mad with the sound as I couldn't get away from it and it would play morning and night. I didn't know how people could live like that!

The horseshoe-shaped beach sloped gently into the blue waters of the Arabian Sea. Tiny rental cottages and funky, shack-like restaurants sat under towering coconut palms. During the day, the beach was littered with scantily clad backpackers from around the world soaking up the rays and swapping tales. Each evening as the sun slid slowly into the sea, restauranteurs set tables and chairs on the sand in preparation for the dinner crowd. I loved the nighttime beach scene with candles twinkling on every table, the eateries aglow with multicolored lights and western music being played at a modest volume!

On New Year's Eve, the beach was alive with revelers. Bands were playing, fireworks were booming, and each restaurant was trying to outdo the other with special menus. We weren't into the party scene so found a quieter place to eat and celebrate our second "anniversary".

"How could it be two years already?" Herm asked.

"It doesn't seem possible," I answered. "What a long way we have come from shoveling snow in Concord to sitting in the sands of India," I laughed.

"Who could have even imagined it?" he chuckled shaking his head.

The holidays passed and many travelers were moving on. We would soon do the same and miss dining on the beach with our feet dug into the soft, warm sand. It was wonderful to have meals that way with the surf pounding a few meters away, the stars twinkling overhead and lights from fishing boats strung along the horizon. I wanted to bottle this peace, quiet and relaxation and take it with me as we dove back into the "real" India.

As we traveled deeper into Tamil Nadu, the pace of life seemed to get slower and slower, the older women wore no under blouses and had very long earlobes stretched by wearing heavy gold earrings. The land grew hotter, greener and wetter with flooded areas everywhere. Large puddles were being used for washing bodies, clothes, cows, trucks and for bodily eliminations all at the same time.

Mahabalipuram was the town where stonemasons created Hindu statues and cut boulders into temples but wasn't the peaceful place we had hoped for. It was back to blaring Hindi temple music starting at 5 a.m.! OMG, I thought I was going to lose it. All the beach calm and peace out the window, the noise made us both grouchy. It was like Chinese water torture, it would get quiet, and we would start to relax, then it was back but you never knew when. Add to that, the rats chewing through my pack to get to some cookies I had forgotten to remove.

While we were enduring the loudspeakers, the United States attacked Iraq. Not knowing how that conflict would affect each of our countries and our travels, created a bond among us travelers. Our days were governed by the TV news broadcasts at 3 and 9:30 p.m. We all gathered in a local house to see what was happening and spent hours discussing plans and helping the Israelis deal with their anxiety. The American Embassy was advising Americans to go home but we decided to continue with our plan to travel to Calcutta.

The infamous Calcutta. I had read so many books about this city and its poor people, I'm not exactly sure what I expected. It turned out to be just another big, noisy, crowded, dirty, smoggy city with the same hassles!

The traveler's area was in the Muslim section of the city and right at the spot our buggy let us off we encountered an anti-war, anti-Bush march with an effigy of George Bush hanging from a light pole. In fact, the dog at our Muslim owned hotel had a sign around his neck reading, "George Bush Dog Boy." We were a bit concerned but soon discovered the owners of our hotel were very welcoming and didn't seem to mind that we were Americans. In fact, Herm joined them each night to watch the news and get the war updates.

We never tired of surprise encounters. We had just finished eating dinner at our favorite restaurant when who walks in the door but our dear friend and travel companion Jock, from the Netherlands! We made quite a scene with our emotional greeting. He caught us up on news of Peter, Sue and Jenny and told us he was heading home in the next few days. We had met this sweet, naive, young man in Sumatra just as he was starting his travels; and now, almost six months later he seemed so mature and worldly. He told us he had loved the traveling but was excited to get home and start his new life. He also gave us an update on what was happening in Calcutta regarding travelers. I guess most were heading to Thailand or Nepal as the threat of violence was building each day. Thankfully, we hadn't encountered any issues and hoped it would continue that way as we had to stay until our mail arrived.

Each misty, cool morning, as we headed to the Blue Sky restaurant for breakfast, we encountered life as experienced by the Calcutta street dwellers. On the bare sidewalks, huddled under thin woolen shawls, slept the dispossessed. Those who were awake lathered their nearly naked bodies and rinsed in the cold water from the hand pumps that stood along the road. Women scrubbed aluminum pots and pans; children squatted in the gutter while men added their bodily fluids to the curbside stream of foul-smelling liquids. I always wondered where the women did their bathroom duties as you never saw them squatting in public!

In stark contrast, a totally different scene unfolded at the restaurant. Over fifty travelers stuffed themselves into the tiny establishment to down a western-style breakfast, talk about the war and exchange travel tips and gossip. Some had just arrived on their journey while others, like us, had been out for a year or more. We would exchange stories of adventure, gripe about the touts, relate experiences about the kindness of the locals but the most talked about subject was "elimination!" Yup, poop and pee were a hot topic. Travelers' diarrhea and giardia were rampant and tales of trying to find bathrooms and enduring hours-long bus rides with crampy guts were griped about incessantly. We never tired of those stories, all told over our pancakes and omelets!

The elimination issue for the women was much worse than for the men. The "bathrooms" at bus stops were a horror show. Most were cement slabs where you squatted amidst others pee and poop. At one such stop, an Indian woman came out holding up her sari and her nose shaking her head at me as I was entering. I didn't have a choice, I had to pee! I always wore flip flops and, in that place, I had certainly wished I had proper shoes. These "bathrooms" were "cleaned" at the end of the day when they sent the pigs in to gobble up the dumps.

The other thing women travelers had to endure was being grabbed by men. Most of the time it was done so covertly you weren't sure it actually happened. A bump here, a hand there, all done quickly. You were left wondering if you were crazy! One day I was grabbed and there was no mistaking the intent! I was buying tickets for the Calcutta Book Fair and as I was reaching one arm through the crowd for the tickets, a young man grabbed my breast!! I was livid and grabbed the guy's shirt, but he pulled away and ran off. It is a good thing he got away because if I had gotten ahold of him, I would have beaten the crap out of him. When I told Herm, he was beside himself and wanted to find the guy but of course, he was long gone. I had to try to calm him down, but I knew how he felt. I had over a year's worth of anger built up from being grabbed in multiple countries. If I had been able to keep my grip on that guy the results wouldn't have been pretty!

The mail we had been waiting for never did arrive and we just couldn't hang around any longer. We were running out of energy and wanted to visit the Buddhist enclave of Bodhgaya and the holy city of Varanasi before leaving the country. India had taken its toll on our bodies and spirit and we were hoping Nepal would somehow resurrect our resolve to keep traveling.

When we reached southern Nepal, we got to return to nature at Chitwan National Park. It was a relaxing time with new friends from France who were biking around the world. We even got to ride in an ox cart, experiencing the slow pace of native life as we plodded through the countryside for over two hours. The guide we had met at the bus stop was taking us to his village which was located adjacent to the park.

It was a fun few days canoeing on the river and walking with the Rhinos in the jungle. It was sometimes a bit scary as our guide kept telling us to keep an eye out for climbable trees in case a rhino came running out of the tall reeds! Thankfully, we were never charged as there weren't many trees!

Kathmandu was where we headed next, to get our permits for trekking. After living on "native" food for over a year, the gastronomic delights in the city were overwhelming! The restaurants catered to the plethora of world travelers who congregated there. They offered simple western food, like burgers, fries, pizza and cakes, to gourmet European dishes. For "foodies" like ourselves, it was hard to resist sampling all that was offered.

Unfortunately, the other thing Kathmandu is known for is giardia. Something about the water and sewer systems mixing? I don't think we talked with one traveler who hadn't gotten sick there and we soon joined the crowd. Of course, Herm had been suffering on and off with it for months, so it was nothing new for him. I had only experienced some occasional traveler's diarrhea but nothing like the giardia.

We hung out for about a week hoping to kick the shits, but nothing was working. It had been almost 14 months since we left the States, and we were tired. When we gave up our 1-year return ticket, we thought we would be traveling much longer but it had all caught up with us. The constant moving, dealing with different cultures, having to make so many decisions each day, the noise and now the shits, it was time to go home.

Thirteen and a half hours on a plane with Giardia is no picnic. We both popped Lomotil and charcoal tablets, to keep us from spending the whole time in the bathroom! We did have some drama, however, to help keep our mind off our cramping guts. A middle-aged man, not too far from us, was sitting calmly in his seat with his jockey shorts perched jauntily on his head. The flight attendants were all in a tizzy about it wondering if the guy was nuts and would do something crazy. Our seats were near the back where the attendants were whispering their concerns. I overheard their conversation and let them know I was a psychiatric nurse and related some ways to gauge if he was a threat or not. They were grateful for my input and kept me informed about what was going on. As I suspected the guy was fine, just a bit eccentric. At least the incident made the trip go faster!

When we were going through customs in San Francisco, the agent who checked our passports said "welcome back" with a big smile. I had a hard time returning his enthusiasm but managed a weak "thank you". At that point, all I cared about was getting to my sister's apartment, sleeping and having a bathroom close by!

Dear Diary....

I'm a mess! We were told coming back to the States was the worst and boy, is that ever right on! I wasn't that excited to come back to begin with, but this culture shock is worse than it was when getting used to Asia! Yes, there was plenty of "in your face" stuff that drove me nuts, but it felt so alive! The US feels dead, angry, depressed and way too civilized. I have never fit into this society but now I feel even more alienated. The excess of "stuff" in stores is overwhelming and I get literally dizzy whenever I have to go into one. Everything is too clean, and the fresh food looks fake with its lack of blemishes.

Do I even belong here anymore? Who am I if I'm not a traveler? What am I supposed to do with my life? I don't feel like I have anything in common with ordinary Americans and just want out! Will I ever feel comfortable here again?

····✦✦✦····

NEW DIRECTIONS
1991-1994

····✦✦✦····

CHAPTER 9

IN AND OUT AGAIN

A month after returning to the US, we were back in our little house in the woods and pretty much reacclimatized to this culture. It was heaven to be off the road and back into nature's peace and quiet. We had a lot of healing to do from our extended time out in the world. Our systems had been stressed by sickness, noise, pollution, vaccinations and parasites. It was time to take care of body, mind and soul and let nature heal us.

We spent the next seven months gardening, working in the woods, visiting friends and basically relaxing in the warmth of summer. As fall approached, we began to get restless once again and started to think about what we wanted to do next. Going back to the old way of being was never an option. We had been radically changed by the simplified life we had experienced and by the people we had met. Even with a lack of material wealth, the cultures we had encountered seemed to be at peace with their lives, something rarely seen in the West. Their deep connection with community, the land and spirit saw them through whatever tough times they faced. We wanted some of that for ourselves, along with the freedom to live each day to its fullest, to trust we would be provided for and led to where we needed to be.

We still had the travel bug and after spending the last year in the tropics there was no way we wanted to hang around New Hampshire in the cold weather. Since I had originally wanted to travel around the US, we decided to check out the places which were supposedly warm in the winter. Florida, Texas and Arizona were the three states that appeared to be our options. I had no interest in going to Florida, so we decided to give Texas a try. We spent the fall planning, getting free campground books, gathering maps from AAA, buying camping gear and getting the car ready to roll. On the morning we left, I "asked" my oracle cards what this trip held in store for us. I figured the angels were with us when I drew the "Vision Quest" card ("a time of new directions"). The trouble was, I had forgotten about the dark night of the soul which comes before finding the light.

CHAPTER 10

EXPECTATIONS

As our teacher in Java, Pak Suyono, always said, "expectations lead to disappointments." Unfortunately, this turned out to be very true. Our free campground book was totally useless, taking us on wild goose chases down questionable roads to places that didn't exist. The weather was cold and rainy, even in the South, and we were both tired and grumpy.

The best part of the trip was being back in our tent. We had slept in it all summer, in the woods behind the kennel. I had missed the feeling of the earth beneath my body and being lulled to sleep by the wind in the trees and the sounds of the animals of the night. I was not new to tent sleeping. Years prior, before selling my farm, I would set up my tent, deep in the woods, behind my house and sleep there most of the summer. Since I liked challenging myself to find my way by feeling, I never took a light. There was no trail, but I was familiar with the lay of the land since I spent a lot of time in the forest. I had put the tent by a stone wall so if I ever overshot the exact spot, I just had to follow the line of stones. I must admit, there were a couple of nights that had my heart pumping when I got turned around and couldn't find the wall.

It was good practice in staying calm, thinking things through and not panicking. With a sigh of relief, I would plop down inside the tent, safe and sound for a peaceful night's sleep.

We made it to Texas but ….it was STILL rainy and cold! Was there no sun anymore? Maybe the beach would have sun, we thought. We had heard Padre Island National Seashore was the place to go for snowbirds' free camping. For some reason, I didn't have a good feeling about it, but we figured we had better check it out. Oh my God, we were disgusted with the RVs, cars, ATVs all running up and down the beach! The sand was covered with trash, some setups looked like slums. There seemed to be no regard for nature or other people, and we couldn't wait to get out of there. It made me so angry and sad that people did this to the earth.

Another place we couldn't get out of fast enough was the Alamo! It was as though we were feeling all the fear of the people who had died there as if that energy had been soaked into the stone walls. It was funny as we were both trying to be cool and look at the exhibits but finally said to each other, "do you feel creeped out in here?"

"Yup!!!" Out the door we went.

We had been on our own for 27 days with only each other to get grouchy at. We were feeling the need to interact with some other humans to take the pressure off of us! Well, ask and you shall receive!!

On the Alamo day, we kept running into one man over and over. Since I don't believe in coincidences, I felt there was a reason this was happening. I finally started a conversation with him and discovered he was a rancher from Montana. He had come to Texas looking for a winter job to get out of the cold up north. We immediately hit it off, so we invited him to join us for dinner. It was great fun and reminded us of our trip overseas connecting so quickly with other travelers. Joe, at age 55, had just gone through a traumatic divorce and was trying to reinvent himself. It was obvious the "Universe" had brought us together that day. We had all been craving human contact and it was delivered. This incident was the start of noticing how the "Universe" works to bring people together at just the right time to help each other. We would experience this over and over in our travels and never stopped marveling over how perfect it always was.

We learned to live our travel life with "signs" and after seeing five coyotes that day, we bowed to the "trickster" and finally got the message Texas wasn't our place. It had been pretty clear since we arrived, we just hadn't wanted to believe it!

We had heard there was something called Long Term Visitor Areas (LTVA) on Bureau of Land Management (BLM) land in Arizona and California. It was said you could camp for months at a time for a minimal fee. That sounded exactly like what we had been looking for! A race across New Mexico, to get ahead of the snow, we arrived in Arizona to find the sun actually DID still exist!

With high hopes, we started with the LTVAs in Yuma. The road to the first one would have destroyed the car, the next was filled with RVs and no privies. The final one was basically a gravel pit filled with motorhomes. That was disappointing but we weren't discouraged as there was one more in California that sounded promising.

NOW we were discouraged, this last site was basically a parking lot full of ORV's (off road vehicles) tearing up the sand dunes. It was another place to get out of fast! It seemed the only other option between us and the ocean was the mountains but they were too cold! Without any other ideas, we pressed on to San Diego to visit my son, Michael, and think about what to do. While there, my sister called and asked if we would spend Christmas with her in San Francisco. Off we went up the coast, with my son soon following, to spend the holiday with family.

New Year's Eve 1991. It was weird to realize this time last year, we had our feet sunk in the warm sand at Kovalam Beach. This motel in Ukiah, California wasn't nearly as romantic, but we did have some excitement! It was 2:30 a.m. when I woke up to a strange noise. I lay there listening, trying to figure out where it was coming from and what was causing it. It sounded as if someone was trying to unscrew the hinges on our door but that couldn't be, as the hinges were on the inside! I got quietly out of bed and drew back the curtain just a tad and peered out. I couldn't see anything, but the noise continued. I went over to the bed and shook Herm. "Wake up. I think someone is doing something to our door."

Herm got up and went over to listen. "I think someone is out there all right!" he whispered. Herm dropped his voice a few octaves and yelled, "who's there?" Whoever it was took off running. We called the office to let them know something was going on and someone came flying out the door and actually caught the guy! Come to find out he was a prankster who was going door to door exchanging the numbers. Our room, which was formerly number 8, was now a dangling 6 since we had interrupted the screw tightening. What an unusual but funny way to start off 1992!

OK, I guess we couldn't live with my sister or son all winter, so we resumed our quest. Record rain and snow pushed us eastward to investigate a couple more places. First was the Salton Sea but it had a highway on one side and busy train tracks on the other. The second was a pretty spot on the Colorado River but trash was scattered everywhere, and the energy didn't feel good at all.

We were at our wit's end. What were we going to do, just keep wandering for months? We had thought it would be easy to find a warm, dry, place to camp in this big wide country but I guess it didn't work so well if you only had a tent! Everyone thought we were nuts camping that way and we were beginning to agree with them! Despite our rest stops in San Diego and San Francisco, we were tired, really tired. We had tried everything we knew, asked at every information office and nothing had panned out. "Please 'Universe', help us find a place to land!"

Our last hope was the BLM's LTVA west of Blythe, CA. Since the previous LTVA's were either gravel pits or parking lots, we didn't have high expectations. The one exciting thing was that area was supposed to have lots of rockhounding which had Herm excited.

With our usual optimism at an all-time low, we headed 19 miles west on highway10. We took the exit by the prison, onto a dusty, rough, dirt road which headed straight into the desert. No gravel pits, no dune buggies or trains, just flat desert with scattered cactus and some hills in the distance. We didn't want to get our hopes up but at the 12 mile mark, we came to the sign for Wiley Well campground. It was beautiful!!! The 15 camping spaces were arranged along a tree-lined wash, making it feel cozy and peaceful. We were so excited; this was just what we had been looking for! We stopped to talk with the campground host and were devastated to discover the campground was FULL! "No! Now what?" The host told us there was another LTVA further down the road which was much bigger and not usually full. OK, the last try, this was it, there were no more!!

The sign by the side of the road read Coon Hollow Campground. We took a right down a long dusty entranceway and parked in front of the host's large RV. Even though the place looked pretty empty we didn't let out our breath until we were welcomed and told to pick a spot! Oh my God!!! After two months of our Vision Quest, we had finally found the light at the end of the tunnel!

CHAPTER 11

COON HOLLOW

Site 29 was at the far north end of the campground. It was very private and backed by a tree-lined wash. Long stretches of flat desert rose into a series of hills in the distance. Each site had a picnic table, fire pit and a grill. A pit toilet was close by and there was a well, where you could get water for washing. Drinking water was available from a tested well at the rest area where we had turned off the highway.

As usual, we were the only fools with a tent. Most folks enjoyed all the comforts of home in their roomy motor homes or trailers and had been coming here for years, to escape winter in their home states. The LTVAs were a good deal as you paid a small one-time fee which allowed you to stay six months!

Due to the almost nonstop winds, we snuggled our tent into a thicket of twisted branches, so we were protected on three sides. We cleared away debris, dragged brush over and piled it up to make a windbreak so we could sit in front of the tent out of the gale. It was so weird how we could sit there in shirtsleeves but if we stood up, we needed three or four layers of clothes. Since we hadn't brought chairs, we fashioned our own. Herm built his out of sticks, but I dug a hole to put my butt in and used my pack to lean on. It ended up being very comfortable, way nicer than the one Herm had made!

When the wind wasn't blowing, it was fairly mild but as soon as the sun set the temperature plunged. Getting into the tent was like climbing into a meat locker and puddles were often iced over by morning. We had no idea the desert got that cold, we thought desert equaled heat! Another belief shattered.

It had been a week since we had showered, and we were feeling the need to clean our bodies. Since there were no showers in camp, I came up with an idea inspired by our overseas travel. I emptied the milk crates we stored our supplies in, lined them with trash bags and filled them with water from the well. In Asia, we had learned the native way of washing by dipping water out of a container, throwing it over us, soaping up and rinsing. We did the same here, finding bushes to hide behind and hoping no one was hiking nearby. As long as we did it in the heat of the day it was tolerable. We also used the crate method to get water to wash our clothes. We got a kick out of draping our laundry all over our windbreaks to dry, just like they did in India. It made us feel right at home!

Born and brought up in New England, neither of us knew anything about deserts so every day was an adventure. We discovered all the rusted ration cans and spent shell casings we were finding, were from General Patton's army during WWII! I guess this area was a training ground for the troops. It was amazing all the detritus from that time was still there for us to discover so many years later! Our guidebook to the deserts of the southwest, helped us put names to the trees, bushes, cacti and other vegetation. It also assisted in identifying the tracks of our animal neighbors. We saw lots of birds and the Gambel Quail with their funny little feather hats frequented our campsite, looking for leftover food. The cute little Kit Foxes we would occasionally see weren't as cute when they stole our shoes if we left them out at night.

Besides the birds that filled the sky, there was also a plethora of military aircraft. With a number of airbases not far away, they used the desert for their exercises, so we got to see some pretty strange sights. Besides the usual jets, there were stealth bombers, drones, helicopters, even a blimp! Helicopters would swing through the campground dangling rescue platforms and young pilots would buzz us in their jets flying so low we could see their smiling faces. I must say, for someone who hates noise, the deafening blast of those jets flying by so close was a real rush. Nighttime brought a light show as flares lit up the sky and the boom of bombs dropping at the nearby practice range shook the ground. It was like the 4th of July at least a few times a week.

With us being in our early 40s, we were by far the youngest people in camp. In fact, most of the long-time regulars were our parents or even grandparents' age. It was a friendly group, and we were warmly welcomed into the Coon Hollow community. They all felt sorry for us camping out in the elements and sort of adopted us. We were included in the group campfires where we cooked "pies" over the coals, and everyone swapped stories. Potlucks, birthday celebrations, rockhounding trips, all came with invites for us "youngsters".

Every day Herm would gather wood for our little grill so he could cook our meals. EJ, our 80-year-old neighbor, was also the cook in his family and many nights at supper time he would call out in his husky smoker's voice, "Herm, is dinner ready?" Oh boy, we loved those calls because that meant EJ had been baking.

"Sure is!" Herm would call back and a few minutes later EJ would deliver either rolls or bread hot out of the oven. Mmmmm, mmmm!!

EJ was a character, tall, white-haired, with a deeply lined face, he was always laughing and joking. A former chiropractor, he would give us adjustments right on the picnic table and when he worked on you, you knew you had been cracked! He and I often had long conversations about alternative health, healing and spirituality, all subjects close to both our hearts.

Exploring the desert to our south one day, we were excited to find a hill full of crystals which we creatively dubbed Crystal Hill! We followed the trail of glittery rocks to discover geodes littering the area. When we got back, our neighbor, Fred, came to see what we had gathered. He, along with many of the other long-term rockhounds, brought cutting and polishing equipment with them so they could process the stones they found. The geodes didn't look like much on the outside, just nondescript, bumpy gray rocks, but many of them held a surprise. Fred kindly offered to cut them open and the moment I saw the delicate quartz crystals inside, I was hooked on rocks.

On one of our weekly road trips, we stumbled across Quartzite, AZ, just on the other side of the Colorado River from Blythe. During the winter months, Quartzite hosts the world's largest swap meet. Thousands of RVs, of all sizes and shapes were scattered across the desert as far as the eye could see! Hundreds of vendors lined the streets with their tables and tents, selling everything from grandma's jewelry to dead animal parts. Rocks to solar equipment, you name it, you could find it there! There was even a used book shop whose proprietor was a small, wiry, deeply tanned man clad only in a thong! Now that was different!

The crowds were large, the atmosphere was festive and in the hours we spent wandering among the booths we barely made a dent in all there was to see. Then we learned the big selling season didn't even start until the following month! At that time, over half a million people would descend on this town of 1700 hardy desert souls.

Since we were getting bored sitting around camp every day and Quartzite had everything a crafter needed, we decided to try making jewelry. We had no idea what to buy so got a little of everything. Some wire, thread, findings and beads. We also bought soapstone to carve and leather to make bags.

Back at Coon Hollow, I became obsessed with creating. There were never enough daylight hours to do all I wanted and way too many night hours lying around. I would lay awake half the night thinking of new designs and then couldn't wait to get up and try them! I was exhausted! I started earlier and earlier each day, but the days still weren't long enough.

By the end of January, the midday sun was so intense we had to put up a tarp to give us some shade while we worked. The weather was getting steadily warmer, and the desert was starting to come alive. Little green plants and grass were poking their heads out of the sandy ground and the trees were starting to bud and leaf! A new world was appearing before our very eyes and a lot of that had to do with the rain.

Contrary to yet another misconceived notion, it actually rains quite frequently in the desert and sometimes quite heavily! On one of those stormy nights, I elected to sleep in the car as I was concerned the wash in back of us would flood. Since Herm didn't relish curling himself into a ball in our cramped vehicle, he opted for the soggy tent. About 4 a.m. the ground could absorb no more and the wash behind us started to roar with a torrent of water. As dawn broke, Herm and I went out to see what was going on. We forged the stream nearest camp but weren't able to get through the next one as it was churning white water with lizards and a tortoise riding debris in the middle of the rapids. It was very exciting, and we now understood why people are warned not to camp in washes!

A few hours later, the sun was out, big puffy clouds drifted in the blue sky and there was a cool gentle breeze bringing us the sweet smell of clean air and moist earth. The water in the wash subsided to a gentle, slow-moving stream soon to become a trickle in the mud.

As much as we loved our tent we were being worn down by the weather when it was cloudy, cool and windy. On those days we spent a lot of time sitting in the car which was not much fun. After spending time visiting our neighbors in their homey RVs, I was lobbying for a new house but alas, there was nothing in our price range. I suggested we go to San Diego to visit Michael and RV shop there.

Many dealers and newspaper ads later, we found an old 24-foot Class C motorhome, who we dubbed "ALF". It had a sleep-over cab, a nice kitchen and a huge u-shaped area in the back with a table and cushions all around which was perfect for working on my crafts. I was so excited to finally have a real home but also a bit sad to see our old life changing. We were no longer pioneers; we had given in to convention. Even though we still slept in the tent and cooked outside, it just wasn't the same.

The best part of having the RV was the refrigerator! Now we were able to buy frozen foods, ice cream, condiments and fresh veggies! The second-best part was having lights at night! The not-so-good part was not understanding how batteries and generators worked. We thought we could run our lights all week, then just turn on the generator to charge the batteries when they were low. We didn't realize in order to START the generator, there needed to be juice left in the batteries. Having no luck getting them charged by hooking them to the truck, we gave up and went to Quartzite to buy a solar panel. At the same time, I bought a Solar Oven, so I could bake with the energy of the sun!! We were excited to get back to self-sufficiency.

By March, the desert was alive. Flowers carpeted the ground and adorned the bristly cacti with magenta and yellow blooms where butterflies dined. Crickets creaked, birds sang, rabbits nibbled, tortoises crawled, lizards scurried and then there were the rattlesnakes. We were careful when walking as we would often hear them rattling their warnings as we passed their hiding places. I love snakes and thought the rattlers were beautiful, but their appearance meant it was time to go.

Alf had been really fun to live in but was a horror show to drive and turned out to be a piece of junk! He swayed like a drunken sailor while moving down the road and we had to death grip the steering wheel to keep him from falling over. AND Alf apparently didn't like being hot. If we shut off his engine, he wouldn't start again until he cooled off. This caused us some embarrassing moments at gas stations as we sat there taking up space at a tank while Alf rested. Our only alternative was to fill him up while he was running which was a bit nerve-wracking. We stopped in Tucson to try to sell him, but it was obvious Alf didn't want to leave us. Every time we got to a dealer he went dead. NOT a great selling point. No one wanted to give us more than $4000 for him and looking back that would have been a good deal since I ended up giving him away many years later.

We switched off driving as we crawled our way to Georgia to visit friends. When we got there, we were total wrecks, our nerves shot! We just couldn't drive Alf one more mile! With a sigh of relief, we unhooked our car from the back and left Alf with our friends. It was so wonderful to be headed home in a vehicle that wasn't trying to kill us.

We learned a lot that winter and had found a home at Coon Hollow but we were looking forward to a summer in our little kennel house gardening and creating. Little did we know our "accidental" discovery of Quartzite had set in motion a new direction in our lives that would color the years to come.

CHAPTER 12

BUSINESS

So, we were home with all this jewelry, stone carvings and little deerskin pouches. Plus, we still had some supplies and were keen to keep creating. What were we going to do with it all? I had sold some jewelry to our neighbors at Coon Hollow which had whetted our appetite to make some money. It would be nice to at least cover the cost of the materials.

Herm saw a flyer for a craft show, which we entered, made some money and before we knew it we were in full production mode. We signed up for every show we could find that summer and fall. Of course, most were outside, so that meant buying a canopy, and then we needed tables to put things on, and then we needed cloths to cover the tables, and then we needed a way to display the items and then we needed a truck to carry it all! So much for keeping things simple!

It was turning into a real business, so we needed a name. One night I had a vivid dream where a voice kept saying, "It's the fire eagle, it's the fire eagle!" I had always had an affinity for eagles, so that name resonated with me. Herm also liked it and after throwing around a few permutations our business became Fire Eagle Productions.

When I wasn't online searching for supplies to replenish our raw materials, I was sitting in our screened porch designing. It was as if my creativity had been repressed my entire life and now had broken free in a flood of enterprise! My whole family is artistic, and I never felt I had gotten that gene so I was amazed when I realized I had some talent as well! I never seemed to run out of ideas and was having SO much fun!

Herm was also making product every day but what turned him on was selling. At first, I went to the shows with him but quickly discovered I didn't like that part. It worked best if I created, did the books and ordered supplies while letting him do what he loved best.

By November, the cold was settling in, and we were ready to head back to Coon Hollow. It was cheap, we had friends there and it was close to Quartzite where we could buy supplies. We were much better prepared than the year before. We knew where the free campgrounds were, what to bring with us and could head straight there instead of vision questing for two months!

CHAPTER 13

ROCKS

We settled into our old campsite and joined the Quartzite Rock and Mineral Club. Once members, we could use the rock equipment for free. They also offered classes ranging from the cutting and polishing of cabochons to various kinds of jewelry-making. We were excited to learn all we could and took as many classes as we had time for.

I love how the "Universe" provides. We had made peace with the fact we would have to spend another winter in our tent but that was about to change. When EJ arrived with his trailer, he asked if we would like to buy it? He said he had a different one at home he preferred and wanted to sell this one.

"Hell yeah!!!" Our new home was 26 feet long with a bed in the back. It wasn't as roomy as Alf, but it would keep us out of the weather and everything worked!

The previous year we kept hearing about a fire agate mine that was not too far from camp but could never find it. Determined to discover its whereabouts, we asked for more detailed directions and took a hike up there. We were welcomed by a friendly woman about our age, skinny as a rail, her long brown hair pinned up in a wild bun. The mine sat high on a hill overlooking our campground in the distance. It was desolate, with chunks of blasted rock around deep holes in the ground. To one side was Nancy's residence, an old trailer sitting under an overhang attached to a weathered shed. Tools, propane tanks, a 4 wheeler, an old truck and a bulldozer littered the area. We liked Nancy right away, she was a wild thing, full of life and laughter. We couldn't believe she lived up there alone all year running the mine, she was one tough lady!

The three of us really hit it off and we spent much of that winter learning silversmithing, rock cutting and mining from her. The mining part was no easy digging in the dirt but was smashing rock with picks and hammers. What made all the shoulder-jarring banging worthwhile, was discovering a pocket of the opalized reds, blues and greens of the fire agate. Mother Gaia sure does hide some gorgeous stones.

I don't know if it was the mining or Nancy's personality that drew people there, but it was a busy place with many folks returning year after year. We met some real characters and also got our picture in a rock and mineral magazine. Since Herm's latent passion for rocks had been reignited, it was great for him to mingle with and learn from all the old, experienced rockhounds who came up there to dig.

As soon as the shows opened in Quartzite, we spent most days shopping for jewelry-making supplies. We stocked up on deerskin for making bags, more carving stones to turn into pipes and stone fetishes and even turtle shells to make rattles. After getting a taste of mining and finding fire agate, Herm was now on the prowl for rock and mineral specimens to buy for resale as well. We would have a full truck going home!

It was a very busy winter, making product, shopping, learning, socializing and hiking the desert. Before we left, EJ decided he liked his old trailer better and bought it back from us. I had a sneaking suspicion this was his plan all along. Selling us the trailer in the first place was his way of giving us a place to live for the winter. Having people like EJ for neighbors was one of the reasons we loved this place so much.

CHAPTER 14

EXPANSION

This summer, in addition to craft shows, we began setting up at Pow Wows. We were making a number of Native-type crafts and thought Pow Wows would be a better venue in which to sell them. We did well but soon discovered if we sold supplies for other people to make things, business was even better!

Always on the lookout for new items to sell, we discovered the New Hampshire roadkill auction. Yup, you heard me right…roadkill! All year, dead animals which were still pretty much intact were collected and thrown into a freezer. In the fall, they were dragged out, sorted into species, numbered and placed on the floor of a huge barn in Concord, NH for humans to bid on. I imagine most of those humans were taxidermists and trappers who knew what they were looking for, not rank novices like ourselves. We picked up a clipboard with a list of the animals and their numbers and walked among the contorted frozen critters not having a clue about what price to write down. All the animals looked good to us, especially the glut of black bears! Herm and I looked at each other trying not to laugh at the whole scene.

We turned in our paper with all the numbers filled in and waited. Would we get anything, we wondered? A while later we were handed our sheet marked with the animals we had "won" and found we had done pretty well! Six beavers, two red foxes, two otters, four bobcats and one bear! "OMG, now what?" we laughed.

We loaded up the frozen carcasses, carted them back to the kennel to thaw out, then skinned them. Herm made a wire enclosure, we called a "rotter", to throw the carcasses into so the bugs could clean the bones. When the insects ate all they wanted, we finished the cleaning process and sold the pieces. The skins we tanned and sold as well but found we had become attached to our young bear and had to keep him. I totally enjoyed all of it, the skinning, tanning, cleaning, it all made me feel close to the spirit of the animals and brought me great peace.

So, Fire Eagle was growing by leaps and bounds and every weekend saw us setting up at one venue or another. Sometimes we split up and I did the Pow Wows while Herm did either a craft or rock show. I loved the Pow Wows and selling there didn't seem to bother me like it did at the craft shows. I felt comfortable with these down-to-earth people. The powerful resonance of the drum, the "singers", the dancing, brought a feeling of deep connection with the earth that filled my soul.

At season's end, we decided we needed a travel trailer. I guess we were getting soft, or maybe smarter. We found a used 17-foot Wilderness and brought it home to fix it up. It had lots of big windows, the dinette in front turned into a bed and the couch in the back did the same. The kitchen was in the middle with a bathroom near the front table. I went to work reupholstering all the ugly brown and orange cushions, covering them with a pretty turquoise design. The linoleum floor we covered with a carpet remnant and Herm put up shelves everywhere. When finished, it was a cozy home, and we were excited to get on the road and try it out! Little did we know at the time, that it would be our dwelling for the next 12 years.

CHAPTER 15

THE TRIBE OF LIGHT

We were soon back at space #29 in Coon Hollow. Each time we crossed the country going west, I delighted in reaching west Texas where the vistas opened wide. I used to love the cozy feel of New England, where I grew up, but now it felt stifling after being in big sky country.

Along with our usual winter activities, something extraordinary occurred that season. Each morning I prayed to the six directions and during that time I started to feel a pressure in my throat and tension in my body. It was almost like something/someone wanted to speak. When I closed my eyes, I could see what appeared to be Native American warriors clothed in feathered regalia. The tension then started to happen in other situations, usually in relation to the natural surroundings or even some events or people. What was going on? Did this have something to do with all the Pow Wows I had been to?

I finally decided to go ahead and just "let it out". When I did, a voice/voices began to speak or sing through me in some unknown language. The singing style was similar to what I had heard at the Pow Wows and the words almost sounded Native as well. It felt like the words and song were some sort of prayer. I could feel five distinct personalities as they all had different "voices". One was a woman who sounded like she was crying for the earth. A deep-voiced, matter-of-fact male felt very powerful, and another man felt calm and very caring.

It was all pretty strange but since I had been studying metaphysics for so many years, it didn't freak me out. I figured I was channeling something/someone, or a group of someones but I wondered why me? It wasn't as if I had asked to channel and what was I supposed to do with this? Since I was well aware negative entities could masquerade as positive, I was anxious to get home and consult my psychic friends to make sure they were the good guys!

CHAPTER 16

SPIRITS

It turned out to be a very "strange" summer in many ways. The voices were still with me when we got home from the desert. I asked my friends to experience what was coming through me and was relieved when they said they were positive entities. I continued to "speak" when I did my prayers and sometimes it happened when I meditated. All summer the voices grew stronger and were especially active at the Pow Wows. The drumming, singing and certain people, animals or regalia appeared to set them off. I asked who they were and heard, Elohim. I had never heard that word before so asked again and they said, Tribe of Light/Tribe of Stars. OK, I didn't know if I was just making this up or not but decided to just go with the name, Tribe of Light. I still didn't know what they wanted from me, but I just let it go and rolled with it.

In August, I bought the book "The Celestine Prophecy", a first-person narrative of spiritual awakening and synchronicity. I had debated for months about buying it but then felt an unknown force directing me to get it. Once I did, I started experiencing my own synchronicities.

At the end of the month, just after starting the book, Herm and I were driving to a rock show in Maine and Debbie Gagne popped into my mind. I thought, "I should get in touch with her and ask her about "The Tribe". Her husband, Paul, had worked at my ex-husband's company and when we went on sales trips, she was the one I hung out with. Debbie was a psychiatric nurse and a Therapeutic Touch (TT) practitioner. TT is a form of energy work, and she was the one who introduced me to it when I was in nursing school. In fact, we had attended some Therapeutic Touch workshops together. She was very in tune with Spirit and was a powerful healer in her own right.

Well, wouldn't you know, who appeared at our booth but Debbie and Paul! Oh my God! After a bit of girl squealing, hugs and introductions to Herm, they told us they now owned a metaphysical shop and were at the show to buy crystals for the store! They invited us to their house for dinner where we caught up on the past nine years of our lives. I told her about my voices, and she wanted to hear what they had to say. She asked them a series of questions which they answered in their language. Even though they didn't speak English, I always felt a sense of what they were saying. I got the impression they were speaking to people's soul-self which would bypass the ego. Debbie felt they were here to heal people and I should find a way to use them to do so. I was thankful for her perspective and after that started to expand on "using" them.

I began with Herm as he was always a willing and supportive guinea pig. Since I had learned Therapeutic Touch, I already knew how to feel and clear energy blocks in the body. I would have him lie down, then scan his body with my hands. This is when the Tribe would step in to help. When I came to stuck energy, they would tone or talk through me. They would sometimes use hand motions, like mudras or Reiki symbols, and also would blow or clap over the area. The crying lady appeared to work on emotional blocks, while others worked on physical issues. It was always interesting and over time, I learned to get out of the way and just let them do their work.

While all this was happening, I began doing automatic writing. You do this by going into a semi-meditative state and just letting your hand write without thinking about it. One day I asked where the "Tribe" was from and they wrote, Electra. I had never heard that name and had no idea where that might be. At the same time, I received a card in the mail promoting the book "Pleiadian Agenda" by Barbara Hand Clow. I thought it was pretty weird getting that card but felt it must be a sign I should buy the book. The day it arrived in the mail I opened to a random page and staring me in the face was a list of the stars in the Pleiades system and there was Electra! I was totally blown away!!! The Seven Sisters/Pleiades was always the first constellation I looked for when I gazed up at the night sky. It always felt like my touchpoint, my home and I had a longing to be there. What did all this mean?

After a difficult day where I was resisting sitting down to do automatic writing, I had an overwhelming feeling I just had to do it. The words poured out as I typed, and I got a transmission which read: "I wonder what you will do when you see us?" As Herm and I headed out in the dark to sleep in our tent in the woods, I was thinking how weird that message was and wondered what it meant.

I had just fallen asleep when I was jolted awake by the sound of something running down the path toward my side of the tent. It started scratching and trying to climb up the side whining and snorting. "Oh my God, what IS that?" Herm cried, quickly sitting up.

"I don't know!" I said, heart pounding as I banged on the side of the tent yelling "go away, go away!" It stopped briefly, then went to the front and started up again. With both of us yelling and banging, it finally ran into the woods. We looked at each other wide-eyed, both remembering the message I had gotten just before we headed to bed.

"I didn't want to look out the front, did you?" Herm asked.

"No way, I was afraid I would see something weird!"

"Me too!" he agreed.

"It sure wasn't scared of us and it came right to my side of the tent too! Would a wild animal really do that?"

"I wouldn't think so. It was pretty freaky," Herm said settling back down. It was a restless night for both of us, half-awake, on guard, wondering if we would get a return visit.

The next morning, while I was getting ready for my daily run, I had a premonition that I would see what was at our tent the night before. My usual jog took me down the road then onto a woods track. This led to a gravel pit and eventually wound its way through the woods back to the kennel. As soon as I reached the gravel pit, I spotted an animal waddling along the path, headed away from me. I thought at first it was a porcupine but once I got closer, I saw it was a raccoon. It turned as it heard me and started walking slowly towards me making the same whining sounds I had heard at the tent. I stopped and it kept coming toward me. "OK raccoon, I don't know if you are a real animal or some kind of spirit but you need to stop right there. You may have a message for me but coming as a raccoon isn't such a great idea. Don't you know they can carry rabies? Even though you look healthy you are not acting like a normal wild animal, and you are making me nervous." I waved my hand off to the right and said, "go on, go back in the woods please." He stared me down, then seemed to shrug and headed into the woods in the direction I had pointed. "Oh my god," I breathed, "what WAS that?"

When I got home, I went right to my bookshelf and opened my *Animal Speak* book to look up what raccoon signified. Holy Crap!! "Spirits coming in disguise!" WHAT? Okay, that seemed to mean my automatic writing may actually be real. I felt a bit disappointed that I hadn't been calm enough to "listen" to what raccoon may have wanted to tell me, as it certainly was no coincidence we had crossed paths that morning. I guess I may have failed that "test". I hoped I would get another chance to interact with whoever/whatever was writing through me. It was all very interesting!

CHAPTER 17

NEW FRIENDS

The "Universe" was on fire that summer! In addition to all the synchronicities and messages coming at us, we met two people who would change the trajectory of our future.

The first was Dr. Marsha Wolfe, an acupuncturist, naturopath and practitioner of Tibetan medicine. We went to her for treatment and ended up becoming friends. Marsha is a great practitioner but eccentric. She is always a bit frazzled, forgetful and almost always late. She had been studying Tibetan medicine for years with one of the foremost Tibetan doctors. She would often bring her teacher, Dr. Dhonden, to the States to see patients. We would volunteer to help and in the process got to know him and his pharmacist quite well.

Late that summer, Marsha told us she would be traveling to south India in the fall to assist at the Kalachakra teachings given by the Dalai Lama. Many thousands of people would attend, and she was going to work with the medical practitioners there to treat any illnesses. We asked if she needed any help and she thought that would be great!

Herm and I were always talking about doing volunteer work. We looked into a number of organizations, but we were both pretty independent. The thought of following orders from some institution didn't sit well with us. In our travels, we had seen first-hand, the damage some of those groups did in Third World countries. We wanted no part of that but helping Marsha in India sounded really great as we were getting the travel bug again. I never thought I would go back to India as I wasn't enamored with it the first time. This time, however, we would be working with the Tibetans, a culture I felt very drawn to. Herm, on the other hand, had a real affinity for India, so he was more than anxious to go. It wasn't a certainty this would all pan out, but we were hoping for the best.

Not long after talking with Marsha, I got a sign it may actually all work out. I was sitting in the woods, reading the book *Animal Speak*. It outlines how to interpret what an animal or nature is trying to tell you. A snake had crossed my path going east. I thought that might mean we were actually going to India since India is in the East. Then I thought, "wait, that's silly, India isn't in the East!" I continued reading and it said, "In the East, India and Tibet especially......." What? REALLY?

The second person who was to figure so importantly in our future, I met at a Pow Wow in New Hampshire. Hawk was a tall, dark-skinned man with a gentle smile. His hair was cut in a distinctive manner, shaved on the sides with a short oval patch on top blending into a long braid in the back. Dangling feathered earrings framed his handsome face. I felt an immediate energetic connection with him and to our surprise, we found we were from the same city in Rhode Island! Since he was younger than I was, we had missed each other in high school but it appeared he had been in my sister's class! What were the odds??

Hawk was a descendent of the Nipmuck tribe and lived with his family in Maine. He was at the Pow Wow selling his beautiful hand-carved flutes and playing them for the crowd. I noticed he also had a didgeridoo which he got the most magical sounds out of it. We had brought one back from Australia but had no luck producing anything but a big fart. That night I told Herm about Hawk and how I would love to give him our didgeridoo since it was only gathering dust in our house. Herm agreed and the next day when I presented it to Hawk his eyes got wide and a big grin spread across his face. He gratefully accepted our gift and immediately started making some good noise with that long wooden tube.

In September, Herm and I attended the Pow Wow held each year at the casino in Connecticut. Native dancers and singers from all over the US and Canada came to compete in their colorful regalia.

A couple of strange things happened that day. When we drew our oracle cards that morning, we had each drawn Fox. Fox means camouflage or being in Oneness. We joked we ought to try being invisible foxes when we walked into the casino and see if the camouflage worked. It did!!! To our amazement, no one looked at us or said a thing as we walked right past the ticket seller. Not believing this could be true, we walked out, then back in again. No one gave us a second glance, not even the security guard. It was very strange!

Herm had yet to meet Hawk and I was hoping we would see him that day. A hawk had landed in front of me that morning when I was doing my prayers, so I took that as a good sign. I had scanned the crowds all day and was beginning to doubt the morning's omen when I literally bumped into him as we were leaving the bookstore. "There you are!" I cried, giving him a hug, "I thought we were going to miss you!" His wife, Lisa and two daughters were there as well, so we all got to do introductions.

Somehow, we got talking about a piece of property they were trying to buy in Maine. They had a vision of a place where people could gather, have ceremony and connect. I resonated strongly with that dream, as it was something I had envisioned as well. We soon said our goodbyes and headed home but I couldn't get the conversation about that property out of my mind.

······◆◆······

NEW ADVENTURES
1995- 2000

······◆◆······

CHAPTER 18

CHAOS

Chaos reigns! Hanging out with Dr. Marsha always involved exasperation and a test of patience. We bought tickets to India and then Marsha decided not to go! BUT she wanted us to change those tickets so we could accompany a Buddhist spiritual teacher and his son back to India. She had sponsored this person to conduct teachings at the Open Center in New York City where she lived. Marsha was very tied to the Buddhist community through her Tibetan Relief project and as a student of Tibetan medicine for many years. Through those ties, she had heard of this Rinpoche. (An honorific title which means precious one.)

That all sounded really interesting, but we didn't want to trade in our cheaper tickets for the more expensive British Air ones. Well, wouldn't you know, as fate or divine intervention would have it, the airlines overbooked our flight! This Buddhist guy must have put out some pretty powerful prayers to get his wish for us to travel with him!

We agreed to go to New York a few days before the scheduled departure to give Marsha a hand with all that needed to be done. The bus from the airport left us 10 blocks from her apartment in Chelsea and by the time we rang her bell we were huffing and puffing from hiking with our big packs. The door flew open, and Marsha pulled us inside. "Hi, I'm glad you are here, I was just going to leave you a note. We have to leave for the Open Center right NOW!"

Before we could even drop our bags, she told us to grab a bunch of boxes and her German Shepherd dog, Gabe. We helped hail three cabs and fill them with all the paraphernalia that was needed. A throne, makeshift altars, boxes, bags, the dog, Herm, myself and a monk. Marsha would be following later with the teacher and his son.

When we arrived at the center, I was handed a stapler and a pile of papers and told to collate and attach the reading material and prayers and Herm was tasked with assisting the monks. As the devotees arrived, I was promoted to ticket-collector and shoe police. Unlike the Buddhist practitioners who were streaming in for Rinpoche's teachings, we had no idea what was going on. This was all new to us, we didn't even know what a Rinpoche was!

Marsha came bustling in followed by an older man dressed in an orange wool hat and long, brown robe. As the teacher shuffled into the room, his devotees stood with hands folded and bowed as he passed. He mirrored their hand position and bowed in return, smiling and nodding. He was a tall, well-built man in his 60s while his son looked to be in his 30s and was dressed in western clothes.

Back at Marsha's, after the lecture, we made up our pads on the floor of the entrance hall, but as usual, Marsha wanted to talk….and talk, which she did until 2 a.m. She finally got the hint we wanted to sleep and disappeared into the adjacent treatment room to sleep on her massage table. The actual living space of the apartment was downstairs but that is where Rinpoche, son Sangye and the monk were staying, so we all had to make do with what was left.

The day we were set to leave was total chaos. Our flight wasn't scheduled until evening, which meant we had many hours to endure Marsha craziness! It started off with her not being able to find Rinpoche's tickets. She ran off to get replacements while I tried to pacify her irate patients, answer her phone and make return calls. Meanwhile, Herm had to take Rinpoche and Sangye to the Indian Consulate to get their passports stamped so they could leave the country.

At last, the patient schedule was completed so we could take a shower and pack. Just as we were calming down from the day, the doorbell rang, yet again! Marsha then informed us it was now office hours for Dr Wu! What? I thought we were going to have some peace for a little bit! The ring of the bell was constant as a stream of patients arrived and crowded into the tiny waiting room. We hauled our bags from one empty space to another, trying to keep them out of the way of the patients and Dr Wu.

Time was moving on and we were trying to get Marsha in gear. Herm and I are very organized people who are always on time, so dealing with the disorganization and craziness had us biting our tongues bloody! It was so annoying!

We found Marsha downstairs with a typewriter in her lap, conversing with Sangye. I was told to take it upstairs and type a note to Tsering, who was accepting the donated clothes we were schlepping to India. As I was climbing the stairs, she yells, "there will be an Italian filmmaker coming any minute to see Rinpoche. Make sure you're near the door to answer it."

It was total insanity, we needed to take control of the situation, or we would never make it to the airport! We got the filmmaker out of there and Herm called a car for Rinpoche. We dragged 12 bags of gear through the packed waiting room and got Marsha and her dog through the door. She careened through the streets following Rinpoche's taxi, complaining the whole time about how bad the driver was while we hung on for dear life!

Right up until the end she had to manage everything and everyone. Taking control of the bags and telling the airport staff how to do their jobs. Oh my god! What a relief to make it through the gate and leave that madness behind!

We had a 14-hour layover in London which could have been deadly had it not been for Herm getting us into the Executive Lounge. He told the lady at the desk that Rinpoche was a spiritual leader and she let us in! Woohoo! Reclining chairs, couches, TV, drinks and food were all provided! Sangye spoke decent English, but Rinpoche's grasp of the language was limited so we did a lot of smiling and nodding. It was all very congenial, and I had to keep reminding myself this was a big-deal guy!

CHAPTER 19

KALACHAKRA

Amonk met us at the airport in Delhi and arranged for cabs to transport us and the mountain of luggage to Gomang Guest House at Majnakatila Tibetan camp. We were provided with a fancy room with an attached bath which Rinpoche insisted on paying for. Everyone we met treated us like VIPs because of our association with this spiritual teacher. It was all very strange!

Since thousands of people would be in Mundgod for the Kalachakra, Rinpoche told us to contact his other son, Jigme, who was a monk there. He assured us he would be able to find us a room. Before we left, he thanked us for our help and made us promise to visit him in McLeod Ganj after the Kalachakra. With that, we bid our new friends farewell and began our next adventure.

Almost thirty-five hours of train and bus travel later, with little to no sleep, brought us to the Tibetan settlement camp in Mundgod. It was made up of nine different camps all miles apart. The bus deposited us in Camp 3, where we spent an hour walking around asking where to find Mrs. Ky. When we were finally directed to the hospital, we discovered our services would NOT be needed. Well, that was typical! Marsha had assured us everything was set up and they were expecting us. Just another fantasy, I guess!

We told Mrs. Ky we needed to find a monk at Gomang Monastery and she kindly put her ambulance and driver at our disposal. At the monastery, we were told Jigme was in town, so back to Camp 3 we went! We were advised to find the information table so they could announce who we were looking for over the loudspeaker. We waited and waited and waited, through several calls for our monk but he wasn't showing up. What were we going to do? We had no place to stay! At that point, we were so exhausted we wanted to collapse onto our bags, right there in the middle of all the hubbub.

But wait, who is that coming through the crowds towards the announcer's table? A savior in red robes looking very much like Sangye! Thank you, Buddha, it's him! We introduced ourselves and handed him the note from his brother which was written on four wrinkled napkins. He studied the Tibetan script, then looked up and said, "I can get you a room, but it won't be until after the teachings." Oh NO! I just wanted to cry. How would we ever make it through the afternoon? We pulled ourselves together and made plans to meet Jigme later that day. Shouldering our bags, we dragged ourselves to the distant field where the teachings were in session.

Under one of the large tents, we found a whole slew of Westerners sitting on the ground listening intently to the translation of the teachings. The voice of the translator was coming through a loudspeaker which was attached to a pole. Very cool, we would at least be able to listen to what the Dalai Lama was saying! We smiled, said hi and tried to find a spot to sit amongst the crowd. No one looked at us, no one smiled, and no one moved. I thought, "had we become invisible?" I was so pissed, and it was hard to keep my mouth shut. What I wanted to say was, "Fuck you holier than thou Western Buddhists! Thanks so much for accommodating us, I guess we will go sit with the monks in the back." Which is what we did and were welcomed with big smiles. Yup, we sure like Tibetans better than Westerners!

Since we couldn't hear the translation, we had started to nod off. Suddenly, our monks jumped up, grabbed the huge teapots sitting beside them, and sprinted across the field to some tents. A few moments later they came tearing back, went to the front of the Westerners and were working their way towards us. As they got closer, we could see they were serving tea. When finished with the tea, they came running back with buckets of sweet rice. We didn't have containers to accept either but the monk beside us wanted to share his food. It had been plopped onto his dirty bag and we said, "no thank you." However, he wouldn't take no for an answer, and we didn't want to insult him. We smiled, thanked him and choked down the offering as best we could, then surreptitiously poured the rest on the ground. It wasn't only psychologically repulsive but tasted disgusting, both sweet and rancid at the same time.

Jigme got us a great room at his monastery. It had western toilets, cold showers and a big sink where folks washed, clothes, babies and dishes. The electricity was iffy, so we spent most nights straining our eyes to read by candlelight. The people staying there were mostly Mongolian and Russian monks along with Tibetan families. With 50,000 people attending the Initiation we were all very lucky to have a roof over our heads.

Since Mrs. Ky had no work for us, the only thing left to do was attend the teachings we knew nothing about. During the next few days, the Westerners grudgingly allowed us to squeeze in with them and luckily, we landed next to Kate, a friendly woman from California. She was very patient as we asked question after question about what was going on. She told us we were very fortunate to be there as this was the most important tantric initiation conferred by the Dalai Lama. It didn't matter if we knew what was going on or not, we would still receive the blessings and the initiation. Wow! Who knew?

On the final day, I had the coolest experience. I was sitting with my eyes closed listening to His Holiness speak when I saw and felt myself inside a decorated temple with thousands of Dalai Lama's walking towards me. I was very moved by that vision and when I told Kate, she said I had visualized myself inside the Mandela! How cool was that! I had no idea His Holiness had been speaking about that when I had my vision! It was a nice way to finish off the teachings. My back and hips were so sore from sitting on the ground for hours each day, I was ready to move on.

CHAPTER 20

SAI BABA

When in south India on our first trip, we had heard other travelers speak of Sai Baba. We didn't know much about him but since we were so close to his Ashram, we decided to go check him out! A preview of strange things to come occurred when our bus driver stopped for a lunch break. I was standing outside the bus when this wild-looking beggar, began speaking to me. He was sitting on the ground holding a piece of cardboard and the inside ink tube from a pen. His face was partially hidden by his matted hair and long curly black beard, but I could see he had kind eyes. He wore only a torn, filthy shirt and…. nothing else. My ears perked up when I heard his almost unaccented English saying something about psychology and being friends. It appeared he was writing something on the cardboard as he was speaking. He was obviously bright and seemed to have a good sense of humor. In fact, I could see a glint in his eye and a mischievous grin as he reeled in my attention. He didn't seem like a real beggar. Was he some kind of doppelgänger of Sai Baba? I liked the guy and gave him what change I had. He bowed slightly and gave me a big smile. It would have been nice to talk with him, but our bus was leaving. As I looked back, I could see him standing in the dust, waving.

It was a bumpy four-and-a-half-hour bus ride to Sai Baba's Ashram. We passed through farm country on potholed roads but once in Puttaparthi the scene totally changed. Devotees of this guru came from around the world to be in his presence and receive healing. If he couldn't fix them, there was always the modern Super Specialty hospital in town. It was built by donations from his wealthy followers as was the private airport and the multi-story buildings which lined the crowded dusty streets.

In contrast, the room we were assigned at the Ashram was bare, I mean TOTALLY bare! It was like a jail cell with a cement floor and block walls. We were told we could buy mattresses in the village, so Herm ran out to get a couple before the 9 p.m curfew. This "cell" did, however, come with a toilet, sink and shower which was a nice touch…we thought. We soon discovered we were sharing our place with a very large rat who called the sink drain home. He didn't seem at all pleased we had encroached on his space but when we blocked the drain he just shrugged and used the window to get in and out instead.

This place was strange and had too many regulations. Men were dressed in white, you had to be silent, the sexes were segregated in most areas and certain pathways had to be followed. I didn't get it. Why the segregation and the curfews, etc? I don't like rules, never have, so all of this bugged me and put me in a pissy mood.

Even more baffling were the Darshans, which means "the beholding of a holy person". Herm and I were split up as we were directed to segregated sections of the temple. We sat on a polished stone floor facing a "stage" at the front. After waiting for over 30 minutes, tinkling music issued from the loudspeakers and in walked a small man dressed in orange with a bushy black afro. The crowd turned towards him with their hands folded, eyes wide. He walked slowly up one of the "paths" collecting pieces of paper from the raised hands of his devotees. It was my understanding they were handwritten notes beseeching the "holy one" for blessings or healings. When the guru reached the "stage", he and a group of women disappeared behind a door.

I was totally confused. Was that it? No talking to the crowd? Since no one in the temple moved, I figured there must be more to the show. Fifteen minutes later, he reappeared, then disappeared again with another group of people. This coming and going act went on for about an hour and I was SO bored, this was ridiculous! Suddenly, we were blasted with music from the speakers, and everyone began singing. The small orange man emerged from the back of the stage, walked through the crowd once again and was gone. Thank goodness, we could finally leave!

Unlike me, with my bad attitude, Herm was getting into this guy and was totally cool with the whole scene. I didn't see the attraction, but kept attending the Darshans each day, with Herm, hoping to figure it all out. Then it happened, I too fell under the spell but immediately devolved into a petulant child. "Why did he walk down every path but the one I was seated near? Why did Herm get to see him walk by any number of times? Why did he not walk near ME?" Seriously Terra, get a grip! I was fully aware of how ludicrous it was that I was so outraged and jealous. I just shook my head at myself but for whatever reason, I seemed to have no control over Miss Pissy Pants.

At our last Darshan, I finally surrendered to what was going on around me. The separating of the sexes, the pushing and shoving, the not knowing what was happening, I just didn't care anymore. Well, it turns out surrender was the magic key! I was seated in the second row, close to the walkway, and here comes Swami directly towards us. A woman in the first row, a couple of people down from me, put her hands out asking for sacred ash. We had heard this holy man could produce ash or even gold rings out of his palm, so I was watching closely as he suspended his hand above hers. There it was! A stream of gray ash appeared to fall out of his open palm! Wow! If that wasn't real, it was a damn good trick! Was he a true holy man who could materialize things or was he a great magician? I had no idea, but what I was certain of was our time there had been a major learning experience for ME!

CHAPTER 21

RAJASTHAN

Sightseeing, bus and train trips galore followed our time at the ashram. Normally, I would be triggered by the touts, taxi drivers, the noise and the crush of the people. I don't know what Sai Baba did to me, but all of a sudden, I was very calm and tolerant. I realized all the folks yelling for our attention were just trying to feed their families. There was only so much business to go around so if they weren't aggressive, they wouldn't get the money. In contrast, poor Herm was now having his anger issues triggered. Ah, India, the great teacher.

One thing about this country that amazes me is how everyone seems so centered, calm and unhurried despite the chaos around them. In the midst of the congested traffic of city streets with buses, trucks, cars, rickshaws, bicycles, and so forth, all moving in different directions, the people and animals don't hurry. They always seem to know when to move and when to pause. This is true for the legless beggars wheeling their dollies through thick traffic to the animals wandering the streets and train tracks. How everyone moves and weaves is like a dance. When we were first in India, we didn't know how it was possible to get across a busy street without getting run over, but with time, we got into the flow.

I found if I centered myself and breathed slowly, I could join the dance. It became almost a meditation where you could "feel" when to take steps and when to stop. It was a transcendent experience and I got to the point where I loved crossing streets.

Pushkar was a small desert city frequented by many tourists and travelers, so had a lot of touts. My good juju from Sai Baba went out the window when a tout kept bugging us as we took a walk around the lake. When we met some westerners looking for a place to stay, we told them about our hotel and the tout was furious. We tried to ignore him, but he kept harassing Herm. I finally told him to fuck off and when he told me to fuck off, I thought Herm was going to slug him. So much for my new tolerance!

The family who ran our place was really sweet. Princess and her 14-year-old daughter, Surita, took a liking to me and we ended up doing all kinds of girly things together. We looked at magazines, talked about men, marriage and a woman's lot in life. We tried on clothes and jewelry, Surita painted my nails and we laughed as we practiced Hindi and English. At dinner time, Princess taught me how to make chapatis from scratch and I do mean scratch! It started with beating the sheaves of wheat onto the stone patio, gathering the kernels into a mortar and grinding it by hand into flour! Princess made plain chapatis, sugar ones and chili ones and they were all SO yummy!

Jaipur was a blast! As soon as we arrived, we were "adopted" by several young Indian men. We were taking a walk when two guys approached us wanting to join us for tea and practice their English. Herm's first thoughts were they were going to drug and rob us but I didn't get any bad vibes. I was in a good mood and thought, "why not?" Vicky was an art student and Johny worked at a jewelry factory as a silversmith! When they offered to be our tour guides, I was all for it. Even though Herm was still suspicious, he agreed to go along.

The next morning, we found four young guys waiting for us, instead of two. I think that made Herm even more nervous, but he joined me in climbing aboard the motorbikes and off we went to visit some forts.

Later, Vicky took us to his house for tea and we hung out on his bed watching TV and talking. I wondered what his mother thought about him bringing two old Americans home.

The four friends were from different economic and religious backgrounds, with Vicky obviously being from the higher class. He was studying traditional miniature art, following in his famous grandfather's footsteps. The close friendship of the boys clearly illustrated that despite what we have heard, relationships across different backgrounds are very common. We had come to realize how the media distorts and sensationalizes the news. What is happening in real people's lives, is nothing like what is reported.

What followed were several days filled with fun and adventure with "our boys". We visited temples, forts and museums. We were introduced to everyone's families and shared tea and dinners. Hung out like teenagers in Vicky's room and attended a nighttime wedding. Since Johny was involved in the stone cutting/jewelry world, he took Herm from factory to factory bargaining for stones and mineral stock for Herm's business.

It was so much fun cruising around the city on the back of motorbikes. I felt wild and free like I did in college, on the back of my ex-husband's motorcycle. Of course, in India, it was more like an amusement park ride, and you had to stay very aware of everything going on around you. The kids wove in and out of traffic, coming so close to other vehicles, I had to make sure I kept my knees and feet in close. Then there were the times they drove under lumber and pipes sticking out the backs or sides of trucks. Duck or get beheaded! One night, it was particularly exciting when we were stuck in a traffic jam amongst huge Lorries and buses. The only way out was to drive into the oncoming traffic. The headlight on the scooter kept going out and many of the vehicles we were dodging had no lights either! Neither did the cows, dogs, camels, people and bicycles we had to steer clear of! It was a real adrenaline rush, SO much fun!

Just before leaving Jaipur, we had our first accident. We were passing a bullock cart laden with some kind of iron contraptions and one fell onto Johny and I. As we swerved, we hit Vicky and Herm. Pieces of both machines flew off as we came to rest on the center island. Taking inventory of our bodies, I had a scraped and bruised knee, Johny had abrasions and Herm had a twisted wrist. Thankfully we were in pretty good shape, we gathered the pieces of the motorbikes and limped back to town.

I guess the accident was a sign it was time to leave. It had been great fun with our boys and they were sad to see us go but we had to keep our promise to Rinpoche.

CHAPTER 22

MCLEOD GANJ

A 12-hour overnight bus ride from Delhi took us into the mountains where McLeod Ganj was located. Sleeping was an on and off affair as the rutted roads bounced us into the metal seat in front of us threatening to knock our teeth out. Accidents galore littered the roadways and many times the wheels of our bus played with air as it rounded mountain curves. I found it best not to look into the ravines below and see all the vehicles which didn't make it.

In the middle of the night, the bus stopped at a tiny chai shop sitting all by itself in the pitch black. Everyone got off to relieve their bladders. As the men scattered along the roadway, I watched what the Tibetan women did and followed them. They stayed close to the bus where there was light and squatted there. I did the same, using my long skirt as some measure of concealment. One young western woman, however, decided she just couldn't pee in the middle of the road. She wandered out of sight and the next thing we heard was a cry for help! In her search for privacy, she had tumbled down a hill and fallen into a ditch full of water. Lesson #1, don't wander around in the dark on the side of a mountain!

We arrived in McLeod Ganj to a cold, bustling early morning village crowded with Tibetans, Indians and Westerners. The Dalai Lama's yearly teachings were about to begin and many of the people who had been in Mundgod had come to attend. We sat in a restaurant trying to figure out how to find a room when we overheard a monk asking customers if anyone needed a place to stay. The "Universe" had provided for us, yet again! The room was a bit expensive and not so clean, but it would give us a base to work from. Since we planned on staying a few months, we would need to find a cheaper, more permanent place to live.

We dropped our bags and were off to find Rinpoche's place. After many fits and starts, we were eventually directed to a tiny house perched on a hillside outside of town. We were warmly welcomed by Sangye, his wife Jamyang and Rinpoche. They insisted we stay for food after they had heard all about our trip. I don't know how she did it, but Jamyang whipped up a veritable feast on her 2-burner kerosene stove in a corner of the one-room house. It was delicious!

We heard from some Canadians that the Indian villages above McLeod Ganj had cheap rooms for rent. We climbed the steep road which dead-ended at a tea stall and from there followed the dirt paths which traversed the mountainside connecting the villages. It was so peaceful, the only sound being the tingling bells attached to the sheep and goats that wandered the hillsides. We tried several places and ended up in the village of Dharm Kot where we rented a room from Lakshmi. It had a sitting room in front, with a wall of windows looking out to the mountains. There was a big bedroom in the back, a place to cook and a toilet downstairs. It was very "us".

Our life settled into a routine of walking up and down the mountain to McLeod Ganj, shopping for food, and visiting Rinpoche and family. In Dharm Kot we hung out at the tiny tea stall on the corner with other travelers, listening to the village gossip. The locals would tell us who was losing livestock to leopards and bears, which families were having weddings and there was a thief and a possible rapist roaming the hills. At home, we enjoyed dinners with our landlord, Laskshmi and family, sitting on the floor around the fire. That was always preferable to cooking on our little kerosene stove and trying to keep warm in the cold Himalayan winter.

Climbing the steep hill to our village was one way we kept warm, but the tricky part was avoiding the roaming bands of monkeys. They would jump out of the bushes and try to snatch the bags of food we carried. If you looked them in the eye, they would advance upon you with bared teeth and you couldn't scare them off. At times a tug of war would develop and if those sharp little nails ripped the bags, it was all over. They would gather the spoils to their chests and run into the bushes. Annoying little buggers! The second thing which was precarious, was navigating the road at night, especially when it was raining. I generally have no problem walking in the dark, but one black night I slipped off the edge into a clump of stinging nettles. I was glad I was fully clothed!! It was always an adventure!

We were living in three cultures, and it was fascinating. We had the Westerners, the Indians and the Tibetans. The Westerners were an eclectic, and sometimes eccentric bunch. Many were serious Buddhist practitioners; some were just passing through and others were living there full time. Teaching, environmental work, medicine and advising the government were some of the jobs volunteers participated in. Other individuals were studying some aspect of Tibetan culture, art, writing books or making films. They were drawn there from all over the world by the mystique of the Dalai Lama.

Jamyang and Sangye had a one-year-old, holy terror of a son named Rinzen who we took a shine to. As soon as I met him, I felt he was special and maybe a reincarnation. One day Herm played a game with him. He sat him down and said, "I'm going to hide the coin in one of my hands and you have to find it." Remember, he was only a year old and didn't know English. Rinzen listened, watched and picked the correct hand every time! How did he do that? Many times, we would take him for walks to get him out of his mother's hair. Herm would carry him in a kid's backpack and jokingly say, "you know, someday when you are discovered to be a reincarnation, you will owe us! "

We had been looking forward to attending the Dalai Lama's teachings but would soon get a rude awakening! It started off okay, even though it was already crowded when we got there. The Westerners were given a special room to themselves with big pillows to sit on, lots of space and a speaker we could actually hear the translation through! After being frustrated in Mundgod, we were thrilled to finally hear what His Holiness had to say!

The second day we took our time and stopped for pancakes, figuring our seats were secure since we had left our pillows to mark our spot. When we arrived, we were shocked to discover the Westerners had been moved outside. Our precious pillows were out on the cement slab somewhere, under someone's butts! I was apoplectic, we were right back to where we had been in Mundgod, no pillows, and no translation. I wanted to cry and say the hell with it. Herm took our pancakes and sat far away while I made a complete fool of myself. I stomped across people's bodies and feet looking under everyone for our pillows. I eventually found all three, put them in a pile and squeezed into the last row of Westerners. I kept making faces and waving for Herm to join me, but I don't think he wanted to be associated with this madwoman. Can't say I blamed him!

I so love the powerful chanting of the monks, but even that didn't shake my crappy attitude that morning. When lunch break arrived, and people left to get food, we moved to an empty space right in front of the speakers. Since I didn't dare leave our spot, I sat there guarding it during the three-hour break, while Herm went off to scout up lunch. It was a tight squeeze when the crowd returned, but at least we could finally hear….AND I had our pillows!

During the chanting, on the third day, a young Tibetan woman appeared to become possessed by a spirit and started singing and gyrating with her arms spread and her body stiff. His Holiness chuckled and told the spirit or God to quiet down, but it wasn't listening. The folks around her finally had to carry her out of the temple. Her body was totally stiff, and she was still singing as they hoisted her over their heads and carried her like a board. It was quite amazing, but the Tibetans didn't seem to find it at all strange.

The day we took Bodhisattva vows His Holiness broke into sobs. It was a very powerful moment and there were a lot of wet eyes in the audience. I imagined he was crying for all us poor, suffering sentient beings. It was just another example of how we had seen him show his compassion over and over again. It was so cute when he would tell the monks to put their robes over their bald heads so they wouldn't get burned in the sun. We so loved his sweet energy.

After six months in India, our visas were about to expire so it was time to head home. We loved this town and had made so many friends among the Tibetans and long-term Westerners we decided to come back after Monsoon season. As usual, the flight home was interesting. This time, instead of a peaceful man with underwear on his head, we had an angry guy verbally abusing a flight attendant. He was taken off in handcuffs by the Feds when we landed. Another passenger was suspected of having TB, so we also had health officials board the plane to check her out! Welcome to America!

CHAPTER 23

RUSSIA

The seven months before we returned to India, were full and interesting. During the summer we took a trip to St Petersburg, Russia to attend a rock and mineral show. The best part was doing a homestay with a sweet older woman named Elizabeta. She lived in one of those high-rise cement apartment complexes just outside the city. She spoke no English but was very welcoming and even insisted she feed us breakfast. It was obvious she didn't have much money, so we felt uncomfortable accepting but didn't want to insult her. We had no idea what the white blob was on the plate she placed in front of us. She looked at us with an expectant smile as we picked up our forks and smiled back as best we could. Oh God, what was I going to be putting in my mouth? I took a bite into the squishy thing which, thankfully, had no taste. I struggled not to gag and just chewed, swallowed and smiled. Thank goodness there wasn't a lot of it to choke down! I'm still not sure what we ate, maybe a glob of fat? Whatever it was, we made sure we went out to eat the rest of our stay.

In addition to continuing our Fire Eagle business, we solidified our friendship with Hawk and Lisa that summer, and I offered to lend them money to buy the house and land they had told us about the previous year. In the fall, they invited Herm and me to a sweat lodge at the new place where I had a very interesting experience. During the ceremony, I felt a hawk's talons grab my arm and a feeling of deep peace and love came over me. In that moment, it was as if my energy field had melded with that of Hawk, the human. It was the first of many such moments I was to experience on that sacred land.

CHAPTER 24

TIBETANS

Well, India hadn't changed in seven months! Sangye had arranged for his friend to pick us up at the airport. Champo left us on the sidewalk when he went to get the car but 15 minutes later came rushing back saying the police wouldn't let him stop to pick us up! We shlepped our bags to the distant vehicle, got in, locked the doors and ....the car was dead! The driver got out, lifted the hood, banged on a few things with a hammer but still no luck. The security guards yelled, "move that hunk of junk out of the way!" Herm got out to help push the car to the side, then he and the driver looked under the hood. Herm asked for a flashlight and to his horror, the man lit a match to illuminate the engine compartment. Meanwhile, Champo found us a taxi that made a terrible racket as we careened through the darkened streets running red lights and narrowly missing oncoming vehicles. It was a miracle we reached Majnukatila in one piece!

The bus ride back to McLeod Ganj was especially interesting. We usually slept fairly well on those overnight trips but this time we were in the front seat with nothing in front of us to lean on. Every time the bus stopped short, we would fall out of our seats and be jolted awake.

In the early morning, when we were on the curviest mountain roads, I noticed we had a tired driver. Since we were sitting in front just to his left, I could see his face in the rearview mirror. His eyes grew heavier and heavier, almost closing before his nodding head jerked him awake. Herm was asleep beside me, but I kept my eyes glued to the driver until we reached our destination. I was prepared to jump up and wake him if those eyes stayed closed. Years later I had a psychic reading where I was told we were scheduled to exit this life in 1996. Fortunately, we had re-upped our contract, but this trip was possibly when we were meant to go.

The craziness continued on our arrival in McLeod Ganj when we had a run-in with a Coolie. After he got our bags off the roof of the bus, we asked him how much he wanted. He replied, "pay me what you want." I handed him a 10 rupee note but he wouldn't take it. I said, "OK" and put the note back in my pocket. He was pissed but I had been in India enough times now not to be intimated by Coolies and Touts. He and his buddies trailed us into a restaurant and stood at our table waiting to be paid, telling us how hard they had worked. "Here you go," I said as I handed him the 10 rp again, "it's this or nothing."

"In your country 10 rp is nothing," he said angrily.

"Yes, but we are not in my country, we are in India where 10 rp is something!" I replied calmly. He snatched the bill out of my hand, ripped it up, threw it at us and stomped out. Ah! Welcome back to India!

While at the Tibetan settlement in Delhi, we were handed a message from Rinpoche. He wrote he and Sangye were traveling, but he wanted us to stay in their home until they returned. That was really nice of him, but it was such a tiny house, we wondered where we would sleep? The building consisted of one small room for the family and another for Rinpoche. The family's room held a twin-sized bed, table and chairs, a large TV and in the corner, a tiny kitchen with only a 2-burner kerosene stove. There was no refrigerator and the only running water was in Rinpoche's bathroom. A small, covered porch connected the two rooms where Rinpoche's attendant, a Tibetan nun, had her bed.

Just to make things more interesting, we found two additional children in residence when we arrived. Herm and I were given the bed, while Jamyang and the three kids slept outside on the floor of the porch. We felt terrible they were sleeping out in the cold, but Jamyang waved off our concern. She said it was no big deal, we were their guests. Of course, the bed also doubled as a couch, so it was where the kids hung out to watch television late into the night! In order to get any sleep, we would curl ourselves into a ball and throw the covers over our heads. Thankfully, we were usually so exhausted, even with the kids sitting on us, we actually got some sleep.

Peace and quiet were what we were used to and the chaos of three screaming kids and a blaring television started to wear on us. We couldn't even get away from the noise by going for a walk as it was the Tibetan New Year, and everyone was setting off firecrackers and fireworks. I learned to escape to the roof of the house where I could look over the Kangra Valley and the series of hills beyond. Hawks, vultures and ravens cruised the thermals in the warm sun and big puffy clouds slid across the snow-covered peaks to the north. Here I could breathe and recharge in order to return to the group, in a better mood.

Rinzen's second birthday was a mix of Tibetan ceremony and Western customs. Traditionally, Tibetans didn't celebrate birthdays, in fact, many people didn't even know their date of birth! With the advent of television, all that changed, and birthdays became a big thing. Rinzen looked like a cartoon Buddha as he sat crossed-legged, sporting green plastic sunglasses and a yellow-billed duck hat. Everyone placed a katak, a white scarf, around his neck as a symbol of respect. We sang happy birthday, and he blew out the candles on his cake but the whole time never cracked a smile or changed expression. It was just another example of him not always acting like a normal child.

Another illustration of this, was whenever we took him for a walk, he would insist upon going to the temple. He would stop at the special rooms and do prostrations and would demand to be lifted so he could turn the prayer wheels. A wild man at home, he was very serious and calm when we took him out. Our suspicions were growing more and more that this was a "special" child.

Ten days of holding it together in the bedlam and the constant flow of people in and out of the house was all we could take! We needed to find a place of our own! Jamyang was sad to see us go but we found a room to rent nearby. We still spent much of our time at her house as Rinpoche and Sangye had asked us to keep an eye on things.

The weather was dank and wet and the only way to stay warm was to walk, hang out at a restaurant or stay huddled in our sleeping bags. Even though walking would warm us up, it was tricky as the mud was thick and slick. Mist blanketed the greasy streets with its icy fingers creating a ghostly fog where the apparitions of hooded figures slid by at the edge of our vision. The gongs and trumpets from the monasteries echoed eerily in the dim light and the chanting of the monks was more dreamlike than real.

The mood in town grew somber and the town emptied of all casual travelers. Those of us left, were sick with the winter scourge which kept Dr. Dhonden busy. We always enjoyed visiting him and even though he rarely smiled, he seemed to like seeing us as well. Twice he invited us to dinner and the second time we encountered a bit of drama.

Hotel Tibet had the fanciest, most expensive restaurant in town. The food was delicious despite the added aroma of stale urine wafting up from the tin-roofed huts below. As we were eating, a waiter delivered one of their famous "flaming dishes" to a nearby table. The fire, however, seemed to have a will of its own as it grew, filling the room with choking black smoke. The waiter beat at the flame as patrons ran for the door, gasping for air. Windows were thrown open and the torched dish was returned to the kitchen to be traded for a flameless version. Just as the customers settled themselves back at their tables.... the power went out. Such is a typical day in India where you learned to roll with the punches.

Rinpoche bought a piece of land to build a house and teaching center. Before starting to excavate, he consulted the Astrology Institute to determine which day was most auspicious for breaking ground and which was best for holding the blessing ceremony. We were impressed this culture would acknowledge and honor the spirits of the land and ask their permission to build. If only all people remembered the earth is a conscious, living being we would have a much better world.

Always looking for volunteer opportunities, we were happy to take on some newly arrived Tibetans who wanted to improve their English. The stories of life in Tibet and their dangerous journey to India were fascinating. They had to walk over the mountains from Tibet to Nepal in the winter as the Chinese army was less active during that time. Hypothermia, frostbite, and capture by the Communists were all serious threats. If walking in winter wasn't bad enough, they had to move at night so they wouldn't be seen. To keep their packs light, they lived mainly off Tsampa, (roasted barley flour), for most of the six-week trek. It was incredible to realize this journey was undertaken not only by young adults but the elderly and small children as well.

Life in Tibet was difficult under Chinese rule. If people spoke out, they were beaten, jailed, murdered and had their land stolen. In addition to enduring the invasion of one's country, the individual tales of illness, injury and family tragedy were heart-wrenching. Two such stories stood out as especially tragic.

Lhundup, a young man in his early 20s, survived being struck by lightning... twice! The first strike, when he was three years old, killed his mother and left him with permanent eye damage. His father didn't have enough money to feed three children, so Lhundup was sent to live with his aunt in another village. With the father working away from home, his ten-year-old sister was left in charge of herding the yak, and the seven-year-old girl to cook and keep the fire. Six years later Lhundup was able to return home but by the age of 16, he wanted an education, so journeyed to India. He was so intent on studying day and night, barely eating or sleeping, he became sick with TB. This started many months of hospital stays, first for the TB, then for emergency abdominal surgery and then for the second lightning strike! After all of that, he was now caring for two friends with cancer!

Norbu, a young man with a sweet soul, basically spent seven years in a hospital. From the ages of two to nine he was sick with some kind of illness the doctors could never fully diagnose. When he was finally released, he was only able to spend four years in school, as that is all his parents could afford. He then took a job as a servant for a wealthy family until a friend helped him get into Astrology school. Two years into his studies he took part in a demonstration which got him arrested, jailed for three months and expelled from college. Because he had been in jail, no one would employ him, and he fell into a deep depression. He began hanging out at bars and drinking too much, until one night, he overheard some people talking about going to India. They told him he would have a chance to study there, so he made the decision to leave. When I met him, he had been working again as a servant and studying hard so he could reapply to Astrology school.

All the new arrivals were homesick for Tibet and their families but if they tried to return, they would be arrested for leaving illegally. They also felt an obligation to get a good education in case they ever did return, so they could help their country. Unfortunately, there were few jobs for them in India, so many were trying to get sponsors to go to the US, Canada or Europe. It was a very sad situation but I admired them for the courage to follow their hearts.

Since I wasn't a trained teacher, I would just wing it and get creative. One method I used was to take them to the library and have them tell me about the pictures hanging on the walls. Another was to use song lyrics. I would write out the verses, we would go over each word, then sentence, then meaning. I then asked them to tell me how the themes related to their life. The ones that spoke most directly to their rural mountain upbringing were John Denver's Rocky Mountain High and Country Roads. When finished, we would sing the song together and then I would have them serenade me with a Tibetan tune and tell me what it meant. It was so much fun!

The neighborhood monkey was coming into our room and stealing food. One day after a nap, I found bananas in the hallway and another day bread on the floor. He was a strange one, living alone and sleeping at the top of a dead tree outside our veranda. When it was bedtime, he would face the mountains, turning his back to the humans and go to sleep. Ravens often harassed him, jabbing at him with their beaks. Mr. Monkey would shake the tree in anger and voice his displeasure before settling back down with a sigh. We felt sorry for the guy as it appeared he had no friends or family. I wondered if he liked being alone or if he was an outcast for some reason?

Being so involved with the Tibetan community we were privy to all the news, both good and bad. When we first stayed at Rinpoche's house, we had met a talented young Thanka painter who lived nearby. He was quiet with a ready smile and always a friendly greeting. One day when we ran into him, he barely spoke and looked haggard and drawn. When we asked what was wrong, he told us the local Indian shopkeeper had raped his cousin, but nothing was being done about it. This man was a known serial rapist, but the police wouldn't arrest him as he had standing in the community. The painter was totally devastated, his whole life had fallen apart. He couldn't paint and all he thought about was revenge. He even went so far as to contact gang members in Delhi about having the guy killed. It was another sad and frustrating instance of the police being paid off. It, unfortunately, happened way too often.

Not long after hearing this story, the town was buzzing with the tragic news of the death of an 11-year-old Tibetan girl. Her half-naked body was found on the side of the road by some passersby. Since she was still wearing her watch, they figured a Tibetan had murdered her because, in their minds, an Indian would have stolen the watch. Police dogs were brought to the scene and followed the scent to a nearby house. Inside they found the girls clothes and a bloody sheet in a plastic bag. The man was arrested and confessed to raping the girl and strangling her when she started to scream.

The community was in an uproar, especially after they found out he was a new arrival from Tibet and had been jailed in China for murdering two people. It, unfortunately, was common practice for the

Chinese to let Tibetan criminals out of jail to infect the exiled communities in India.

It was the middle of May, and I was getting bored and depressed. All my students had finished their lessons and I was sick of trying to learn Tibetan. I was a terrible student as I was too embarrassed to say more than hello, how are you and what is your name. Rinpoche was disappointed as he was hoping I would learn more so he could converse with me. Herm, on the other hand, was great at practicing and not at all shy.

"Come on, we are going exploring," my Aries man said as he grabbed my hand and pulled me off the bed. I had been sitting around sulking and he knew I needed a nature boost.

We descended the steep hill across from our guesthouse to the river far below the road. I don't know why we had never gone down there – it was beautiful! As we rested on the rocks near a small waterfall, I was thinking about the book I was reading. It was about looking for a guide and we needed one to find our way out of there as we didn't see any path. Poof! Our guide materialized just as we were trying to make our way up some slippery rocks. He took us to the trail which led to a water-powered mill where local farmers brought their grain to be ground. How cool was that to be able to grow your own grain and have it processed with no electricity? This was right up our alley! Tour over, questions answered, the man pointed to a path that led up the mountain and we proceeded onward.

Unlike the dirt paths, we were used to following, these were constructed of big blocks of worked stone. I couldn't believe how quiet and peaceful it was down here, such a contrast to the racket of vehicles far above on the road. We passed through several small stone cottage villages where everyone greeted us with a smile and a Namaste. A couple of men we met on the path spoke to us in their local dialect which of course we didn't understand but we found it interesting they didn't speak Hindi.

We crossed the river following a calf bawling for its mother and followed a man carrying a plow over his shoulder, herding two cows ahead of him. He wanted us to sit with him in the shade for a while, and then follow him to his village but it was getting late, so we reluctantly said our goodbyes. It was magical down there and I hated to go back up top to the noise and hectic pace but up we went. It appeared the paths would take us further from our destination, so we bushwhacked upwards over the rockslides. Amazingly, so many hours later, we came out to the same village we had passed on our way down! Thanks to Herm and nature's healing energy, my sour mood had disappeared, and I was smiling again!

Soon, it was visa expiration time again and the rounds of goodbye dinners began. Our Tibetan friends all stuffed us with great food and regaled us with gifts. Rinpoche went all out and gifted us with a Dramyin (6 stringed lute), Tibetan carpet, Mongolian bowl, Thanka and a bunch of other small things. He also gave us a list of things he wanted us to bring back when we returned in the fall.

We had quite a crowd at the bus stop. Most of our students showed up bearing small keepsakes and draped us with Khatas. Lobsang came with a beautiful Thanka from Dr. Dhonden; and Sangye, Jamyang and other friends were all there to see us off. We were very touched by all the love and were happy we would be returning in a few short months.

As we boarded the bus, draped with dozens of khatas, it started to pour. Of course, the bus leaked like a sieve, soaking everyone and there were no windshield wipers. Oh well, in India, you just learned to trust all would work out. There was never a dull moment.

CHAPTER 25

HAWK

Not long before leaving India, I had received a "message" one morning as I was doing my prayers on the roof of our guest house. An internal voice had said, "Look for the hawk, he will call you." At the time, I thought it was pretty odd and had no idea what it meant but was soon to find out.

During the months we were away, my son Michael had moved into the "kennel". After living in San Diego for a number of years, he felt it was time to come home and we were thrilled to have him. I was even more excited on the day he showed up with a tiny puppy someone had given him. When he said the people had told him it was half wolf or coyote, I just rolled my eyes as I could see it was no such thing but no matter her background, we welcomed Miss Wya with open arms. I had so missed having a dog.

Spending time in India had shifted our focus away from our business. We loved living in McLeod Ganj, had many Tibetan and Western friends so we were planning on spending most of our time there. Because of that, we offered to sell Fire Eagle Productions to Michael. He was excited to do something new, so we spent the summer getting him up to speed. We taught him about the business, accompanied him to shows and introduced him to his fellow vendors.

When we weren't doing that, we were spending time at Hawk and Lisa's house getting to know them better and becoming fast friends. That Fall, before we returned to McLeod Ganj, they suggested we move our trailer to their property. At that moment I realized what the message I had received in India had meant. The "Hawk" had "called" and a whole new chapter in our lives was about to open.

CHAPTER 26

RINPOCHE

No power, frozen water pipes…. we were back in McLeod Ganj in winter. During those times, people melted snow for water or filled buckets from a spring near our guest house. I loved our little community, where we all suffered the cold and inconveniences together. I smiled when the power would be restored, and you could hear everyone in the neighborhood yelling "yay"!

Snow shovels were unheard of, so we improvised with various objects. A dustpan, a piece of metal, a frying pan, a tray, even a cleaver! We and our fellow tenants would grab whatever we could and gather on the roof to clear the snow, so we had a place to sit in the warm sun. Working together was fun and a great way to get the blood moving.

Rinpoche's new house was finally done, and we were the first ones to move into one of the three guest rooms on the bottom floor. We had a sitting room/bedroom, a kitchen area and a western-style bathroom with toilet, sink and a shower with hot water! We were in heaven! Our family lived upstairs where there was a large open area in the middle, a huge kitchen in the back and bedrooms on each side. A third story would be finished in the future which would be Rinpoche's temple/teaching area and a place for visiting monks to stay.

Rain, cold and snow preceded the dark news of a triple murder that winter. The director of the Dialectic School, Geshe Lobsang Gyatso, and two monks were found stabbed multiple times. The light had gone, and darkness had descended on that once peaceful town. The inhabitants were worried for their safety and that of their leaders. Sangye was afraid to move to the new house and Jamyang didn't like us to walk the back way home. The feeling of inner-city America had come to McLeod Ganj.

People in town speculated that paid assassins, hired by Shugden devotees, committed the atrocities. The director had written a book condemning the worship of the negative deity, Dorje Shugden, and the Dalai Lama had spoken against this God as well.

Even though suspects were arrested, Sangye believed the real culprits were long gone. The evening of the murders, he had seen two taxis speeding away but he wouldn't talk to police. I was sure someone must have seen or heard something as the Geshe's room was on the corner of a busy street, across from the main temple. Five or six men covered in blood, during daylight, would have been hard to miss. Sangye and others, however, were afraid of reprisals and didn't trust the authorities to protect them. Apparently, the Shugden group was very powerful, had a lot of money and was purportedly backed by the Chinese.

The Dalai Lama's yearly teachings had started just as the murders happened and he spoke about the Shugden practice and how negative it was. As he talked the wind lifted the tarps, the thunder rumbled, and it felt very much like Shugden was there and not very happy. I got a really eerie feeling, and it wasn't at all pleasant.

Poor Sangye was under so much stress. He was worried his father might be in danger and then discovered his longtime friend, who was staying in the new house, was a Shugden practitioner. Sangye noticed the monk never went to the teachings and was beginning to suspect he was a spy. A short time later, his suspicions were confirmed when the police came and took the monk away.

Kate, our American friend, told us there were many Shugden practitioners in the States and things were getting nasty there as well. Much
of what was happening was coming out of Bloomington, IN where
Rinpoche had many students. She had a message for us to pass on to him
from another Rinpoche which was: "I command you not to come to the
States. This is a secret message to be told to no one. There will be no more
messages from me if you do."

Wow! Now we were passing secret messages in addition to being
bodyguards. Yes, Sangye had asked us to guard Rinpoche in his walk
to and from the teachings! Of course, we could do nothing if he was
attacked, but since we were Westerners, we figured there was less danger they would go through us to get him. Herm and I would flank him
and try to keep the crowds at bay as he passed through. It was difficult
as many people wanted to talk with him and receive his blessing. We
were like CIA agents, constantly scanning the crowds looking for danger.
One day Rinpoche asked Herm if he had a gun and when he said no, he
laughed and said, "what good are you then?" Very true!

On top of all the Shugden stuff, Jamyang was told by the CID
(Criminal Investigative Department) that Palden, the young man staying in their house, had done bad things in Tibet and they should get
him out. I knew there was a reason I never felt comfortable around him.
He was already on my shit list for throwing water off the second-floor
deck which splattered on us when we sat outside. Asking him nicely
had gotten me nowhere, so I had to resort to yelling which he didn't
like one bit. If all that wasn't bad enough, there was a monk hanging
around sowing dissension within the family! What a crazy place we had
moved into!

I couldn't sleep and had a dream about a bad storm coming. In the
dream, the wind howled and blew trees down and the sky was as dark
as night in the middle of the afternoon. The weather report was that the
worst hurricane in history was coming, and we didn't know if we could
get back home in time. I was soon to discover that a storm WAS coming
but it had nothing to do with the weather.

I had always wanted to visit an Oracle and Rinpoche invited us along for his yearly audience. An Oracle is considered to be a fully enlightened being, a God, and we were told this one was the 3rd most important to the Tibetans.

At 4 a.m. nine westerners and several Tibetans headed to the temple for the gathering. We were told the small, unimposing man, entering the room was a shopkeeper in town. It was hard to believe he would be the channeler for such an important entity.

A suitcase and hatbox lay open on the floor. Within, were robes, a headdress and breastplate. The shopkeeper had his back to us, while the monks dressed him in this gear. As he was being attired, one group of monks smudged him, while another chanted prayers.

The minutes ticked by with nothing happening until we noticed the shopkeeper's head beginning to vibrate. The tremor spread to his whole body which then went into spasm and a monk had to grab his elbow. With a beastly, deep guttural sound, the man in the tall, pointed hat, red robes, and round mirrored breastplate turned stiffly and lurched towards us. His arms were outstretched, his face contorted, his mouth slathering like a rapid animal. The monks shoved us against the wall as the Oracle reeled past into the adjacent room. With the help of two attendants, the God prostrated himself twice before the ancient statue of Buddha. He staggered by us once again before being settled into an ornately carved and decorated wooden chair.

Rinpoche immediately went over to him and placed two yellow khatas around the Oracle's neck. He grabbed Rinpoche behind the head and pulled him roughly to his shoulder. Rinpoche whispered his questions and the Oracle responded in a loud raspy voice, speaking a strange form of Tibetan.

When the questioning was finished, Rinpoche motioned for some of us to come forward and present the Oracle with a khata. The monks put orange barley grain in his hand for him to bless and present to each person. I was the last to go and when I bowed and laid the scarf on the Oracle's lap, he clutched my hand to put some barley in it. I didn't know what he was doing so he had to grab it a couple of times. When I went to stand, the Oracle reached out and seized the back of my head and shoved it into his knee. His grasp was so strong, I couldn't move. I had no idea what was happening and was afraid I had done something to offend the God. I kept very still while the oracle bent over me and whispered in my ear. It felt like I was in his iron-clad grip for minutes before he finally released me. I was stunned and shaken, stood with difficulty and backed away from the seated deity to stand against the wall.

As soon as he freed me, he stood, let out a gasp and went stiff as a board as his two attendants caught him and carried him from the room. I was the only one he had talked to, in fact, he treated each person differently. When Steve went up there, the Oracle pulled his hair, with Molly, he put the khata around her neck and he did nothing with Herm.

Everyone gathered around me to ask what had happened? "I have no idea!" I replied while looking around for Rinpoche. I knew he had been recording his conversation with the God and wondered if he had caught what the Oracle said to me.

When I found him, a quizzical, but worried, expression crossed his face and he said, "Terra, Terra, Terra, while slowly shaking his head.

"What's the matter, did I do something wrong?" I asked.

"Not at all," Sangye translated. "It is a real honor to be spoken to by the Oracle and it doesn't happen very often."

"Why me then?" I asked.

Rinpoche said, "It might be because you are a student of mine and close to the family."

I thought, well that was also true of Herm, but the God hadn't spoken to him!

Rinpoche continued, "The Oracle recognized you are a kind and generous person, with a pure mind and faith in Buddhism."

"Did you hear anything he said to me?" I asked.

"The only thing I heard was if you totally believe in the lama and follow him the Oracle will remove all your obstacles."

Wow, I couldn't wait to hear more, too bad it took weeks for the translation to be done!

I was having a hard time realizing the Oracle had actually spoken to me! It seemed like a dream! I was so grateful to Rinpoche for inviting me to go and I was flying high but that look he had given me was something I couldn't get out of my mind. It hadn't been a happy one and I wondered what was going on. Had he told me everything he had heard?

Barbara, a student of Rinpoche's who lived on our floor, totally pushed my buttons! She seemed very unstable, almost manic at times, friendly one minute, reclusive and morose the next. She spent most of her day sitting in, or just outside, Rinpoche's room and one time stated he was her only friend. Their relationship was decidedly odd, and I felt something untoward was going on. I tried to stay out of her way as she seemed to be especially jealous of me because I had known Rinpoche and his family so long. She told me she was a private person and had a lot of things going on and she didn't always like to talk. We were soon to discover what "a lot of things going on" really meant!

One night, not long after we saw the Oracle, Herm stepped outside on the balcony to look at the full moon. Ten minutes later he was back, looking like he had seen a ghost!

"What is it?" I asked.

"I think I just saw Rinpoche going into Barbara's room."

"No way!" I said.

"Please, go to her room and see if you hear the same thing I heard."

I crept down the balcony, paused outside the open window and listened. The sound of soft groans and panting sent me scurrying back to our room in shock.

"It can't be," I exclaimed, "it must be someone else."

"But she never sees anyone else, and I am sure it was him, although the moon was behind the clouds at the time." We decided to sit outside our room and wait to see who came out, even if we had to wait all night. No way it was our beloved teacher! I wouldn't believe that he was one of those gurus who slept with his students.

We didn't have long to wait as we sat in silence under the full moon. Twenty minutes later, Rinpoche tip-toed quietly out the door and up the stairs to his quarters. He didn't turn our way but Barbara, who had followed him out, spotted us and quickly ducked back into her room. Herm and I looked at each other dumbstruck. We felt as if we had been punched in the stomach. "What are we going to do?" I cried, "I just can't believe it!" Many of the pieces of the puzzle of Barbara's mysterious behavior, had just snapped into place.

I couldn't sleep, I kept going over everything in my mind trying to decide what to do with the information. I was angry, hurt, confused and disillusioned. The Oracle had said to put my total faith in the lama and just as I was about to do that, this happens! Was this supposed to be a test of my faith or had the Oracle been warning me? Since Rinpoche never told me what the translation said, who knows what the God had actually whispered? I knew something was off that day when Rinpoche gave me that look, it was as if he heard something he didn't want me to know.

I was obsessed, I couldn't stop thinking about this. Authority figures taking advantage of students and patients was one of my triggers. As a psychiatric nurse, I had worked with victims of this type of abuse, and it made me furious. I wanted to make sure no other students would be taken advantage of. How could I do that? Should we tell the Dalai Lama? I felt I needed to do something, but what?

I needed an objective perspective, so I went to see our friend Joyce who had been in Dharamsala for over 30 years and was very involved with the Tibetan government in exile. When I told her she wasn't at all surprised. She said, unfortunately, it was a fairly common occurrence. His Holiness had preached against it, but the monks and lamas did what they wanted. She said the best thing was to let it go, everyone had their own lessons to learn. I knew she was right. The letting go part was MY lesson.

Jamyang and Sangye were relieved we finally knew. They had wanted to tell us but had been too embarrassed to say anything. Sangye had begged his father to listen to reason but was told to mind his own business, he would do as he pleased. They knew Barbara was disturbed and now that Jamyang's mother, Pema, was visiting she was having fits of jealousy. Pema and Rinpoche had been friends for years and Barbara didn't want her anywhere near her "boyfriend".

I was starting to lose it! I was angry all the time and kept thinking of terrible things to do and say to Barbara and Rinpoche. My dark side was being confronted big time. Where had my compassion gone? Paranoia was also rearing its head. Rinpoche was performing a lot of pujas and we wondered if he was putting some kind of hex on us. We smudged each other with sage and put protection stones around us, just in case. Even my dreams seemed to be sending me messages. In one, I was trying to understand Tibetan code, in another, I was trying to translate a message that was in Tibetan. Was the Oracle trying to communicate his real message to me?

To add to the madness, our next-door neighbor, who was married and in his 50s, appeared to be an exhibitionist! He would stand on the veranda in his tiny, tight underwear talking to the girls in the street. We never felt very comfortable with him, but this was just too much! The wackos were everywhere in that house!

Making up crazy cynical jokes became a pastime of ours, to deal with our conflicting emotions. We so wanted out of that madhouse, but Sangye and Rinpoche were getting ready for a trip overseas and Sangye asked us to stay and keep an eye on things. We weren't thrilled but we knew Jamyang needed us there with everything going on. At least Rinpoche would be gone. We hadn't visited him since "that" night and we heard he was wondering why. Since it was common for us to see him almost every day, our absence was noted.

I was reading a book on gurus and students which had me re-thinking the whole situation. I had been hurt, angry and disappointed but now just felt sorry for everyone. So many Westerners give their power away to people who they think are wiser than they are. I had tried to do that many times but, in each instance, "someone/something" stepped in to "save" me. I was reminded I am my own guru and have all the answers if I just look inside.

I woke up at midnight laughing out loud from a dream. There was a big catholic church wedding planned with a very uptight priest. I was in a room with the groom and the priest, trying to get the father to loosen up. When I succeeded in getting everyone relaxed, I told the cleric something strange may happen during the ceremony. In fact, things could get pretty wild and very weird. I said he should pay no attention to what was going on but stay centered and do his thing. The two people must be joined together no matter what. Even if the bride was exchanged with another person, he must remain unconcerned and continue. Hmmm, I wondered what the message was?

Walking down the road that morning two strange things happened which made me feel as if I was still in the dream. I heard a grunt coming from the area of a big tree below and saw a young man facing me. He had his hand in his pants and was obviously jerking off so I immediately turned away and kept walking. A little further along, a man in a school uniform with a book satchel passed me and said, "good morning". I thought he looked pretty old to be going to school and when I heard him calling, "madam, madam" behind me, I just kept walking. My feeling was if I turned around, I would have seen something other than a human. It felt like I was being tested to see if I could remain centered, just like the priest in the dream. What a crazy time!

When Sangye called to say he and Rinpoche were back in Delhi, we got the first bus out of McLeod Ganj! We had no intention of seeing Rinpoche but had written a letter outlining our displeasure and disappointment with his behavior. Our plan was to have Sangye read it to Rinpoche and that would be that for our relationship with him. I was NOT thrilled when Sangje told us Rinpoche refused to hear the letter and wanted to see us in person. I was tired, had the shits and SO didn't want to talk with him but when I heard he was blaming Jamyang for us being mad, I had to set the record straight.

I was nervous as we walked into Rinpoche's room. I was trying to remember what we had written in the letter in order to compose what I was going to say. Rinpoche was seated, a table with a pile of long sheeted prayers before him. His eyes were downcast as we took our seats across from him. I took a deep breath and began by thanking him for all he had done for us and how grateful we were he had considered us part of his family. That now we had to move on as we disapproved of his relationship with Barbara. He said he didn't understand what was wrong with that. I explained how it is looked upon in the West and that behavior could jeopardize him from being invited back. He made all kinds of excuses for himself, listing a number of lamas who had married their students. He said His Holiness had never told him not to have affairs and anyway, he didn't have to go to America again. I tried very hard to stay centered and not get angry. I could tell he was trying to control himself as well as he never looked at me, just kept his head down, angrily flipping over the pages of his prayer book. It was obvious he was beyond reasoning, so we got up to leave. As we were standing, he told us in a strained voice, we were still members of his family and were welcome in his house.

As soon as we got out the door I burst into tears, not so much for me but for Sangye and Jamyang. I now saw how stubborn he could be and all they had to put up with. Sangye reached out and put his arm around me and said, "forget about it, it's over".

CHAPTER 27

MAINE

Returning to Maine and our dear friends was such a relief after all the drama in India. It took me weeks and lots of working in the woods to lift the shadow hanging over me. The whole Rinpoche thing had done me in, I had put such faith and effort into that relationship over the last few years, it was difficult to let go. Nature, however, has a way of healing open wounds and it soon worked its magic, bringing me back to a sense of peace and equilibrium.

Hawk and Lisa's tiny home sat on a hill in the woods at the end of a long driveway. Our trailer was parked next to the barn just down the slope from the house. We enjoyed meeting the many Natives and non-Natives who came from around the country to visit or attend the many gatherings. There was one frequent guest who made an especially big impression. A huge Arctic wolf whose owner would let roam the property as he chatted inside. I was always impressed at how well behaved, yet aloof this big guy was!

We each found odd jobs to make extra money and I eventually got a housekeeping position at some oceanside summer cottages. I cleaned, changed beds, washed linens and eventually the out-of-state owner had me checking people in and managing things during the week. I loved welcoming the guests, getting to know them, and dealing with any issues that came up, it was great fun!

During that time, we were blessed to have Zuna enter our lives. When we decided to stop traveling, I really needed to have a dog again. I was still heartbroken over leaving my best friend Zuri with her breeder when we left on our big trip. It was the first time in my life I had been without a dog. I wanted another Ridgeback, so I contacted Diana and thankfully, she had a litter! Herm, who had only had dogs with his former wife, fell head over heels for this lively eight-week-old puppy. I was smitten as well, and this bundle of energy was to become a huge part of our lives.

We were also honored to become friends with Marjorie Spock. When we met this tall, ruggedly built 98-year-old, she was still tending her goats and gardens on her oceanside biodynamic farm. We also discovered she was the sister of the world-famous baby doctor Benjamin Spock. She loved her brother, but she was the black sheep in her family following a totally different path in life. His advice on child-rearing went against all she had learned by teaching in Waldorf schools for most of her adult life.

Marjorie was the last living person to have studied with Rudolf Steiner in Austria. She had spent years learning all she could about Steiner's philosophy on teaching, biodynamic farming, anthroposophic medicine and the therapeutic movement called Eurythmy. I had never heard of Steiner but was soon avidly reading all the books I could get my hands on. I also attended the weekly Steiner discussion group held at her house. It was great fun and a good brain workout.

Most days when I visited, she would be sitting at a tiny table in her kitchen either translating Steiner books and essays from German to English or working on books of her own. She never ceased to amaze me with all she did at her age. This woman was an inspiration of how to live life a day at a time, with a great attitude. She was as astonished as her doctors that she made it to the ripe old age of 101.

It was time to settle down and get a piece of property of our own. We wanted to stay near our friends, so we bought the 40 acres adjoining their place. The problem was it was landlocked, so we needed to get a right of way. Susan, one of our abutters, was willing to sell us one but couldn't until some legal matters were cleared up. She did, however, offer to let us set up the yurt we were buying on part of her property.

Our 20' diameter "tent" went up in the fall of 2000 and we lived in it for almost a year and a half. There was no road to the site, so we hauled all the building materials about a quarter mile through the woods.

We were under the weather gun to get things up and functioning before the snow flew. We had to build the platform, with no power tools, erect the yurt, install a woodstove and furnish the inside. We then had to cut and gather our winter wood supply so we wouldn't freeze and also dig and build an outhouse.

We hauled water in buckets from the nearby brook, dug our cooler into the ground for a refrigerator and cooked on a small propane stove. It was very cozy, and I loved living in the round and hearing all the animal noises outside. Our woodstove heated the space nicely, but we learned as fast as it heated up it cooled down just as quickly. That meant stoking the fire a few times during the night, so we didn't freeze in the 20 below winter nights.

During that year and a half of having a "house", I dove into taking courses. I am a perpetual student and love learning new things. A Certified Intuitive Healer program and one to become an animal communicator kept me busy for six months. With time on my hands after the courses, I took a job tutoring individuals preparing for their GEDs. The teaching end of things ended up being the least important part of the job. I found myself back in the role of counselor, reminding me of my days at Family Strength in New Hampshire working with families involved in the court system.

Unfortunately, the legal issues with Susan never worked out, so we were back to square one. This started a search for new land and a trip to an astrocartographer who pointed us toward eastern Canada. Our trips to Nova Scotia and New Brunswick didn't end with finding our place but it did get us thinking. Things didn't seem to be working out in Maine, it was like we were shoveling shit against the tide with everything we were trying. We knew enough about energy to understand when that happens, it is time to do something different. We thought – we loved Canadians and their way of life, what the hell, why not immigrate?

We contacted an immigration lawyer and mailed our application. When we were told it would take about a year to process, we decided to go back on the road and see if we could find a place that felt like home.

Just like that, we sold our land, packed up our yurt, hitched up our little trailer and became nomads once again.

····+◆+····

SEARCH FOR HOME
2001-2003

····+◆+····

CHAPTER 28

VOLUNTEERS

January 23rd and we were leaving Maine at a snail's pace with the roads a sheet of ice and our new used truck barely pulling the trailer. We were thinking we may have made a BIG mistake buying that truck! We resigned ourselves to traveling slowly and wondered if we would even make it over the small hills we would encounter, never mind the mountains!

We planned on a two day stop in Tennessee to visit friends, but our truck and trailer put on the brakes, so to speak! Herm was out shopping when the brake light came on and when he took it to a garage, they discovered a broken brake lining! We sent a silent prayer to our guardian angels that it hadn't happened while we were pulling the trailer! In addition, the garage found transmission problems in the truck. Sigh! Our used truck deal wasn't turning out to be such a good buy after all!

Thankfully, Nick and MaryAnn were happy to have us there for as long as needed. It seemed the "Universe" had this all planned as Nick needed me to do healing work on his knee and MaryAnn had some personal issues I helped her with. We even discovered it was better we didn't arrive at my sister's right away, which was our next stop. Her kitchen was torn apart, and she would just as soon have us come later rather than sooner.

After two weeks, the machines and humans were fixed, and it looked like we had "permission" to move on. As we said goodbye, Mary Ann was in tears and told me I had "saved her life". I had to smile as the "Universe" always seemed to guide us to where we were needed. It was just another indication all happened the way it was supposed to at just the right time.

It seemed we were on a two-week cycle of "volunteer" work. It was another fortnight with my sister and family, where my brother-in-law put Herm to work rebuilding their kitchen. Then another stint with my aunt and uncle in Dallas when our refrigerator died, and we had to wait for a new one. We certainly seemed to be needed and we were just going with the flow. We trusted we would be moved on when each job was done.

At my aunt and uncle's house we helped with the cooking, Herm did some maintenance work, and I did healing work on my uncle who had cancer. He invited us to attend his cancer support group where a lecture was scheduled on natural foods. When the speaker never showed up, I was aghast as I heard my uncle turn to the group leader and say, "my niece is a nurse and very interested in holistic health, maybe she could speak to the group?"

"Oh, that would be wonderful," the leader smiled as she turned to me and asked, "would you be willing to do that?"

Crap, I thought, my mind reeling. I'm no expert, what can I possibly say? I took a deep breath, put on a smile and said, "sure!" I have no recollection of what I said, it was all a blur. I think it was something about having a positive attitude and how people can heal, and things like that. Whatever it was, I guess it was okay as I received lots of smiles and positive feedback. Just another little "push" from the "Universe" to get out in the world and do my work. Sometimes, I don't like its sense of humor!

CHAPTER 29

MARRIAGE

With our visiting done, we kept heading west. By the time we had hiked in Guadalupe National Park and toured Carlsbad Caverns it was the end of March. I thought we should head south until it got warmer, but Herm wanted to head north. We turned to our trusty coin flip which we used when we couldn't make a decision and the flip said south.

The truck was developing one problem after another, and I wondered if it was just telling us to stay in one place for a period of time? Maybe it was actually a magical truck and not just a piece of junk as we thought. It appeared to break down in places where we had wonderful experiences and met interesting people. Three Rivers Campground turned out to be one of those extraordinary areas.

It was a long uphill climb into the mountains of New Mexico and as we struggled higher the truck kept losing power. I held my breath and kept saying, "I think I can, I think I can", as we putt-putted upward. Just like the "little engine that could" our enchanted truck made it. With a sigh of relief, we pulled into the first empty spot in the campground.

Again, the angels were with us because that spot turned out to be the perfect one for our stay.

Over the next weeks, Herm did his best to get parts and fix the truck but no matter what he did, our vehicle wasn't having it. He finally quit and brought it to a mechanic who assured us it was all set. Nope! We definitely weren't being allowed to leave Three Rivers which was fine with us. We were very happy there. Except for weekends, it was peaceful, incredibly beautiful and we enjoyed the company of our campground host, John, and family.

It was only a short walk from our campsite to the entrance of the main hiking trail. Entering the forest of ancient pine, spruce and fir was like setting foot into an enchanted cathedral. The river adjacent to the trail, with its rushing water, added the hymns. I was enthralled and felt totally at peace each time I ventured in. Additional trails sprouted off the main one. Some led to mountain meadows, already clothed in spring wildflowers, while the higher trails were still coated in winter snow.

The day we were out hiking and Zuna found an elk leg, changed the whole focus of our stay at Three Rivers. We searched the area for more parts and discovered most of the elk carcass in the stream bed. Scouting further upstream, Herm found half an antler rack and a jawbone. We were excited as we had never found elk parts before! When we showed John, he told us if we found fresh "horns", he would buy them from us. Since the going rate was $12/lb, we were intent upon finding all we could and became obsessive "horn hunters".

Every day we were in the woods, scouring the ground, canyons and streams, climbing to 10,000 feet sometimes covering nine to ten miles a day. This was right up our alley, exploring, looking for treasure and making money to cover the truck expenses…woo hoo! It became our new job and some days we would split up, going in different directions, in order to cover as much ground as possible. Meeting back at camp in the afternoon, we related our adventures and compared our finds. We were having a ball!

One day, Herm went out alone while I stayed in camp doing crafts. As I saw him walking towards me, after a day of hunting, I knew something was up. He was carrying some horns he had found, and he had a little grin on his face.

"What's up?" I asked smiling.

"You are never going to guess what I found," he said very quietly.

"What?" I said excitedly.

"I was hiking this trail when I spotted something strange in the middle of the path." He stopped talking, unzipped his pack…. "This is what it was," he said as he slowly pulled a very large brown bird out of his bag. "Is this what I think it is?" he asked.

"Oh my God, it's a young Golden Eagle!" I said in excitement.

"That's what I thought," he said as he put it back in his pack.

Eagle "medicine" is something we had always wished for, but we knew the possession of feathers by non-Natives was illegal, so we had to be careful. Since the campground was empty, we decided to quickly dismantle the body and hide it in our trailer. Like thieves stashing their stolen gold, we feverishly stripped the feathers, cut off the wings, head and feet, then stuffed them into plastic bags, giggling to ourselves the whole time.

Our immigration lawyers contacted us and said we would have a better chance of getting into Canada if we were married. I never wanted to do that again and told myself after my divorce I never would. There were too many stories of people who had lived together happily for years and then broke up after marrying. I loved our relationship and didn't want to jinx it. On the other hand, I wanted to immigrate. After much soul-searching, I decided to go for it and hope for the best. As fate would have it, John's wife was a minister. She was happy to sign our marriage certificate which made the whole procedure very easy to accomplish.

On April 22, 2001, Herm and I climbed to our favorite meadow, high above the campground. We exchanged vows and the special gifts we had made for each other, with sweet Zuna, as our witness. I couldn't have had a more beautiful wedding or married anyone else but Herm, my best friend, and soulmate. To celebrate, we went horn hunting and the "Universe" presented us with three special wedding gifts. A horn, a skeleton and a skull!!

It was the last day of April; the truck was finally fixed, and it was time to find our next adventure. We sold the horns we had collected to John, had a goodbye dinner and reluctantly left our friends and that beautiful healing place behind.

CHAPTER 30

BRITISH COLUMBIA

It was May 13th, my birthday, when the "magic" truck started making noises and pulling severely to the left when braking. It was a tense ten miles to the first garage and when the mechanic took a look, he said, "Wow, you guys must have a guardian angel, that rear wheel is about to fall off and you have a broken brake line. You are REALLY lucky!" Holy crap! Just the day before we had come down the long, steep road off Mt Hood! If our angels hadn't been with us once again, I may not have made it to my 54th birthday!

We were excited to get to Canada and look for land. Since our immigration application was in process, we had to decide where we wanted to live. The plains weren't for us, and we had decided against the East Coast, so British Columbia and Alberta were the next places to look.

When I lived in New Hampshire I had crossed the border to Canada many times and it was always easy and friendly. Not so much in 2002! I should have known something was coming when the oracle cards I had drawn that morning were harmony, peace and power. I get triggered easily when someone doubts my integrity and boy was I triggered by the border guards that day! They didn't ask only once if I was carrying any guns but kept asking over and over until I was totally pissed! I finally yelled, "NO I don't have any guns, I don't like guns and have never owned a fucking gun!" I must say, it wasn't one of my better moments.

To add insult to injury, they then insisted on inspecting both the truck and trailer. I felt totally violated with border agents tramping through my "home" and I just wanted to cry. THEN…they took the turtle shells I use to make crafts, saying they were an endangered species!!

"You have GOT to be kidding," I said furiously! "They are common, painted turtles farmed in Louisiana for meat!" I was about to totally lose it when Herm stepped in before I got myself arrested. He followed the officers into the building and soon emerged carrying the bag, as someone saw they obviously weren't an endangered species! It wasn't a very auspicious welcome to the country we were trying to immigrate to! I should have recognized the signs then and there.

The scenery in BC was breathtaking with raging rivers backdropped by snow-covered mountains, interspersed with gentle farming country. I should have loved that but something about it unsettled me and made me feel very tense. Of course, the constant rain and fog didn't help, maybe it was just that. I needed the sun!

We did meet some wonderful people, however, which could have changed my mind about staying in BC. In Nelson, we discovered a friendly community of laid-back old hippies, who were into the earth, organic food and healing. Herm even set up at a Saturday market where he sold our crafts and rocks. We considered looking for land in that area but found the prices were too high for our budget.

On a remote, winding, bumpy road, through the mountains, a leaf spring on the trailer broke. We picked up the pieces, unbolted the broken part so it wouldn't drag and prayed we would make it the 30 miles to Kaslo. Our prayers were answered yet again, and we coasted into a municipal camping spot on the lake.

Kaslo was a cozy little town surrounded by massive pinnacled snow-capped peaks. It felt like a safe haven from the rest of the world, almost like a place out of time. When we took Zuna for a walk on the beach, we came upon a labyrinth and a group of women in tie-dyed clothing performing some sort of ceremony. Had the "Universe" led us to a possible landing place? It certainly had brought us an angel in the form of Maggie!

"Went for a swim, did she?" I said smiling at the woman on the beach drying her wet dog.

The woman laughed and said, "yes, she loves to swim." We got talking, I shared our predicament with the trailer and she said, "Let's go meet your husband." When Herm showed her the issue, she immediately had us hop in her car and took us to the local junkyard. Unfortunately, they didn't have what we needed but Maggie offered to call Nelson the next morning to see if she could find the part.

Maggie came in the morning to tell us she had found some parts and to call from her house to order them. She also invited me to work with her and three other women in the community garden. The others were ex-pats from California and Oregon, and they told me how much they loved living in Canada. I wondered if that was a sign we were doing the right thing? Getting my hands in the dirt again was heaven. I have always gardened and one of the reasons I wanted to settle down was to be able to do that again. Hanging out with four like-minded women for the morning, talking and laughing was a balm for my soul. I was falling in love with that town!

A busy week socializing with Maggie, her husband and friends, left us feeling welcomed and wondering if we should stay? We checked out some places for sale but as much as we loved the town, the people and the area, the constant dreary weather just didn't do it for us. We reluctantly bid farewell to our friends and headed to Alberta hoping we could leave the rain and fog behind.

CHAPTER 31

ALBERTA

As soon as we crossed the border into Alberta the sun came out and the view from the pass through the Rockies was magnificent. The combination of massive mountains transitioning to green rolling hills of grass was exactly the type of landscape that made me happy. To me, it was the perfect blend of male and female energies. I was instantly at peace, more so than any other place we had been. It was big sky country where I felt so expanded but a vibrant green, unlike the brown desert.

We were the only ones at Cripple Creek Campground, just outside of Waterton Lakes National Park, not far from the Montana border. The wind was howling, and it was hard to stand up, but hiking in the woods among the trees brought some relief. We had often talked about being campground hosts and this place was so gorgeous, it seemed just the place to do it, so we put in our applications.

June 8th and we were in the middle of a blizzard. Two and a half feet of snow with a topping of rain had us stranded. The wind was so strong it had the trailer rocking and blew away most of the warmth our tiny heater was putting out. A trip to the bathroom meant dressing in all of our winter clothes, head down, plowing through the blowing snow and sloshing through standing water which swamped our boots. The campground host told us he had never seen such a storm so late in the season. He said it was especially bad for the cattle, as they had already been put out onto summer range.

It was a long three days sitting in the storm with our outerwear and boots soaked. The inside of the trailer was wet, the power was off and the river beside us was rising. Food and drinking water were running low before the skies finally cleared. Once the water on the road receded, we headed east to explore more of western Alberta.

A dead pheasant in the road triggered a meeting with a friendly buffalo rancher. The bird, which we stopped to pick up, was in front of his ranch. Always looking for animal parts for crafts, we wanted to see if he had any buffalo skulls for sale. Len invited us in and told us the story of how he went from running cattle to ranching 200 buffalo! He used all the parts of the animals he butchered. The meat went to health food stores and the skins were tanned for gloves and robes. Bones, rawhide and skulls were purchased by Natives or people like us who use them for crafts. I showed him some of the native-inspired crafts I made, and he asked me to do a scrimshaw design on a buffalo jaw for him. I was happy to oblige and in exchange, he gave us three jaws. We gave thanks to the pheasant for guiding us there as we wouldn't have stopped otherwise.

CHAPTER 32

HOSTING

At the end of June, we returned to Waterton to begin our hosting position at Belly River Campground. It was located several miles from the main section of the park, adjacent to the river of the same name and within walking distance of the US border. Thirty campsites, in two separate areas, were scattered amongst the trees. Our assigned space was in the first grouping closest to the entrance. The sites in our section were arranged in a horseshoe shape with a big field in the middle and woods behind. The remainder of the campsites were situated further down the access road.

It was a tranquil place, especially when there were no campers. Wildlife abounded. There were deer, elk, moose, marten, fisher, our resident red fox and lots of bears. The river was also alive with beaver, otter, cranes and other waterfowl. Sitting in cool rippling water doing my laundry became one of my favorite things to do. As I scrubbed clothes amongst the tall reeds, under a cloudless sky, I felt one with the river and all of the natural world. This was heaven.

In order for us to contact park headquarters, we were given two-way radios. They were to be used to check in each morning and for any issues that might arise. Meeting the people and making them feel welcome reminded me of how I had done that in Maine at the seaside cottages. My favorite thing to do each day was to walk the campground greeting each new arrival and seeing how everyone was doing. I handed out park information, dealt with any issues and answered questions. Of course, with people came issues. Plugged toilets, no toilet paper, running out of firewood, noise problems and illegal camping. Support from the park was great, whenever we were out of an item, it was soon delivered. If something needed fixing that Herm couldn't manage, an expert showed up. If we had rowdy campers, a Mountie came to take care of it. If we had wildlife issues, a warden arrived. It was very comforting to be part of a team of people all looking out for each other and the campers.

The game wardens were called often because of the bears. The first time was to clear away the carcasses of a cow elk and calf which were half in the water. We discovered them when we were clearing the trail through the woods that led from the campground to a beautiful meadow by the river. While we were surveying the scene, we noticed the bodies were surrounded by VERY large bear poop which was a bit disconcerting. We immediately scanned the surrounding trees for bears and beat a hasty retreat back to camp. This was grizzly and black bear country and even though I wasn't afraid of black bears, I had no experience with grizzlies and they made me nervous.

No matter how many times I preached to people NOT to leave food in their campsites they just didn't listen. They would then freak out when a bear showed up to feast on their goodies or to poke around looking for more. This would result in the bear being trapped and relocated, which the game wardens told us was basically a death sentence. The wardens said the relocated critters were either killed by resident bears or driven out and starved to death. It made me so sad and angry that people thought only of themselves with no regard to the lives of the animals. After all, it was the wildlife's territory THEY were encroaching upon.

It was 7 a.m. when we heard the screams. A car with its horn blaring came screeching into our campsite with two people in total panic. The woman was hysterical saying a bear had attacked her. We saw no wounds, so calmly asked exactly what had happened. Apparently, she had been asleep in her tent when she felt a nudge and when she moved, the bear had swatted the tent. That was the "attack". We calmed her down, then called the wardens who set up a bear trap close to our site. We had seen that bear around camp for several days but as far as we knew it hadn't been in trouble until then.

It was late afternoon when I looked across the field to see our bear slowly sneaking up on a man who was sitting in a chair reading. I walked over and said very quietly, "Don't be alarmed but there is a bear right behind you, so you may want to get into your camper." At that point, the bear was about 10 feet away, so thankfully he didn't panic. He slowly got up and walked to his vehicle while I went and called the warden.

We watched the bear amble toward the trap, sniffing it all over trying to figure out how to get the meat inside. She found the entrance, dashed in, grabbed the meat and ran out before the door could close. When the wardens got there, they re-baited the trap and waited. Sure enough she came back for more but wasn't quick enough that time and the door slammed shut behind her. I say she as the wardens told us later it was a two-year-old female. I sent a prayer for her to be safe wherever they sent her.

On one of our last days there, we had our own close encounter while we were working outside at our picnic table. I turned towards the trailer to get something and there was a bear right in front of it. "Herm, bear," I said quietly as I grabbed Zuna, who thankfully hadn't seen it. Once inside, Herm opened the door to take a picture, but Mr. Bear was right there on our steps ready to come in for a visit. We yelled and clapped our hands and he finally ambled off, but not before trying to get into our sun oven.

Gordon, our local Royal Canadian Mounted Police (RCMP), was a sweet guy who took good care of us. The times we had rowdy drunks who wouldn't listen to me to tone it down, or illegal campers who didn't want to move or pay, Gordon would be called to sort things out. He seemed to take a liking to us. If he was patrolling in the area, he would often stop by to see how things were going. He was quite a talker, and we always enjoyed his visits and the many stories he loved to tell.

Pincher Creek was the small town where we did our shopping. It was cattle ranching country but also drew nature lovers, writers, poets, old hippies and back to the landers. Those friendly folk tended to gather at the small health food store or the cafe where everyone knew everyone. Since we didn't have to be in the campground during the day, we were hoping to pick up some paying work. Elizabeth, who ran the health food store, cleaned houses on the side and told me I could help her with a big job the following week!

The job was at my dream place. Hundreds of acres of rivers, ponds, woods, rolling plains all with a gorgeous view of the mountains. Elizabeth thought the daughter of the owner and I would hit it off and introduced us. Joan was a lover of nature and animals and like me wanted to build a retreat center. Herm and I ended up spending quite a bit of time visiting there and sharing meals with her and her husband. We even earned some money when Joan hired Herm to clear brush and when she bought $200 worth of my crafts!

One of the fun parts of being a campground host was meeting interesting people from all over the world. We met folks from back home in New England, we met people who knew people we knew, we met bikers who were pedaling across Canada and the US, and others from Europe and Asia. It made us feel right at home, like we were traveling again. There was one woman who made an impression on me. She was an 83-year-old botanist, who lived in New Mexico. She told us she loved to just throw all her stuff in her car and drive around for months at a time. She was a free spirit and I hoped I would be just like her at age 83!

When Herm attended a local Pow Wow, he made a connection with some Native people who were selling ammonites they had dug on the Reservation. When they learned of Herm's interest in rocks, they invited him to dig with them. He was thrilled and his association with those folks ended up being a lucrative one. He bought a number of the beautiful iridescent fossils and made good money re-selling them at rock shows.

Alas, our two months of hosting was up and new hosts were coming to fill our space. It had been an incredible summer meeting new people, making friends among the locals and soaking up the energy of that special place. I knew if I could settle anywhere, it would be there. With no word from our lawyers about our application though, we would have to move on.

CHAPTER 33

NOMADS

The next 15 months saw us crisscrossing the country. We set up at rock and mineral shows, met new people, visited family and wondered what the hell we were doing with our lives. The Canadian application appeared to be going nowhere and even though we were always on the lookout for "our" place, it was eluding us. I had always wanted to do a vision quest and thought maybe that would give me some direction. In the fall of 2002, we were camped in my son's yard in NH. While searching online for vision quests, I came across one scheduled for just after Christmas near Death Valley. Since that was good timing for us, I signed up and we hit the road at the beginning of December.

The vision quest group was scheduled to meet in Tacopa Springs, a very popular "snowbird" place we had never heard of. There were hot springs and a very active community center. A variety of classes offered, dances were held once a week and a daily meal was served. There were even massage therapists and healers on hand to keep everyone in good shape. Tacopa also seemed to draw an interesting cast of characters. Since Herm and I aren't exactly normal, we tend to gravitate to those who march to a different drum. The three guys we met at Christmas lunch were just such people.

Herm and I were standing with our trays of food, trying to decide where to sit, when we saw three men seated together away from the main diners. Without speaking, we automatically moved in their direction. The old birds of a feather thing.

It was hard to miss Jake, who appeared larger than life, even while attached to a portable oxygen tank. He was an ex-biker, and looked like one, with a massive body covered with tattoos. An avid pot grower, he had been the chef for a number of rock bands and traveled with them all over the country. Even though he was facing major surgery to remove blood clots from his lungs, he was full of exuberance and good cheer.

Bob, 76-years-old, was equally as upbeat even though his nose bled every time he laughed, which was often! He told us he was on blood thinner and 18 other medications because of multiple heart attacks. At 15, he started smoking and growing pot and would be going to northern Idaho that summer to cultivate a new stash. Stints in the army, merchant marines and working as a mercenary in South Africa had occupied most of his life. "Nothing is going to keep me down," he said with a laugh, "I'm going to continue to travel, camp and smoke pot until I kick the bucket." I so loved the attitude of this character!

The third guy was a different breed, and I was happy he was hanging out with the other two. He was only in his 50s but looked beaten down by life. Stooped and skinny, his life force felt especially weak. The only thing that seemed to bring light to his eyes was talking about his dog. I was relieved he had his dear canine friend to comfort him.

It was a true Christmas blessing to share time and space with these folks. Good cheer, good conversation, inspiration and lots of laughter.

CHAPTER 34

VISION QUEST

The 28th was the day seven questers and two guides gathered for preliminary teachings before heading to our questing spot. I was a bit nervous as I had been feeling tense and anxious lately and I knew the rites of passage ceremony would be bringing up some deep issues.

The moment I met Tim, the ruggedly built, dark haired young man, I knew we would be friends. He was wearing a cross and even though I have never been religious, there was something about that cross that brought up deep emotion in me. In a past life reading, I was told I had been an Essene and a follower of Jesus. I always wondered if that was the reason I felt so drawn to him and to the cross symbol. The other interesting thing she told me was, since the Essenes were being persecuted, we would draw the fish symbol in the sand in order to signal each other. I was shocked when she said this as I had been doodling that sign all my life and had no idea what it meant.

The next day flew by with getting us ready to do our solo fast for two days and nights. Part of the preparation was finding a buddy, which, in my case, was Tim. This system was meant as a safety net for our time in the wilderness. We would set up a stone pile central to our spots and each day would place a stone there to let the other know we were okay.

In search of our places, Tim and I wandered far from camp and when he peeled off, I continued on. I knew I had found my area when I came to a slit like opening in the smooth red rocks. I squeezed through and followed a narrow winding passage upward where it eventually opened to a wash at the base of a cliff. Oh yeah, this was SO me, secret entrance and all! I left the gallon water jugs I had been carrying and looked forward to returning in the morning to begin my adventure.

I was to discover short days, combined with long cold nights on hard ground wasn't a fun adventure at all! Add to that being hungry and feeling weak, I was wondering if this was just a big waste of my time and money. I was bored silly and reduced to watching ants, flies and anything else around me that moved. I guess it was all part of the process, but it totally sucked.

The second day was definitely more interesting. I was attempting to nap in the warm sun when a fly kept bugging me. It was so annoying; I eventually got the message I should get up. Even though I had little strength, I made my way slowly up the dry, rocky canyon. Each time I stopped to rest, Mr. Fly came to urge me on. I realized with a start this insect was taking me on a medicine walk! First, I had stopped at a yellow rock, then a red rock, then at a sand shelf with a white rock which had three other stones piled against. Those stones were black, red and yellow and hidden in the middle of that pile was a 5th rock with a design on it that looked like a cross!! Holy crap! Rocks with the colors of the 4 directions AND one with a cross? This was just too wild!

I continued haltingly up the canyon which kept splitting into right and left byways. I figured I would stick to the left as left symbolizes the feminine. I stopped when the little voice told me to and moved when it felt like the wind was nudging me on. Feeling weak and nauseous, I collapsed on a stone facing a red rock wall pockmarked with holes. As I stared at the wall the wrinkled, weathered face of a Native American woman appeared in one of the holes. It then seemed to move from one space to another across the face of the cliff. I shook my head, fearing I was hallucinating but felt I was meant to look in the holes. I approached the section of the cliff where there were two cavities side by side about chest height. In the one on the right, the male side, I saw a snake vertebrae sitting on top of a pack rat nest. It was funny, as just before I got to that fork in the canyon, it came to me I would find something there to bring to Herm. Just as I reached in to retrieve the vertebrae, two dancing butterflies appeared near me. I knew butterflies were a symbol of transformation and they reminded me that Herm and I were dancing together, transforming our souls. No matter how challenging things seemed at times, we were bound together. We are each other's teachers, brought together to grow our souls and become the highest expression of ourselves.

The last night of a quest, you are supposed to sit up all night praying for a vision. I am usually the person who says, "I will show you how tough I am!" but instead, I decided it was more important to take care of myself for a change. I guess it was the right call, because as I lay there looking up at the stars, a feeling of joy washed over me. I then heard, "whatever you encounter in life, face it with joy and a sense of humor." I smiled and immediately fell into a deep sleep.

In the morning, I was to receive two gifts. The first came when I opened my eyes and saw the rock high above me had what looked like a cross carved in it. I just grinned and said, "thank you." The second came when I was walking out to meet Tim. One of the things I had asked for in this quest was to be given a medicine name. I was thinking how disappointed I was none had been presented, when I heard a voice say clearly, "you are Pathfinder". I smiled and shook my head in agreement.

CHAPTER 35

WESTCLIFFE

The summer of 2003 was busy. Rock shows, a month of campground hosting at Belly River and almost buying a piece of property in Colville, WA. By fall we were in Colorado and found ourselves not far from Westcliffe. This was a town our friends Nick and Mary Ann had told us about years ago. Each time they saw us they asked, "have you gone to Westcliffe yet?"

I said to Herm. "You know, I think we should swing through Westcliffe so we can tell Nick and MaryAnn we finally went there." Herm agreed.

The Sangre de Cristo Mountains, even in the clouds, were spectacular. The small ranching town sat in a broad valley between the Sangres to the west and the Wet Mountains to the east. There was one main street with about ten real estate agents, a health food store, restaurants, art galleries and a rock shop! Since we never bypassed rock shops we stopped in and met Steve and Peggy, a couple about our age. As Herm was selling rocks to Steve, I quizzed Peggy about the area. Hmmm, I liked her answers, had Nick and MaryAnn found our place and we never listened? We walked around town looking at the posted properties for sale in real estate office windows and picking up brochures in outside containers. We figured when we got back to NH, we would do some research and maybe stop back here in the Spring.

Research we did and I found a place for sale that piqued my interest. There was no way I could wait until spring, I needed to see this place now! Since Herm is always ready to travel, he was game. We booked a flight to Colorado Springs the first of November, told the real estate agent to line up properties for us to look at and off we went.

CHAPTER 36

WILLIAMS CREEK ROAD

It was a cloudy, cool day as Lisa, our realtor, turned her Jeep onto the bumpy gravel road. This former 20,000-acre cattle ranch had been broken up into 35-acre parcels almost 20 years ago, but it was still undeveloped. Herm was seated in back while I rode shotgun. We had spent the day looking at properties and were getting discouraged with the dry feel to the land with only scattered Pinyon and Ponderosa pines. We needed a place with water and trees, a bit of New England in the West. I kept asking Lisa all day, "when are we going to the place by the creek?"

She said, "I really don't think you will like that place; it is very remote, and I have taken some pretty hardy people there, hunters and the like and they felt it was too far away."

Of course, she had no idea how simply we had been living for the past 14 years. Off grid, no running water, in our 17-foot trailer. She just saw two middle aged folks from back East and couldn't fathom we would want to live that far out in an unfinished cabin.

We didn't say anything as Lisa drove through the Ranch and told us the realtors called Centennial Ranch, "Kansas with a view". The first few miles were just that, flat dusty, dirt with scattered leafless bushes.

Eventually, we came upon rolling hills covered with dried grass and abandoned mobile homes. Most were old, trashed and many had their roofs peeling off. As Lisa chatted on about the Ranch, I turned to look at Herm and we both raised our eyebrows in a message of "this doesn't look very good!" I also knew when we were 10 miles in and still hadn't reached the property, Herm would be thinking this was just too far out. The air in my balloon of excitement about this property was slowly leaking out the further we traveled.

After following the winding road through the bare hills, slowly gaining in elevation, we emerged to an open vista and a T in the road. Behind a short wooden post stretched flat fields with long dried grass, interspersed with bare aspen trees and pine covered hills. Just in back of these small hills we could see the tree covered Wet Mountain range. "OOOH, this is really nice," I said to Lisa excitedly!

I turned to see Herm also smiling and agreeing. On the post there were two hand lettered signs with arrows, one pointing right to "Mission Wolf" and left to "Greenhorn Mountain".

Lisa stopped the car and I asked, "what is "Mission Wolf"?

"It's a wolf rescue that was one of the first properties on the Ranch. You would love Kent and Tracy; they are great people and do great work educating the public about wolves. They have volunteers from all over the world who come to help."

I was excited and said, "Oh wow, I love wolves, that is so cool, I would love to go there!"

As we started up again and Lisa turned left, Herm asked about Greenhorn Mountain. Lisa explained it was the tallest peak, at over 12,000 feet, in the Wet Mountain Range. She then said, "this road we turned on is called Gardner Road and it runs from the town of Gardner, 15 miles away and then through the San Isabel National Forest for another 20 plus miles to come out on the other side of the Wets."

I was all smiles, and my heart was starting to race as I was already falling in love with this place. Wolves, trees, National Forest, no other houses! This was definitely the best place we had seen all day!

The road curved around towards the trees passing a side road with a sign that said Adams Ave. We could see an old log cabin perched on the hill to our left, the Gardner Rd continued straight towards the National Forest and we turned right. Only the bare outline of a road was visible running through a huge field with the remains of old cattle pens.

I said to Lisa, "is this a road or are we just driving through a field?"

She laughed and said, "I told you it was remote but yes, this is a road, it is just rarely used so it grows in during the summer."

I turned around to Herm with wide eyes! We chugged up a long gradual slope which turned steep at the top with a higher bald peak with an old mobile home on our left. As we rounded the first bend at the top I gasped as the vista below us opened to a remote hidden valley dotted with trees. It was so beautiful, and I found a deep sigh relaxing my tense body, "yes, this is what I have been looking for."

After a few more downhill turns with steep drop-offs to our right, we turned left onto a faint dirt track. Lisa stopped on the flat field at the top of the driveway and pointed out the property lines. I was breathing in the cool mountain air and feeling totally at peace in the stillness when the mournful strains of howling wolves broke the silence.

"Oh my God, we can hear the wolves from here!" Just then a second sound joined the chorus. A weird high-pitched scream/howl echoed off the hills to our East. Wide-eyed, Herm and I turned to Lisa with startled looks and asked, "what was that?"

She laughed and said, "it is elk breeding season and that was a bull elk bugling."

Wow! Wolves, elk, what else was hiding in those hills? Wow, Wow, Wow! I think I am in heaven! I turned to Herm and we both smiled and said, "this is SO cool!"

We got back in the Jeep and headed down the very scary, steep, winding driveway. We crossed a culvert over the creek and stopped in a broad field with hills rising to the west and east.

"The driveway dead ends before the house, so we will have to walk from here, it is about a quarter mile." Lisa said.

"Awesome," I replied, "I can't wait to get out and walk!"

Lisa pointed out the willow lined creek to our right which ran north to south the length of the property. We passed through a stand of aspen, walked by some large Bristlecone pine then out in the open again where I could finally see the outline of the cabin through the trees ahead. I could barely contain myself and just kept saying over and over, "this is so cool, this is so cool!" As we entered a second aspen grove, I could hear the sound of water tumbling down a slope to our left. I was excited to discover there was a second creek on the property and the house was sitting at the junction of the two! I didn't think this could get any better! I was just all Wows! We crossed a plank bridge, climbed a short steep slope and there it was!

Plywood siding, rolled roofing, plastic windows, weird protuberances, additions attached willy-nilly, I didn't care, I was already in love. I wasn't fussy about houses, only about land and this property was awesome! I didn't dare look at Herm as I didn't want to see him hating it. In my mind it was already ours.

We followed red paving stones past a small extension to a "rustic" porch fronting the original building. Set back from this to our left was another, larger extension with an open covered area. Tall aspens surrounded the house with the west and north side dropping steeply to the two creeks. A plywood outhouse sat at a distance to the south.

We stepped onto the crumbling porch and entered a dark room smelling of rat and mouse pee. A small propane stove and counter took up one wall, a food cupboard the other. A large wood stove sat in a three-sided alcove made with OSB walls which looked ripe for burning the place down. To the right was the empty addition we had passed on the way in. We walked straight ahead to a room lined with plank benches with a sleeping loft overhead accessed by a ladder. Before us sat a shower stall which we had to squeeze by to enter the new larger addition. The addition was just a shell with an upstairs room accessed by a ladder. There wasn't much to look at inside, it was dark and creepy and would sure take a lot of work to make it livable.

Lisa said, "I'm not sure I told you, but this house isn't permitted. It has no well or septic and the owner never got a building permit. I'm not sure you can get a permit for it, but we can check."

Hmmmm, that could be a problem, but I was sure we could find a way, the land was just too perfect. We had been looking all over the US and Canada for two years and this was the type of land we had been looking for. Seventy-five acres, bordering National Forest, no neighbors, no noisy roads, trees and water, it was perfect for the healing center I had envisioned. In all the places we had looked we met people who kept telling us "you will know it when you find it" and they were right! I just knew in my bones this was our place.

Of course, it wasn't quite as easy as that! I had to convince Herm that living eight miles from any maintained road was a good idea. After all, we had turned down multiple other places that were less remote which Herm felt were too far out. Thankfully, he also loved the property despite all the downsides. We spent the flight back to New Hampshire exploring the pros and cons. Looking for "signs" and synchronicities was how we had lived the past 14 years and it had served us well. I got out a pad and pencil and we started making a list. 1. Our friends Nick and Maryann had told us years ago we should check out Westcliffe as it was a cool place. 2. The property was on Williams Creek Rd and Nancy Williams was my friend and college roommate who now lived in Denver. 3. The seller lived in Canada, where we were trying to immigrate to before our application was lost. 4. There was a rock shop in town and the owner set up at shows like Herm did. What were the odds such a small town would have a rock shop? Hmm, "maybe we were stretching the "signs", we laughed. Pros: Mission Wolf nearby; peace, quiet, no neighbors, trees and water, we could probably afford it, we can hike out our back door. We are ready for a project after being homeless for so many years. Herm could finally have a shop and I could have a garden. Cons: the road, no permit on the house, 24 miles to nearest town and two hours to city shopping. After we finished the list I said, "clearly, all signs point to this being our place, don't you agree?"

Herm said, "Well, when you look at the list, the cons have a lot more weight but let's do it, let's make an offer."

"Yay! Thank you, thank you!" I smiled, giving him an awkward hug in our airline seats.

When we got back to NH, we called Lisa and put in an offer. It was immediately accepted. The seller even gave us an extra $1500 towards getting the house permitted! We were going to be landowners together for the first time! It had been a long-haul consulting psychics, astro-cartographers, roaming this country and Canada searching, searching, searching. If we had just listened to the message sent by the "Universe" through Nick and Maryann so many years ago, we could have made our lives easier. We sure did miss THAT message, but I know that everything happens for a reason in the time it is meant to happen. If the "Universe" doesn't reach you the first time, it will keep sending messages until you figure it out. It is much more patient than I am!!

CHAPTER 37

FAREWELL

I t made no sense for us to move to our place before Spring, so we headed back for our last winter at Coon Hollow. We did our usual winter things, crafts, hiking, visiting, doing the Quartzite show. It was a bit sad at Coon Hollow that winter. The people who had been there for years and taken such loving care of it were slowly dying off. The energy of the place was changing. People with ATVs were tearing up the desert, throwing trash everywhere and causing havoc.

It was also sad to see our friend EJ going downhill. He was blind in one eye and didn't look good at all. Even so, he still found the energy to crack our backs on the picnic table and call to Robert, "is dinner ready yet?" In return, I did some healing work on him and could feel his life force was leaving. I understood, he knew this as well and was living each moment to its fullest.

One night, we heard ambulances screaming down the road to the campground. Herm and I turned to each other and said, "oh no, it must be EJ". Herm went to see what was going on, but I knew and couldn't bring myself to go out. What was interesting is when the ambulance left, it got "lost" and came all the way down to our end of the campground. I think EJ was directing them so he could say goodbye as I was the only one not at his trailer. This husky voiced, mischievous, incurable flirt would be sorely missed. He lived and died his own way. When I went outside later that evening, I heard the coyotes celebrating EJ's transition under a sky of shooting stars. A perfect send off to a very special friend.

It was time to end our nomad life and settle down. I was anxious to get to our new land and start the new chapter.

COLORADO
2004-2017

CHAPTER 38

HOME?

Only 12 miles left between us and the home we had dreamed of for so long! I just wanted to get there but the roads were so rutted, Herm had to creep along at a snail's pace, or we wouldn't have a trailer left! If the potholes weren't bad enough, we still had that steep, downhill bit to negotiate. Poor Herm was a wreck by the time we finally pulled into our driveway.

We got the trailer situated in a lovely spot with a view and discovered we had parked directly above the house! We stood there gazing down the steep hill at the red rolled roofing of the weirdly configured structure. We turned to each other and said, "what were we thinking?"

"It seemed like a good idea at the time," I laughed. "We're here now, I guess we should go down and check out what we bought!"

The next few days were spent cleaning rat poop out of the house and trying to figure what was what since this place came with no instructions! What it did come with though were ladders, solar panels, building materials and a hidden bonus! Behind a plywood door, set into the block wall foundation, was a veritable hardware store! Nuts, bolts, screws, nails, carpentry tools, rakes, shovels, everything we needed to get started on the house.

The next surprise was discovering we had a gravity feed water system! We were puzzled by the pipe sticking out of the ground near the door as we knew there was no well. Upon scouting around we found a coil of plastic pipe and Robert, with his engineer's mind, knew right away what it was for. He stretched the pipe upstream and voila, we had running water! Woohoo!!

Over the next two weeks we were to discover how little we knew about living at elevation. First of all, even though we were in good physical shape, we could barely breath walking up hill. Each evening, we hiked up the steep, winding trail to the trailer but it was a stop and go affair. Step, step, stop and breathe and repeat, it was a slow process. The second thing we discovered really quickly was if you didn't stay hydrated you got a headache. Who knew living at 10,000 feet came with learning a whole new way to function?

The next lesson came as quite a shock. It snows in April; in fact, we were to learn it can sometimes snow in June! One morning I opened the curtains to find 12" of the white stuff had fallen overnight. Of course, we had no winter boots, so basically slid down the hill to the house that morning. Thankfully, we had stored some dry wood for the stove and found some winter jackets which the previous owner had left. Being from New England, where snow lasts forever, we were really concerned. We were running low on food, we needed to do laundry and our income taxes had to be mailed. We only had a two-wheel drive truck, and no snowplows would be coming to rescue us any time soon. What WERE we thinking?

Discovery #4 was this wasn't New England! Spring snow melts REALLY fast here! We were shocked to discover it was all but gone by evening but thrilled we could finally go shopping! Nope, said lesson #5, we weren't going anywhere! Mud, slimy, snot like mud! It was a good thing the kitchen cupboard was full of food. Old food but still food!

Each day we walked to the road to see if it had dried up. On one of these trips, we were shocked to see a Jeep creeping down the steep hill before our driveway. It was the first vehicle we had seen since being there, so went to ask the driver about road conditions. The vehicle stopped beside us and out staggered a white-faced young man. "What's the matter?" we asked.

"Oh my GOD! I didn't think I was going to make it down that road! The car kept sliding towards the drop off and I couldn't control it, it was horrible."

"Oh no," how will you get back out?"

"I'm visiting my brother, down the road and there is no friggin' way I am moving until that thing dries up!"

As he drove slowly away, I said, "Well, I guess that answers our question about the road!"

It was April 14th, and come hell or high water, we had to get out. In the cool, early morning hours, while the mud was semi-solid, we made our escape. Except for a few hairy spots, we got to the highway in one piece.

During the two weeks we had been at the house, we had batted around the idea of putting the property back on the market. As much as we wanted a home, we were finding the adjustment to this place more difficult than expected. We loved the land, the solitude and the peace and quiet but the house gave us the creeps. The snow and mud incident had shown us the reality of what life would be like there, so we decided to list it.

As we told Lisa the news, she just laughed and said, "you aren't the first people to try the Ranch and change their minds, but I think you should stick it out. The best time of the year is coming, why don't you give it until the fall and if you still want to sell it then, I'll put it back on the market."

Oh crap, we weren't expecting that! We were on the fence as it was, this wasn't helpful at all! We paused, not knowing what to say!

She saw our hesitation and said, "Listen, why don't you guys sit here and talk about it, I have to go out for a minute, and you can let me know when I get back."

"Okay," we said.

As Lisa walked out the door Herm turned to me and asked, "What do you want to do?"

I sighed, "I don't know.... I guess I don't want to keep wandering around, maybe she's right, maybe we should give it awhile longer. We talked about building somewhere else on the land and we can still leave if we find we don't want to do that."

He sat there thinking then said, "yeah, I don't feel like wandering either and I'm kind of enjoying working outside. I guess we could give it a try for a while, what do we have to lose?"

Taxes mailed, laundry and shopping done, we decided to stay at a motel and do another early morning run at the road. Hot showers, clean clothes and restaurant food were a real treat but when I called my parents to check in, I received some disturbing news. The day before, my father had emergency abdominal surgery and was in the ICU. My brother assured me dad was expected to make a complete recovery and I could probably speak to him in a few days. I was relieved, but this meant we should probably break down and buy a cell phone so I could stay in touch. We had resisted that expense by using pay phones all these years, but it looked like we were starting to become "normal"! Property, phones, what would be next?

A few days later I talked to my father in the hospital, but he didn't sound good. "When are you coming home?" he asked. That question sent a chill through my bones, he never asked that.

"I don't know, are you okay?"

"I don't feel right at all, but no one is listening to me," he said.

"Oh no, that isn't good! Can you have Bill talk to them for you?"

"I guess," he said.

He asked me about the property, and we talked for a few minutes about that before I said, "I'm going to let you rest, make sure you get the doctors to listen to you and talk with Bill. I will call you again soon and you get better!!!!"

"Okay," he said, "come home soon and thanks for calling."

I hung up with a huge knot in my stomach, I had a bad feeling. I had worked in hospitals, and I knew first-hand how medical staff missed things and didn't always listen to "difficult" patients. My father was an "evening alcoholic" who drank whiskey at night to numb his back pain and I don't doubt emotional pain as well. He was normally a very kind and sociable person but with no alcohol he was obviously detoxing and irritable. I had been a nurse in a drug and alcohol rebab facility and knew first-hand how difficult people could be when they didn't have their drug of choice. I felt terrible I wasn't there to be his advocate.

Two days later I got the call from my brother telling me my father had passed. He had been rushed into surgery again but when they opened him up they found his intestines had died and there was nothing they could do. I was so pissed! I knew it! If they had only listened to him, they would have caught it in time. If I had been there, I would have made sure they had listened! I was crushed, I felt I hadn't done enough to help, I should have called and talked with the doctor myself!

Unfortunately, there was no time to grieve, we had to pack and get out of there as the funeral was only four days away. We drove like maniacs and almost lost a wheel in St Louis! Thankfully, our angels were with us once again. The hubcap and most of the lug nuts flew off leaving the tire wobbling on the axle. A day sitting in a repair garage slowed us up but with extra driving time we got there the night before the funeral.

I was pretty numb and couldn't believe he was gone. Even though my father and I had our issues when I was a teenager, he was always my hero. When I was growing up, I loved helping him build and fix things. My constant questions probably drove him crazy, but he always took the time to answer them patiently. He was interested in what I was doing in my life, was always supportive and was a great listener. I also loved how devoted he was to my mother, he totally adored her. I would really miss him.

The next month was hectic and exhausting, both physically and emotionally. Herm and I were either in Rhode Island, helping my mother, or in New Hampshire sorting through our stuff. We had decided to give that creepy cabin our best shot. That meant trading in our truck for a 4-wheel drive variety and hiring a moving van. It had been fun being foot loose and fancy free but, at age 57, we were ready for a change and a new challenge. What could go wrong?

Sure, there was no snow plowing, but we didn't have to go out too often and it seemed to melt fast. Yes, the roads got muddy but now we had a 4-wheel-drive truck. Yeah, it was hard to breathe, but we would soon get into shape, and it wouldn't be an issue. No well, electricity or bathroom, no worries, we had lived that way for 14 years already. So, what if there was no road to the house, we loved to walk! Looking back, I have to laugh at our naiveté. We were more prepared than most but had NO clue as to what we were up against!

CHAPTER 39

VISION GUIDE TRAINING

Once we got home, I had no time to ponder our decision to keep the property. In two weeks, I was scheduled to leave for a month-long vision quest teacher training in California. The ceremony I had experienced in January, sparked my interest in becoming a guide. It would fit in with my goal of creating a healing center on our land. With my lifelong affinity for Native American beliefs and my background as a family therapist, I knew it was something I could be good at.

On a warm June day, ten of us sat under tall trees on the eastern slope of the Sierras. As I looked around the circle, I discovered I was by far the oldest of the six women and four men. Most appeared to be in their 30s except for our teachers, who were more my age. We were there to gain the tools and wisdom to guide others on rites of passage ceremonies and, in that process, would find our lives changed as well.

Each day started with a council circle where we gathered around the central fire pit. We were tasked with both speaking and listening from the heart. We weren't required to talk but were encouraged to share what we were experiencing on both a mundane and spiritual/emotional level. Our guides would then take us through various teachings before sending us off with homework. These assignments were always interesting and fun but sometimes quite challenging in ways that were unexpected.

The first day we were told to "go find your place on the land". Always wanting to do things BIG, I intended to climb the mountain across the road. Instead, I was drawn to a large pine, while searching for a walking stick. I sat down and leaned up against the tree and "heard", "it doesn't have to be hard, it's really simple." As I looked around, I realized the view from where I was sitting, was similar to one on our land where we were thinking of building a new house. I then heard: "it is close by." I wondered if that meant we should keep the house we had instead of building a new one? Or could it mean we should build closer to the road to make it easier to get in and out? Conversely could it simply mean I didn't have to make it hard on myself by climbing the mountain to do my assignment? Hmmm, many things to ponder but I guess this tree is my place!

The second day's homework was: "Be childlike near some water and find someone to play with." That was an easy one! I went directly to the river, took off my clothes and jumped in! After splashing around for a while, I explored downstream and discovered a hidden cave tucked in the riverbank behind some bushes. I crawled into the cool darkness and crouched, peering out through the tangle of branches.

Downstream, I noticed a fellow "player" and when she spotted me staring, we locked eyes. In that moment, I heard this message, "let's meet in the middle". I crawled out of my cave, and we ran towards each other laughing, as we plunged into the river splashing and giggling. It was great fun to let my joyful inner child out to play.

Over the weeks, my friendship with two of my fellow students truly warmed my heart. When things got tough emotionally, they were always there for me. Peter and I had an instant connection the moment we met. He was a handsome, personable young man from Germany, with a deep love of nature and a passion for personal growth. His easy smile and gentle energy made him comfortable to be around. We would find ourselves in deep conversations about life, love and spirituality far into the night. Christian, a tall, thin Austrian, was more reserved but his quiet exterior hid a strength and compassion that was palpable. When I told my story in circle about looking for a walking stick, Christian took it upon himself to make me one which touched me deeply.

On day three, we were told to: "go into the underworld and find a "wound" in nature and converse with it." Euchaval, a ruggedly built, middle aged German with thinning hair, had a strong warrior energy which I had found intimidating. When I saw we were both headed toward the dump, I immediately turned around and went in the opposite direction. I found a burned area to converse with and it spoke of "burned hearts, deadened senses and new growth". I wasn't sure what that meant, but wondered if it had to do with Herm and I and our new home?

When I rose to leave, I saw Euchaval headed toward me, and we passed in the road without making eye contact. The brief encounter made me anxious, and I wanted to escape to my safe spot by the river but couldn't find the path. I kept hitting dead ends and obstacles and felt stuck in the underworld and …. there he was again! He was standing directly across from my swimming hole peeing on MY sacred tree! I was angry and wondered what the message was. Did he represent my warrior self? Did that self keep my heart from opening, was it guarding my heart? Why was he triggering me?

I needed to know what was going on. Even though we weren't supposed to talk, I stalked over to him and asked briskly, "are you still in the underworld?"

"Yes," he replied calmly.

"Why are you following me?" I asked angrily "I am really upset that you were peeing on my sacred tree!"

He stared at me for quite a while then said calmly, "I saw you going to the dump, and you would have been welcome there as well but you turned away. The second time I saw you, I didn't think much about it. The third time I was looking at the wound in the tree and when I saw you walking towards me, I thought, "here comes a wound".

I stood there shocked, trying to take that in, then thanked him and quietly walked away. Wow, he was right, anger was definitely a wound I carried.

When I shared the story with the group that night, it triggered a lot of tears, but I wasn't sure where they were coming from. When the next day's assignment was to: "find something that represented your gift, your giveaway to the world." I just couldn't do it. I didn't feel I had any gift. When Peter discovered I wasn't doing the homework, he found me at my tent and gave me an apple. That small kindness got me crying again so he sat me down and made me talk. I talked, he listened, we both cried and through that interchange I realized I hadn't properly grieved my father's death.

That night, when we were supposed to tell the story of what our gift was, I felt compelled to act it out instead of speaking. I rolled in the dirt, I crawled like a snake, I grabbed the earth and rubbed it all over me. Gradually, I stood up and up with my arms raised to the heavens, a beatific smile spreading across my face. I felt really powerful and knew then I was the giveaway, I was the gift. There was nothing I had to do but be me.

The group had been challenging me to accept my elderhood/grand-mother role, but I didn't want to. I didn't see myself that way at all, I didn't feel any different from them! It was difficult to believe I was an elder. It wasn't a persona I wanted even though it was considered one of honor and respect. How could I be old already?

We were all experiencing deep emotional clearing and after two weeks we were exhausted. I missed Herm, I couldn't sleep, was cold at night, was having anxiety attacks and I cried a lot. I started to withdraw, as I tend to do when I get tense. Whenever the group went out, I stayed home and hung out with the insects and lizards! I wasn't looking forward to our upcoming four-day vision fast, at all!!

Before our initiation, we had to verbalize our intent, our "I AM" statement. To inspire us in this exercise, we would spend the night on the nearby 700-foot Eureka sand dunes near Death Valley. We arrived at dusk, grabbed our water and scattered along the steep slopes. I took off my shoes and climbed, my feet sinking deep into the loose sand. As the sky darkened, I dug a hole on the slope and settled into the warmth of the dune. As I lay there smiling up at the vastness of the night, the stars whispered, "You are a powerful, courageous elder woman who guides her people with love, compassion, joy and humor." My heart started racing, 'there is no way, I can say that!' I thought. But as I let the statement settle, I could see that indeed I was that person, when I was functioning as my soul self. It was my ego self who kept me from embracing it. As I pondered those thoughts, I drifted off to sleep, warmed by the beads of brown sand that encompassed my body, protecting me from the chill of the desert night.

As we headed to the landing area of our fasting place, I wondered where all that peace, magic and "embracing all that I am" had gone. How could I sit by myself with my anger for four days and what or who was I angry at? I wasn't embracing my femaleness, my elderhood, or my ability to lead. I was doubting my marriage, my relationship to Herm, my ability to be accepting and nonjudgmental. All of it was swirling in my body making me totally anxious. I was afraid I would go off the edge! After almost a month of stirring up emotional blocks and shadows, this was going to be challenging.

I just shook my head and smiled when it was announced Amy would be my stone pile buddy. Of course, she was, she had been driving me crazy for the past month! I had been determined to overcome my annoyance with her but hadn't been having much success. I asked the "Universe" for help with this issue, so with its usual sense of humor it gave me what I asked for!!

Well, the quest was on and here I was. Sitting under a tree on my sleeping mat watching the ants, dreaming of eating. I just wanted to calm my anxiety with food like I always did. ARGH! No food for four days, I just had to sit with feelings without the usual distractions. I thought I would go freakin nuts! I paced, I scratched bug bites, I dumped ants out of my sleeping bag, I watched the lizards sit in the sun, I was totally bored. At least I didn't have to stay rolled up in my bag like a burrito for 12 hours, like the last quest!

We had each been challenged to perform a death lodge ceremony during this time. This is where you invite people from your life to appear before you to process any unresolved issues with them. When I did that, I was surprised to find that the anger I was carrying was mostly directed at Herm. I had trusted him with my heart and in the blink of an eye he had crushed it. I could still remember the day, standing with him in front of a museum in Solo, Java in Indonesia. It was something he said that had cut me so deeply that I stuffed it into the remote corners of my being. I couldn't even retrieve the words; I was just left with the feeling of deep betrayal. I am sure whatever he said was never meant to hurt me. He is a kind, empathic soul who wouldn't intentionally injure anyone, but our traumas sometimes override our true inner selves. I "talked" with him, cried, swore and did what I could to forgive but I knew the scar was still there. It was a wound I felt could be opened again all too easily. I carved a heart from a small piece of soapstone I had brought with me. Its surface imperfections symbolized damage we both needed to heal. I smiled as I remembered those dancing butterflies from the first vision quest. No matter how painful it could be at times, I knew my Herm and I were deeply connected on a cosmic level.

The two days after our quest were powerful and emotional as we each related what had happened to us on our fast. Those experiences were then mirrored back to us by our teachers. This is the most compelling event of the entire ceremony. Deep insight is gained as each thing that happens has significance and is a metaphor for our lives. Imagine my shock when Amy's story appeared to be intertwined with mine! It seems the items I had left her each day at the stone pile were direct reflections of things she was meditating on that day. The morning we finished the quest, she went back to the pile to retrieve what I had given her. While there, she asked the grandmothers to give her a gift for me. She was guided to a rock under which was a scorpion with no stinger! She picked it up with her bandana and brought it back to show me, but it had since disappeared. What made the story so fascinating was she had no idea I had also found a scorpion with no stinger. It was under my tarp and, I too, had grabbed it with my bandana. Coincidence? I don't think so. Scorpion means transformation. What had I asked the "Universe" to help me with? Transforming my annoyance with Amy to one of acceptance. Ask and you shall receive!

That month in the desert took me on the most powerful journey of my life. I made deep connections with people and felt seen and accepted for who I was. The journey into my shadow-self had been totally supported which allowed my light to shine. It was the most fulfilling, most perfect time in my life, and I felt totally at peace. The morning of departure, the word "compassion" was whispered in my ear by some unseen guide. I would carry that word back home with me as a gift for my Herm.

CHAPTER 40

FIRST SUMMER

"You're wild with that thing," Herm joked as I swung the sledgehammer into the rotting walls of the old porch.

"I sure am, I love knocking things down," I laughed. I wasn't a stranger to demolishing walls. I had done a lot of it when renovating my 1840s farmhouse in New Hampshire. It felt good to finally be home, back with Herm and outside in the sunny, cool Colorado air starting to create our dream. I was refreshed and at peace after my time away.

That first summer was all about preparing our house for winter so we wouldn't freeze. We took walls down and put up others, which created a cozy, if rustic, interior to get us started. The kitchen stayed the same, with the welcome addition of a propane refrigerator and the small addition became our bedroom. The adjoining room, which had the bench seats, became our living room. We moved the wood stove into there with a futon couch nearby for cold winter nights. With three small rooms to heat and the big addition closed off, we hoped to stay warm. To feed the stove, we cut, split and stacked five cords of wood, trusting that would be enough.

Since I had been waiting so long to garden, the first thing I did when I got home from CA was to dig up a patch of earth. I was so excited to plant vegetables again, I had missed having my hands in the earth while being on the road. Because the growing season was short, I stuck to cold weather veggies and bought one potted tomato plant to satisfy my fresh tomato addiction. I lovingly tended this small patch of earth each day and when things started to grow, I could just taste a nice veggie stir fry in our future.

It was August and Herm was away at a rock show when one afternoon, the sky suddenly turned totally black. The most ferocious thunderstorm I had ever experienced descended upon me. It was like something out of a doomsday movie, and I was scared shitless! Flash bang! Flash bang! Flash bang! It was a constant deafening roar. Trees were falling left and right as the fierce wind bent them horizontal and hail slammed into the side of the house adding to the racket. I paced from window to window, praying we wouldn't be hit by lightning. The balls of flying ice were shredding everything in sight. The leaves on the trees, the colorful wildflowers I had just raved to my sister about, and more importantly my beautiful vegetables. I stood at the window in despair as I watched my precious tomato plant get beaten to death. I wanted to run out and rescue it but was too afraid of being shredded myself!

Just as fast as it came, it left, leaving destruction and piles of hail in its wake. The trees were all but stripped of their leaves, the flowers and vegetables gone. I just stood there crying. I didn't want to live in a place where this kind of thing happened, I just didn't!

Of course, mother nature has a way of bouncing back. The flowers did return, albeit not in their former glory, but enough to spawn the next generation. My greens also bounced back, before the mice and chipmunks took their toll. The last straw came the day I was going to harvest the kale and found the pack rats had beaten me to it. I discovered its wilted leaves piled neatly on top of the stash of other items they had stolen from us. I was so discouraged. All those years waiting to have a garden again and now this. Would it even be possible here?

Except for the disappointment with the garden, it was a full and happy summer.

We explored the thousands of acres of National Forest just outside our door and connected with our wonderful neighbors at Mission Wolf. By the time fall rolled around we were all buttoned up and ready for snow. At least we thought we were!

CHAPTER 41

WINTER

The two winters spent in our yurt in Maine had taught us a lot about living rough in cold weather. Just as in the yurt, we had the wood stove for heat, an outhouse, hauled water from the creek and snowshoed our supplies in and out. Having solid walls kept the house warmer, and a refrigerator versus a cooler buried in the ground certainly was a convenience. Of course, butts sticking to a cold toilet seat was pretty much the same. The big difference came with the distance we had to hike everything in and out. In Maine, it was a flat quarter mile to a cleared route and here, two miles of up and down, then eight miles of snow packed roads!

The Homeowners Association we were a part of provided no snow plowing for its 50 plus miles of dirt tracts. Once a summer, it did scrape the roads with a grader, but that was about it. When we bought our place, we didn't think we would have any issues since there was a county road within two miles of our house. We figured we could hire a neighbor to clear the other two miles or eventually get a plow for the truck. Boy did we have a LOT to learn!

First of all, we were 15 miles from the town in charge of clearing the county road. Since we were only one of four families living up there, we weren't exactly a priority. In fact, if we needed plowing, we had to call and we never knew if or when they would show up. Most of the time they were pretty good, but we learned it was wise to provide incentives. Now and then our neighbor would leave a case of beer sitting in the snow and Herm would often stop at the town garage and leave "gifts".

With that one road open we were still left with six miles of unplowed snow between us and freedom. Sure, we could get to the town the road was open to, but there was nothing there. A school, church and a general store which was mostly closed. All of our business was in the other direction. Occasionally, another resident might plow a section, or someone might have gone out ahead of us and made tracks to follow. Most of the time though, we were flying on a wing and a prayer and four chains.

The road issue was a constant source of stress and conversation. "I wonder how the road will be?" "I wonder if anyone has gone out?" "I wonder if it has drifted in?" "I wonder if we should put two or four chains on?" Even if we succeeded in running the gauntlet and got out for a day of shopping, there was no guarantee we would get back. If the wind blew, which it did all the time, the roads could be packed in and impassable when we returned. We had to make sure we always carried shovels and snowshoes. Even with chains, sometimes you had to dig your way out and if you didn't, then you had to snowshoe home. The never-ending road issue took its toll.

Then there was the two mile stretch between our house and the county road. That whole, "we will have our neighbor plow us out" thing? Didn't quite work out according to plan. He told us it wouldn't be a good idea, but we didn't believe him. We were used to New England snow that stayed put and didn't move with the slightest breeze. Colorado snow, we found out, is so light you can drive through almost a foot of it with no problem. BUT when the wind packs it? It's like cement and you can barely make it through a couple of inches. When you plow and make snowbanks, you create a nice trough for the wind to fill up with concretized white stuff. After throwing a lot of money at trying to keep that stretch open, we finally surrendered to mother nature and parked our truck on the county road. We were used to lugging building materials down the driveway to the house, but snowshoeing laundry, propane tanks and groceries to and from the truck was a little different. It was always an adventure.

Back from a day of errands, we parked the truck and strapped on snowshoes. Herm bungeed our bags of clean laundry to the sled and I stuffed our food into my big backpack. The wind was howling as Herm started up the tract and I shouldered my pack to follow. We bent our heads against the gale to keep the flying granules of snow from piercing our eyes. I could barely see as I plodded along atop the solid piles of plowed snow at the edge of the road. Suddenly, I was hit by a huge gust of wind. It spun me around and threw me to the ground and I was stuck! I couldn't even get to my knees as wherever I pushed on the snow my arm would sink to my armpit. Herm was up ahead and couldn't hear me in the fierce wind, so I had to figure it out myself. Thankfully, our faithful dog Zuna had stayed with me and was hovering nearby looking worried. I called her to me and by grabbing onto her I was slowly able to disentangle myself from the soft powder. Once upright, I was very careful to keep myself as low as possible for the rest of the hike. I kept chuckling to myself about how comical the whole thing had been. It would have been fun to have a video of the big turtle trying to right itself.

Another time I wished I had a camera, was when the sled full of groceries took a joyride! It was a beautiful Colorado winter day with the snow sparkling brightly in the sunlight. As we crested the hill and started down, the sled somehow broke free and off it went. All we could do was cheer it on as it picked up speed, luged around the first corner, then the second, only to lose it on the 3rd and fly off into space. We rushed to the crash site and peered over the edge. Far below we could see our poor sled up against a tree surrounded by crushed eggs, exploded Rice Dream and produce. "That sled sure did have fun," I laughed as we slogged through the deep snow to retrieve what was left of our groceries.

"I thought it was going to make it around that last curve. It was SO close to being home free," Herm smiled, shaking his head.

Other than our adventures getting to and from the truck and obsessing about the roads, we worked most days on the interior of the house. We cut in windows, built a staircase, put up walls, installed wiring, and much more. The days flew by. When not toiling away we would either snowshoe to our neighbor's house to exchange stories and complain about the roads or go for a hike in the mountains looking for wildlife. It was a quiet, simple life and even though it was challenging at times, we had lived that way for many years, albeit not with the snow and road issues.

CHAPTER 42

SYSTEMS

Nomad's Rest is what we called our Colorado ranch, but we didn't rest much those first few years! Once we decided to keep the cabin, we got down to work. It was a tough decision to stay by the creek because it meant we would never have a permitted/legal residence. The cabin was squeezed into a slice of land between steep hills, the two creeks and the National Forest boundary which left no room for a septic system. Besides that, there was no way to get heavy equipment across the creek. The good news was we didn't pay taxes on the house and had no building inspector hanging over our shoulder during renovations. Since Herm was an engineer, everything was built safely but we could be creative with other things which the code police may not have liked.

Over the following months we transformed that tiny, run-down shack into a beautiful, unique, comfortable home. We did, however, learn a few expensive lessons along the way. The first was the solar system. You think we would have known better after using the one panel on our trailer for so many years. I guess the concept of a battery bank versus one battery didn't compute as we killed that first set. The next lesson was not to set up solar panels near trees that can fall over and crush them! After that expensive incident, we installed a new array at the top of the hill where there was no vegetation. With the new panels and an upgraded inverter, we were able to run almost everything we wanted, even a small freezer. Big power items, like a vacuum cleaner, anything requiring heat or large power tools, we only used in the middle of bright sunny days. Living off grid and being energy independent was really satisfying. It was a bit more labor intensive than being plugged into the power grid, but we didn't lose power in storms like the town did!

Since we weren't able to install one of those large propane containers, we had a number of 50-pound bottles we hauled to town to fill at the hardware store. We set up our tank farm under the deck and Herm ran a pipe from there to the stove and refrigerator. Sure, it would have been nice not to lug tanks to town, especially in winter, but it was nice to be in charge and not have to depend on a delivery truck.

Water in the summer, was from the aforementioned pipe in the creek, that gravity fed to the house. It worked great until it rained heavily and the pipe washed down the brook and got plugged up with debris. There was many a time spent unplugging and repositioning pipe, but when it worked it was wonderful!

Herm also had a great time constructing dams to form deep pools where we could easily fill our buckets. Of course, the heavy rains tended to wash the dams downstream as well but playing in the water was always fun. The big problem came when we had a dry summer. We never totally ran out of water but came close a few times. The pools became puddles and we would have to dig out more and more gravel to make them a bit deeper. We were sometimes reduced to filling buckets a cup at a time throughout the day. The creek water we used for drinking was run through a ceramic filter and the rest was used for washing dishes, clothes and so forth. To water our gardens, we had a rain barrel catchment system and three large tanks we filled from the creek in the spring.

I lobbied for an indoor toilet, so I didn't have to wander in the dark to the outhouse and leave my skin on a frosty seat in the winter. Herm constructed a box with a toilet seat, under which sat a 5-gallon bucket.

Shavings, which were in an old wastebasket, were used to cover our waste. Each day we dumped the bucket into a compost pile and covered it with leaves. We were following directions given in the *The Humanure Handbook*. Even though we were a bit skeptical at first, it worked great, and the compost was an awesome addition to our flower beds.

Our gray water, we dumped on the ground. A bucket sat under the bathroom sink, and another was located in the basement under the shower stall. A hook in the shower held a bag we filled with hot water to wash ourselves. Dishwashing was done in a plastic tub set in the kitchen sink and the dirty water thrown off the deck.

Not able to solve the vegetable gardening issues, we realized if we wanted to eat, we needed a greenhouse. A company in Pagosa Springs sold dome greenhouse kits and advertised they could be used year-round to grow food! This was just what we needed!

We ordered an 18-foot diameter but then had to make a level place to put it. With no heavy equipment to help, it was all up to us. We cut trees, dug out stumps and roots and pried up boulders. Once that was done, the instructions were to prepare a gravel base. Hmmm, how are we going to get gravel? Herm had a lightbulb moment and said, "there is gravel in the creek, we could dig it out and use that!" And that is what we did!

Level pad, check. Puzzle pieces assembled, check. Water tank in, check. Beds built, check. Now came the next hard part, filling the beds with dirt! One wheelbarrow at a time, we dug up our dark, rich soil and eventually got them full. Voila! A greenhouse ready to plant by the first of November!!

I was thrilled to have an inside garden. During summer storms, I would sit in the house grinning smugly when hail was beating the leaves off the trees. No more ruined gardens for me! The added bonus of growing food year-round was a real blessing, especially since we couldn't always get out. What a treat it was to work in the warmth of the green house on cold winter days. With snow piled high outside, the smell of the warm earth and the sound of the bubbler for the goldfish soothed the soul. Getting that greenhouse was, by far, the smartest thing we ever did.

CHAPTER 43

RENOVATIONS

In order to keep the house renovations on track, Herm and I had morning construction meetings. I made drawings of my ideas and Herm was the skillful one at bringing them to life. I have no patience for fussy work, so I did all the easy stuff like framing, putting in windows, sheet rocking, painting, flooring and tiling. I even learned how to do wiring with my handy electrical do-it-yourself book. Herm built all the cabinets, bookcases, desk, kitchen table, dressers and more.

Aspen logs from our property were used to construct a beautiful deck, which overlooked the creek. A sliding glass door led to the dining/kitchen area where Herm fashioned cabinets from blue-streaked beetle-kill pine. I made the knobs and drawer pulls out of Douglas Fir and tiled the counters with black slate adding pieces of ancient Native American pottery we had found in the desert. Arched window openings in the wall between kitchen and living room lent interest and allowed the heat from the wood stove to filter through.

Hidden compartments, a secret room, all added to the fun. I even dug out the basement, which had started as a crawl space. It was a slow project, with pickaxe, shovel and one bucket at a time, but a great place to store our canned goods and potatoes. Plus, I got enough rocks to make another stone wall!

To get to the cellar, from the kitchen, you had to duck through a unique arched hobbit door. On the face of it, I wood-burned an image of the dragon of the underworld. This portal led to the space in back of the refrigerator where you lifted a trap door and descended a log ladder into the darkness.

Not only was the house magical but so was the surrounding nature. We learned everything we needed was provided. Medicinal and edible wild plants and berries abounded. Firewood was a short walk out our back gate. Mulch for the gardens was easily dug out of rotten logs. Wood for our deck, ladders and staircases was plentiful and gravel for the foundation of our greenhouse was right there in the creek. We grew much of our own food and our only bills were for cell phone and satellite internet. It was a good life.

CHAPTER 44

ZUNA

On September 11th, 2006, my life changed forever. I believe it marked the beginning of the end of our marriage.

A love of nature and animals has dominated my life and I have always had a special affinity for dogs. At the age of three I got my first dog, a black and white male Cocker Spaniel named Brig. That puppy and I were inseparable from the first day until he died at the age of twelve. The 1950s were the days when dogs and kids still ran free. My parents always knew which neighbor's house I was at because Brig would be lying in that yard waiting for me. He and I spent many of our days exploring the woods behind our house, a packed lunch and nature guidebooks in hand. I loved my dog, and he was very patient with me as I told him all my woes and problems. He was my best friend and a real comfort while growing up.

Many dogs would follow Brig. German Shepherds in my teenage years, Irish Wolfhounds, Greyhounds, Cairn Terriers and Dobermans in my twenties and early thirties. Except for one exceptional German Shepherd, no dogs were as special as Zuna. She was my second Rhodesian Ridgeback and the first dog Herm had gotten really close to.

Zuna had traveled with us around the US and Canada charming everyone she met. She was a great travel companion, never causing any issues, always friendly to strangers and diving into new situations with nary an issue. She visited zoos and wildlife areas with us, she helped us campground host at Waterton, and she hiked with us in more states than I can count. In New Mexico, she helped us find "horns" and was the witness at our wedding. I was so happy she could finally be off leash all the time when we got our land. She was in heaven.

Herm adored Zuna, and he being a natural worrier, was always concerned with my rather casual attitude of letting dogs be dogs. Ridgebacks were bred to hunt, guard and herd and have a high prey drive, so when bears came in the yard, it was Zuna's nature to chase them out! I let her do that much to Herm's dismay. I had gone to a lecture in town given by a bear expert, and he said bears will almost always run from dogs. He said they weren't a threat unless it was a mother bear with cubs. We had only seen lone bears around our place, and they all took off when Zuna gave chase. She had such fun going after them and was so proud of herself it always made me smile. I did agree, however, it would be dangerous for her to tackle a momma bear with cubs.

Herm was away in Denver at a rock show and Zuna and I were outside staining the new siding I had just put up. It was a typical fall Colorado day with the sun shining in a deep blue high-altitude sky. It was warm and the birds, who hadn't left for warmer parts, were singing. It hadn't been a great workday for me, not much had gone right. I was trying to finish putting up some of the siding and was frustrated as I kept cutting the boards incorrectly. I got the "message" I wasn't supposed to do that job, so moved on to staining. Then I spilled the gallon of stain all over the patio blocks which was totally annoying. At that point I should have taken it as a "sign" and quit but I tend to get stubborn and focused on a job and want to finish. I told myself I would just get one side done, then go have lunch.

As usual, Zuna had been out with me all morning but uncharacteristically asked to go in the house around noon. I thought that was odd and looking back I should have taken that as a message as well, but Miss Stubborn ignored all the signs.

I was getting close to finishing up when I noticed it had become very still all of a sudden. What popped in my mind was I should stay aware of my surroundings as a bear could sneak up on me. I have no idea why I would think that, as I never worried about bears. I continued staining but kept hearing a strange noise and thought maybe my cat Tricky was nearby. A little while later, I felt the urge to turn around and not 20' away stood a small black bear and two tiny cubs watching me work! I was surprised, but not scared. I was more upset that this momma was obviously accustomed to people and was now introducing her kids to humans. I knew it was a very good way for bears to end up dead!

I yelled for them to scram, and they started to slowly make their way up the stone steps towards the trees which bordered the yard. That should have been the end of it, but I felt a "force" moving me towards the door of the house. As I was walking, my mind was screaming, "DO NOT open the door!" It was the most bizarre thing, I didn't seem to have control of my body, it was like a war going on between my body and mind. Unfortunately, the body won. As soon as I opened the door, Zuna dashed out, running up the hill after the retreating bears and disappeared into the trees. I screamed for her to come back, almost before the door opened, but of course that prey drive was stronger than my voice. I ran up the hill in a panic yelling her name when I heard her scream, then scream again. She came streaking towards me, the momma bear hot on her heels. I immediately stepped between them and screeched at the bear to GET OUT OF HERE! I would have tackled her if I had to, momma bear against momma bear. I guess she caught my vibe because she turned and ran back to her babies.

Zuna was standing nearby gasping as I turned shakily to examine her. Her right side was caved in, there were claw marks on her ribs, a puncture wound was spurting blood and a sucking sound came from a punctured lung. Thankfully, she was still standing and could walk, as I would never be able to carry her up the hill to the car.

In a panic, I dashed into the house, trying to think what I would need. I grabbed phone, car keys, checkbook and the Vet's number but totally forgot my wallet. Both of us shaking, we made it to the car and with her still in shock she was able to climb in. I tore up to the top of the hill where I had phone reception and called the mobile Vet but got no answer. Answer or not, I was going to town. I drove 50mph over the 12 miles of rough gravel roads to the highway where I stopped to call again. This time he answered, and we agreed to meet in town, another long 12 miles away. Thank goodness that highway through the valley has almost no traffic. I made it in record time, the whole way praying and talking to Zuna.

He examined her in his mobile van in the parking lot of the small supermarket. He confirmed she had broken ribs and a punctured lung. Since he had no stationary hospital, there wasn't much he could do. He could tape her up, send me home with pain meds and hope for the best. My other option was to drive her to the emergency hospital in Colorado Springs two hours away. I was totally conflicted about which course to take. I had worked for veterinarians for several years in high school and learned animals are amazingly resilient and sometimes less intervention is better than more. But what if I took her home and she died! I so wished Herm was there to help make the decision, but I couldn't get ahold of him. I thought, "what would he do?" He would say, take her to the Springs, so that's what I did.

I knew she wasn't going to die right then so I took a few minutes to breathe and take stock. I was an emotional mess, I was dressed in stain covered, ripped jeans, an old flannel shirt and I hadn't showered in a while. My dirty hair was stuffed under a baseball cap, I had no license, no credit card and I was almost out of gas. Since it was too far to go home to change and get those things, I called a friend in town to ask if I could borrow a clean shirt and a credit card. She readily agreed and insisted on coming with me as I was in no condition to drive.

It was such a long ride, and I was so worried, but I tried to calm down as there was nothing, I could do but wait. Zuna was lying in the back seat, obviously in pain but holding her own. I could just pray she would be okay.

It was four hours after the attack when we finally pulled into the emergency Vet clinic at 5 p.m. I had called ahead, so they were waiting with a stretcher to get her into the hospital. Becky and I sat in the deserted waiting room while the vets did ultrasound, blood work, x-rays, and placed a chest tube. I couldn't sit still and paced the lobby.

A grim-faced vet finally emerged from the back to report Zuna had four broken ribs, a punctured lung and soft tissue damage. They described her injuries as the same as being hit by a car and said there was also trauma to her heart. She obviously wasn't going home that night, so I went out back to see her. I was trying to hold back the tears as I told her she had to stay and I would be back for her soon, to be a good girl. I was happy she was sedated as we had never been apart in seven years. She never liked me leaving her.

As Becky and I walked to the car, lightning flashed, thunder roared, rain beat down and all my anguish poured forth. The storm seemed to be mirroring my devastation. I had done this to my baby girl, I may have killed her! I just couldn't stop sobbing as Becky drove to her friend's house where she wanted me to stay the night. I just wanted to be alone and home. I also needed to get the cats in for the night, so nothing happened to them too!

While waiting for the test results at the hospital, I had finally gotten ahold of Herm to tell him what happened. He was almost as much of a mess as I was. He asked if he should come home and as much as I wanted him to, I said no, there was no point. He was four hours away and his show was going on and I didn't want to burden him. It was my old, "I can take care of myself" stepping in when I should have just allowed him to come take care of me. ARGH! Why did I do that?

I don't know how I got home safely that night. Between the intense thunderstorm, the downpours, flooded roads and my own tears and screaming, I could barely see where I was going in the dark. I thought back to that morning when Zuna had given me a tiny kiss. I had thought it strange as she rarely gave kisses! It almost felt like she was saying good-bye, that everything was going to be okay. Then I remembered lately I had been having feelings that something was going to happen to her. Why hadn't I remembered that and not opened that damn door? What force had compelled me to do that?

The next day, I emailed everyone I could think of to send prayers for Zuna. I called some of our best friends and kept phoning the clinic throughout the day to see how she was doing. The chest tube was out, and they said she was up, and the wounds looked good so I made plans to go see her the next day. I just wandered around in a daze totally preoccupied with thinking of Zuna and sending prayers. I was at a loss with Herm away and my pal Zuna not there.

My neighbor John drove me to the vets the next day. Oh my God, she looked awful! She was still heavily sedated and whimpering. Her whole body was swollen and full of air, it was horrible! The vet I talked with didn't give me much confidence when she said the various vets on her case couldn't agree how to treat her! One wanted to close the hole in her chest to get the air out of her tissues and the other wanted to leave it open so the wound wouldn't get infected. I left with no confidence in them and not knowing what to do. Maybe I should just bring her home? I don't know if she knew I was even there! I was devastated and cried all the way home.

The next day the clinic said she was a little better and if she started to eat and drink on her own, I could get her on Friday. I had all my holistic healers ready to work on her when she got back, and I was preparing the house for her return. Herm had gone to visit her the night before and was also upset about her condition.

Friday came and no Zuna, she was still filling up with air and not eating. I had seen snakes on the path the past two days and their meaning is rebirth, transformation and change. I wasn't too happy with those symbols. I considered going to the hospital and bringing her some chicken as I was sure she would eat for me, but I just couldn't bring myself to drive to the Springs. I will always regret that. I will never forgive myself for not pushing through my anxiety about driving and going to her. She was my baby; I was abandoning her!

I thought about Zuna all that Friday and decided I would call first thing in the morning and tell them I was coming to pick her up. She wasn't getting better there, and I was sure if she was home, where she was comfortable, she would recover. I couldn't bear the thought she was feeling we deserted her. We had never left her anywhere before.

Everyone in the vet office knew me by now and they all loved Zuna, so when I trudged up the hill to call first thing Saturday morning and the receptionist asked me to hold, I had a bad feeling. The vet got on the line in tears saying Zuna had gotten up to drink at 5 a.m. and dropped dead. They figured it was a clot or air embolism.

NOOOOOOOOOOOOO!!!! I had killed our heart dog, our baby, our best friend. I hadn't listened to that little voice that said to bring her home earlier in the week. She had died alone without us! I hung up the phone and just screamed and screamed and screamed, tearing my hair out. No, no, no! It was all my fault! I let her out and I promised I would never let her chase a momma bear. On top of that, I didn't listen to the inner voice that said to bring her home. I would never forgive myself and I didn't think Herm would ever forgive me either!

Amidst my sobbing, I called Herm to relay the horrible news and he was shattered. He had never given his heart to an animal before the way he had Zuna. She was so much his girl and had trusted me with her and I had let them both down. He wanted to come home but again, I told him to stay. Nothing could be done, and he would be home the next day anyway. Once again, I rejected his wanting to help, to be with me, to grieve together. Another humongous mistake on my part. I was screwing up left and right.

I was getting ready to head back to the house, after making my phone calls, when I saw two Vultures land on the ground and disappear from view, not far from where I was standing. It was such an odd occurrence, it knocked me out of my sobbing, and I walked over to see what was going on. One took off and flew toward the house, circled once, came back toward me and the hidden vulture rose to meet it. I watched the two of them circle the yurt but when I turned away for just a second and turned back, they were gone! Just disappeared, vanished into thin air! Was the first vulture Zuna's spirit coming to say good-bye? Circling the house one last time? Was the second one her angel guide? The grief hit me like a ton of bricks, and I collapsed on the ground. I didn't think I could bear the pain.

Vulture means: "death and rebirth. That the suffering of the immediate is temporary and necessary because a higher purpose is at work, even if it isn't understood at the time." This, and the messages I got from salamander and snake would turn out to be prophetic. I had seen a spotted salamander the night I returned from leaving Zuna at the hospital. I had never seen one before, and it was in such a strange place, at a strange time, I felt I needed to find out what the message was. It meant: "a new direction was needed, my present environment may be suffocating me, affecting my health and creativity." It also meant: "a transformation coming from outside circumstances." The snake, I had seen while Zuna was in the hospital, was also at a strange place and time. It meant: "a quick change, death and rebirth or a transition happening somewhere in your life." All of this did come to pass.

Herm returned the following day and we were up until 2 a.m. talking about Zuna and processing our grief. It was so hard, I felt so responsible, and I was!! Even though Herm said he didn't blame me, I know he did. He never liked it when I let her chase the bears, was always worried she would get hurt and he was right! I had let my ego be in charge. It was cool to have a tough dog who chased off bears. Herm so loved her, it was as if I had killed him too but even more importantly, I think I killed our relationship.

People who don't have beloved animals would not understand the devastation the death of a dear companion brings. It is even worse than losing a loved one. Your pet fills your very soul with the unconditional love and devotion we all search for in life. There aren't too many humans who can demonstrate adoration and faithfulness which opens the heart and brings such intense joy. When that gets taken away, there is an incredible emptiness.

CHAPTER 45

DOGS

The only way I could cope with my pain was to get a puppy as soon as possible. I know many folks who can't get another dog for years after losing their best friend, but I knew happy puppy energy would soothe my soul. No dog could ever replace the bond we had with Zuna, but I didn't know how I would go on if I didn't get another dog.

I emailed Zuna's breeder in New Hampshire to let her know what happened and see if she had any pups. She didn't, so I contacted every person on the national club's breeder's list. I had no luck except for one breeder in Oregon who was expecting a litter that week. She said I could have the pick puppy but would have to show it to its championship. I used to breed, train, and show Irish Wolfhounds so I knew what that would entail. I wasn't sure I wanted to get back into that scene, I just wanted a companion. With that being the only option for a puppy, for who knew how long, I reluctantly said yes.

Three weeks later we got Zuna's $6300.00 ashes back and buried them under an apple tree just outside our living room window. At the same time, her breeder emailed to say she was getting a six-month-old pup returned from her last litter. Did we want her? YES! I jumped at the chance to have a relative of Zuna's and we were soon packing for yet another cross-country trip.

It was difficult returning to Diana's where we had picked up our sweet Zuna a short seven years earlier. I was having a hard time holding it together and when Diana introduced us to Zuna's mom, I lost it. She looked so much like our girl. Thankfully, the silly antics of the pup was able to pull me out of my despair as she tore around the living room playing with the other dogs. Zoe was a spunky, confident little girl and Diana told us she was returned because her former owners weren't able to housebreak her and had kept her mostly in a crate. She said since Zoe's arrival she had had no such issues, in fact had found the pup to be exceptionally intelligent and well behaved. She laughed and said, "I think Zoe just didn't like where she had been placed and wanted out!" I laughed but couldn't help but think maybe there was more to it than that. After all, why had she been returned just when we needed a pup to help heal our hearts? Everything happens for a reason and as the "vulture" had said: "a higher purpose is at work, even if it isn't understood at the time."

As soon as we returned to Colorado, Herm had to head out on another trip and as I walked him to the truck, I couldn't help but flashback on what had happened the last time he was away. Even with the new pup, I was very depressed while at home and only felt better when I wasn't there. I just wanted to climb in the truck with him and get away from the horrible memories.

I still had to decide on whether to get the pup in Oregon and wasn't sure what to do. In hindsight, I should have let it go but I had been so destroyed by losing Zuna that I never wanted to have only one dog ever again and be left with nothing if something happened.

In the middle of November, we drove to Oregon to get Kia which began my dog obsession. At this time, the house was pretty much finished, and Herm was busy with his rock shows. I had failed to get the retreat/healing center I had envisioned off the ground so what else was I going to do? As salamander had said: "a new direction was needed."

As Kia grew, she turned into a fine specimen of the breed, and I soon found myself back into the dog show scene I had left behind so many years before. This led to joining dog clubs and gathering dog friends. I had always loved training and when I discovered the sport of agility I was hooked. I made a set of equipment and started training Zoe then put an ad in the local paper looking for others who also wanted to work dogs. Jane responded to my ad and before you know it, we had a group of us training together. Most were only interested in doing it for the fun but both Jane and I were seriously into competing, not only in agility but obedience, rally and tracking as well. Over the years, Jane and I traveled to shows and seminars, trained together and cheered each other on at trials and events. I loved the challenge of working with my dogs, figuring out how to get past blocks in their learning and especially appreciated how it strengthened the bond between us.

CHAPTER 46

WILDLIFE

Walking the dogs some mornings was challenging. One day, when I was alone with Zoe and Kia, I came across an elk leg lying in the road. I thought that was a bit odd until I saw a large male coyote sitting on the hillside. Ridgebacks are big enough to take down a single one, but the problem is, coyotes will lure dogs to their pack, where they will attack and kill them. Because of this, I was always nervous when we had close encounters with the rascals. Before I could stop her, Zoe took off after the big guy on the hill but thankfully, returned when I called. What I hadn't seen was the female on the opposite side of the road who began enticing the dogs with her yipping. With difficulty, I finally got the dogs to follow me and we proceeded on our walk.

On the return trip, I kept an eye out for the critters and thought they were gone, until we were almost on top of them! As we crested the hill, there was the female, standing right in front of us, yipping up a storm! That was too much for Zoe and off she went with puppy Kia following. Shit!!! In a panic, I called and called even laying on the ground to get their attention. FINALLY, they turned around but that wasn't the end of it. That sneaky female followed right behind them, yipping and turning to run, over and over trying to lure them. She was persistent and she was winning. In desperation, I grabbed the elk leg as a lure, swinging it while calling their names, attempting to keep their attention on me! That coyote was talking a good game and it was a tough choice for the dogs to choose me and the elk leg over that enticing trickster. Eventually, we were able to move out of range and leave those troublemakers behind but the rest of the way home I was paranoid at every corner, expecting them to reappear.

Zoe turned out to be a very small Ridgeback with a huge will. Nothing fazed her. One day she took off after a huge herd of elk before I could stop her. I ran up the steep hill as fast as I could and watched her disappear over the rise. I thought surely, she would be trampled. When I reached the top and peered down, there she was in the valley below very much intact. In fact, she had that whole herd rounded up into a big bunch and had no intention of leaving no matter how much I called. I just had to stand there holding my breath until she got bored and came trotting up the hill with a big grin on her face, as proud as punch.

That herding instinct came in quite handy with all the free-range cattle who trampled through our yard. Zoe and I became a well-oiled team in chasing those buggers out and driving them down the road. These cattle weren't anything like the docile dairy herds I knew from my animal science days at college. They were like wild animals, suspicious and fiercely protective of their babies. If they felt their young were threatened, you better watch out as they would charge. I taught the dogs to walk quietly through the groups of cattle when we were on our daily walks, but if they saw a cow give me the evil eye, they would give chase. At those times, I was happy to have the dogs in protective mode.

CHAPTER 47

DECISIONS

When I bred and showed Irish Wolfhounds in the 1970s, I loved the whelping and raising of puppies, so it was a foregone conclusion I would get back into breeding. After Zoe's health testing, at age two, I had my first Ridgeback litter. I kept a female, then was coerced into taking a male pup from a friend. That meant we had 4 dogs. We briefly got down to three when Kia was returned to her breeder because of elbow dysplasia but then I was beguiled by cute puppies from two more litters. Five dogs and Herm was asking why I needed so many?

I secretly agreed we had too many dogs but got angry with him just the same! I didn't say he had too many rocks, or that he went to too many shows! I knew it was ridiculous to compare the two, after all, he made money and I just spent it! But I loved showing and training and being with my dog friends. Just like he enjoyed hunting for rocks, selling at shows and interacting with his rock buddies. Who was he to tell me what to do? He was hardly ever home anyway!

In reality, I had felt him slipping away for a while. He had shut me out of his rock life which hurt. After all, we had been partners when we started so many years ago, but now he just wanted to do it himself. I tried to involve him with the dogs so we could at least do something together, but it wasn't his thing. I was disappointed, but I understood. He had his thing and I had mine but that didn't mean we couldn't support each other in our passions.

I don't believe there are any wrong choices in life. When you come to a fork in the road, whichever path you take, will bring you the lessons you need to learn. Sometimes, however, I wish I had taken the other path! After four years of working on the house and fighting the roads we were at one of those forks. We were burned out and didn't know what to do. Should we sell, stay, try to get the house legal, stay illegal? We looked into getting a well and septic for the house, to pursue legality, but it just wouldn't work. The house was situated too close to the creek and the property line. In an attempt to move to a place that wouldn't be so difficult, we looked at other properties. It was hard, as our land was so much nicer than anything we looked at! We probably should have settled for something less, but instead, we opted to go all in at our place with upgrades.

A quarter mile from the house, we constructed a legal building which would serve a number of needed functions. A well and septic allowed for running water, so we could install a shower, flush toilet and even a washing machine!! Solar water panels gave us hot water and a large array was used to power Herm's tools in his shop. We also added indoor/outdoor kennels for the dogs. We now had everything we were missing at the house. We just had to walk a quarter mile to get to it!

At the same time, we added even more conveniences. A road to the bridge below our house gave us easier access for carrying in heavy objects. A phone booster, let us call from inside, instead of hiking up the hill. We even splurged on a tractor to keep the roads clear, some of the time, in the winter! A 40X80 metal building, allowed me to train my dogs out of the weather and a second, larger greenhouse made us more food independent. We were definitely all in!

I knew full well if we didn't address underlying issues, no amount of added conveniences was going to change anything. When we built the shop, I had thought Herm and I would work together there, like we had in the past. I was looking forward to getting back to silver smithing and sharing the space as Herm worked on rocks. I thought it was something we could enjoy together as a couple and hoped it would keep us from drifting further apart. Unfortunately, it soon became obvious Herm wanted that space for himself. No matter how many times he assured me I was welcome, it was clear the real sentiment was, "keep out". I got the message loud and clear. Instead, I stuffed my hurt and disappointment and concentrated on training my dogs.

I was angry Herm complained about taking care of our critters when I went to competition weekends. What the hell? Did I complain when he left for weeks at a time to do his shows? Could he not support me so I could do what I liked to do? He also bitched about not being able to do anything because of the dogs. Of course, when I came up with solutions, he didn't want to listen. It soon became obvious it was me he didn't want to do things with. The dogs were just an excuse. Besides shopping and working around the house, we were pretty much leading separate lives.

My inner discontent began to manifest outwardly when I started to be plagued by terrible headaches. One of the dogs then ran into me and blew out my knee, hobbling me for months. If that wasn't bad enough, my eight-month-old female tried to kill Zoe and was then accidentally impregnated by our male, RJ. That resulted in a litter of 10 pups, one of which I kept, bringing us to seven. I didn't realize at the time; I was collecting all those dogs to fill the growing emotional emptiness inside me.

My anger, frustration and despair were manifesting as impatience with almost everything he said and did. Every time I turned around, he was pushing my buttons. He was driving me crazy, I just wanted to shake him! What was going on? Why was he being like this? Why was he pushing me away? Why wouldn't he talk with me? I wanted "US" back but was getting no cooperation. It felt like he was negative about everything. I had suggested counseling over and over again, but he didn't want to do it. Why?

CHAPTER 48

SEPARATION

The summer of 2016 was another one of those turning points. We put our property on the market, in a last attempt to start fresh somewhere else. I didn't want to do it but if it would make Herm happier, I would give it a go.

We also tragically lost our dear friend Jason to suicide. Just two days before, Herm had been helping Jason prop up the shipping container which had been delivered to his land. He and his wife, Lexy, had met several years before, as volunteers at Mission Wolf. Their permanent home was near Boulder, but they loved the area, so bought the lot next to ours. Even though they were young enough to be our kids, we had a great relationship. We viewed the world from the same lens and would sit and talk for hours about, life, the world and spirit. Herm and I loved spending time with them and on this last visit, Jason had seemed happier than we had seen him in months, full of ideas for the future.

Lexy never called me, so when her name appeared on my phone I was surprised. "Hi," I answered brightly.

"Jason is gone," she said in a monotone.

"What do you mean?" I asked, totally confused.

"He's dead, he hung himself from a tree in the woods," she said in a deadened voice.

"What!?" I cried dumbstruck.

How was this possible, how could he have killed himself? We just saw him two days ago and he was so happy! We hung up with Lexi saying she would let me know when his funeral would be. I was devastated!

Jason was a complicated guy but really sweet. The day we locked eyes at Mission Wolf a few short years before, we felt an instant connection. Only recently, I had visited their home, where he and I had discussed possibly working together. We also talked about jointly buying a piece of land if things didn't work out with Herm and me. Now all of that was dead and it seemed like another nail in the coffin of my marriage.

Herm finally agreed to counseling that summer but wanted to see a man, not the woman who was recommended. I didn't have a good feeling about this guy and Herm eventually acknowledged the therapist wasn't doing much. By that time, however, Herm had decided he wanted to separate for a few months.

I wasn't at all happy, as I didn't see how being separate would accomplish much. We needed to work on things, not just run away and hide! I went along with it for a few weeks then called and gave him an ultimatum. "Come home and work on our relationship or move out." He relented, but moved into the yurt, giving us a partial separation. We finally began seeing the woman therapist in town, but it seemed his mind was already made up. There was still no discussion of feelings, just that he wanted space. I didn't see much sense in continuing with counseling if that is all that would be talked about!

He got his space from August through October when he was away doing rock shows. During that time, I struggled with my feelings and didn't know what to do. Part of me wanted nothing more to do with him. He was emotionally unavailable and said he wanted no commitments. What did that mean? I just couldn't wrap my head around it.

While he was away, I dealt with my confusion by joining a small women's group in town. This was helpful and supportive as was talking with my sister and other female friends. It was the first time in my life I had women friends and it was very soul-affirming.

One afternoon, I sat in the living room reading a book on how we create things, and about times we regret. The incident with Zuna and the bear immediately came to mind, and I started thinking about how I would redo that day. I soon drifted into a light sleep until shocked awake by a sharp bark. I opened my eyes to see a cinnamon-colored bear galloping across the yard with something hanging from its mouth. The dog door was located to the side of the house where the bear was headed, and the dogs were racing in that direction. I jumped up in a panic, yelling "come, come, come" which of course they totally ignored. Visions of a repeat Zuna event, with all my dogs killed and injured flew into my brain. I wrenched open the front door and dashed out, still yelling. I stopped short totally confused, there was no bear only the dogs standing there staring at me! What the fuck??? What had just happened? The dogs DID bark, so I couldn't have dreamt it! Did I just create that bear/dog thing again so I could do it differently?? Totally baffled, I walked the entire fence line looking for the bent wire which would indicate where the bear had gotten in. There was no bent wire, and nothing looked amiss anywhere in the yard. How did that bear get in? What did it have in its mouth? Was this even real? What I didn't know at the time, was this was just the first of a string of weird events that would happen over the next few months.

Why is it when the man of the house leaves everything breaks? That happened when my first husband left, everything broke down. Was it something about my broken energy that caused it? My computer died and the new one I ordered kept getting delayed for weeks! Our precious phone booster crapped out, so I was back to climbing the hill if I wanted to talk to anyone. I was being isolated; I was out of touch with the world. Was this a sign I needed to look inward?

My mood was all over the place, high one minute, in the pits the next. I was short with the dogs and had no patience for training and no desire to do much of anything. I felt spacey and out of touch with reality, so much so that one day I left poor RJ outside the gate all day. I never noticed he was gone until bedtime when I went into a panic, calling and calling. I finally found him waiting patiently at the shop. Oh my God, I was losing it and even putting my dogs at risk! I needed to get grounded.

In December, Herm decided to take a two-week vacation to Florida to visit friends, leaving me to deal with a snow and windstorm which damaged both greenhouses. He was back for a couple of weeks then off again to Arizona for five more weeks. I felt like telling him to go away and stay there. Just get a divorce, get it over with and move on. I felt SO stuck!! Stuck with the house, stuck with him, stuck not knowing what to do with my life. If the property sells, stuck with not knowing where to move to or if I would be going alone or not? It all sucked big time!

CHAPTER 49

DIVORCE

It was the final countdown of 2016, a year in which people I knew were going through major life transitions. Death, divorce, moving, confronting fears and insecurities, and going bat shit crazy. I certainly had been confronting MY insecurities, SO much had come up. Abandonment issues, feelings of not being good enough, fears of being alone. Fear of not having enough money, of not finding another nice place to live, of not doing my work in the world. Fear of not having anyone to love me. The emotional roller coaster was exhausting. I was terrified one minute, the next I could handle anything. Then I was plunging back into the depths of despair, not wanting to go on. I felt in my soul all would turn out okay in the end, but the process of getting there was grueling!!

I tried to stay in my higher self, but it wasn't easy. My small-self preferred to blame Herm for where I was at. That he was the one in the wrong, that he was selfish to want to do his own thing. How could he leave me here to do everything myself? I sure was into the "poor me" thing big time! I could feel my higher-self smiling and shaking her head about all my drama.

Looking for answers and some sort of higher purpose to it all, I immersed myself in books. Some were by authors who channeled the Hathors, Pleiadians and Arcturians. I could feel entities or energies around me, but it was all kind of amorphous. I didn't think I was imagining it but even if they were there, so what? If this reality wasn't real, as the books said and the other world was out of my reach, what was the sense? No wonder so many folks were going crazy and killing themselves. They were dying to get out of this madness. I couldn't say I blamed them!

I had been home alone for the past nine winters when Herm went to Arizona, but each year got a bit more difficult. I was in good shape from all the walking and working around the property, but I was close to 70 years old. Chopping ice, hauling water and wood, shoveling snow and hiking a quarter mile to the shop multiple times a day, took its toll on me. I also had the stress of plowing, always worrying if I would get stuck or if the tractor would do something weird. I would have preferred to snowshoe out to my car rather than plow, but I was feeding my dogs raw food. That meant hundreds of pounds of meat to get home and I wasn't about to carry that on my back!

I wasn't sleeping well, and I was getting sick of reading channeled and self-improvement books. I was mostly sitting, watching the days of my life roll by, roll by, roll by and going totally fucking nuts. In order to find guidance through the morass of my emotions, I bought a deck of Oracle Cards. The card came up over and over again was, "write!" Seriously, what was I supposed to write about, my life was on hold, nothing was going on! I tried automatic writing, I edited some of my journals but none of it made me feel any better. There were certainly not any aha moments, that's for sure!

With no one around to please, or to judge me, I turned into a hedonistic crazy old hermit. I went to bed late and slept until I felt like getting up. I didn't get dressed if I didn't feel like it. I didn't even wash until it got to the point where I couldn't stand myself anymore. I just did what pleased ME all day, it was actually very liberating. It didn't mean those judgmental voices weren't still trying to get through, but most of the time I was able to hold them at bay.

During that Arizona period, Herm and I had talked or texted almost every day and it almost seemed like old times. I always tried to be upbeat when communicating and he seemed happy with how his shows were going. I was finally feeling somewhat stable emotionally and wasn't as angry as I had been just weeks earlier. In fact, I was actually feeling very loving towards him, but that was at a distance. What would happen when he came home? I had gotten used to being alone and wondered if I even wanted him back.

As I expected, I was thrown totally off balance when he got home. He, unfortunately, had this awful habit of acting cold and distant whenever he returned from being away. This time was no different and when he pulled the usual routine, I just wanted him to leave but he was sick and wanted to stay at the house. I reluctantly agreed but had him sleep downstairs. I tried staying positive, loving and upbeat but it was hard to maintain as I was feeling hurt by his unloving attitude. When he asked to stay another night, I told him it wouldn't be a good idea.

I fought my guilt, telling myself he's the one who made the choice to move out. He couldn't have it both ways and just come and go when it was convenient for him. It would have been different if I knew he wanted to be with me, but I knew he just didn't want to get up in the night to tend the fire at the yurt. I felt he had put me in a tough spot. We tried talking it out, but it was the same old, same old. It seemed we had to do a drama dance before we could get back on an even keel. Of course, after he left, I felt totally lonely and wished I had let him stay. I couldn't freakin' win.

I couldn't stand it and went to the yurt to tell him how much this all sucked. I was all tears, and he was all hugs and loving. I felt as if I was back to square one again. Why couldn't I be stronger? I thought I had gained some equilibrium while he was gone. I guess it was back to the drawing board.

A few weeks later, Herm left for shows in New Mexico and I went to dog shows in Kansas. I came home with a high fever, horrible headache and coughing that wouldn't stop. I was barely able to make it to the shop to feed the dogs and haul wood to keep warm. I basically lay on the couch for four days and didn't eat anything. Herm checked on me the first 3 days but then…crickets! What the hell? I had gone out of my way to let him stay at the house when he was sick. Now, he just leaves me hanging.

My ever-swinging pendulum of emotions was back to feeling I needed some resolution to our stalemate. I just couldn't deal with being in limbo and having my life on hold. Herm had been at the yurt for several months but still wanted no commitments and had no answer as to how he wanted to proceed. Most of his stuff was still in the house and it just seemed weird. Was he in or out? It appeared to me he was out, so one day I emptied his dresser and closet and put all his clothes into bags. When he came to the house and saw them, he said in shock, "What's all this?"

"Well," I replied, "I figured if you aren't living here, you should have all your clothes with you."

"I WAS going to come back!" he said, the hurt in his voice very apparent. He was? Had I made a huge mistake? He never said he was going to come back!

I guess I was in a, let's get this resolved once and for all mode, that day. The next thing I heard coming out of my mouth was "let's get a divorce". I had been paying all the bills and received only $400 a month from social security. I had read if we divorced, I could get more. If it hadn't been for the money or if Herm had offered to help with the bills, I think I would have hung in a little longer. Or maybe not? What was the point in staying married to someone who didn't want to be with me? Who didn't talk about his feelings or what he was thinking? Yes, I still deeply loved the man but wasn't I just butting my head up against a wall?

"Okay, if that's what you want," he said sadly picking up the bags. That impulsive piece of me that just needs to have things neat and clean had started the ball rolling. That first week after Herm left, I felt powerful and back in control of my life but like that day in New Zealand when I looked left instead of right, I had no idea a collision was coming and this time, I had no one to save me.

ALONE
2017-2018

CHAPTER 50

BETRAYAL

The meltdown came when I was sitting in the living room filling out financial forms for the divorce. When I read the section Herm had filled out, I felt gut punched and actually thought I would be sick. Almost 30 years together and I never knew he had all that money! I knew he came from a secretive family and kept things close to his chest, but I didn't think he kept anything from ME! Because I had money from my first divorce settlement and an inheritance, I had paid for almost all the big-ticket items over the years. Cars, trucks, tractor, travel trailers, our property, greenhouses, his shop, my dog training building! I never minded paying for everything as they were for us! I am always about sharing anything I have. He never offered to help, not even when it came to buying the trucks he used for his business! I felt totally betrayed! Who WAS this person I had been with all these years? I stomped around the house crying, screaming, swearing, going wild and scaring the dogs! I was so hurt and angry, it was something I just couldn't wrap my head around. It would never occur to me not to share and to keep secrets from my spouse. What the fuck! I punched Herm's number into the phone and when he answered, I tore into him. He was basically silent and said he had no excuses, he was sorry, he had been wrong. Damn straight he was wrong! ARGH! At that point I wanted nothing to do with him ever again! Good riddance!

It took a while for me to regain equilibrium and a modicum of forgiveness after that financial trauma fiasco. So, a month later, when he asked if I wanted company for my birthday, I was conflicted. I did want to see him but was also trying to create some distance and stand on my own. I plucked up my courage and told him I didn't think it would be a good idea as it would just upset me. Well, I guess the "Universe" had a different plan. Two days before my birthday, we got 10 inches of snow on top of 3 inches of rain. This combination brought down dozens of trees, blocked the driveway and took out the solar system at the shop. I was scheduled to spend the weekend with Lexi but without help, I wasn't going anywhere. So, I called Herm.

Unfortunately, despite each of us promising ourselves we wouldn't do our usual "routine", we fell right into it as soon as he arrived. He was cold and unfriendly, I tried to stay centered and upbeat, failed, and started crying. He told me he had no idea why he did that and had promised himself he wouldn't, but the ugly just seeped out. I continued crying as we moved the trees off the driveway. I then stomped angrily up to the shop and spun my vehicle through the snow and mud to the top of the hill. I was determined to get out of there no matter what! When I went back to the house to get my things, Herm was apologetic, also part of the usual drama. The last part played itself out when he asked me to stay the night and I caved. Man, what a pair of dysfunctional, fucked up people!

CHAPTER 51

STRANGENESS

I had Maurice, from England, do an energy reading on the property in case some "force" was keeping it from selling. Lo and behold, he found a curse on the house and two portals that were letting in dark spirits. He also found black magic had been placed around our bed! No wonder things had gone to shit!

Maurice did a number of clearings on his end, then instructed me how to close the portals. We always knew the energies on the land were intense, but never knew about those openings. Their approximate localities were marked on the plot plan, but I had to find the exact spots. I walked around each of those areas until I felt a change of energy. I then did a ceremony with prayers until I felt them close. It was pretty cool! I sure hoped this switch in energy would help the house sell!

I don't know if there was any correlation, but it was after the clearings that strange things began happening. Finding pennies or feathers was supposed to be a sign your guides or angels were with you. I had been finding many of each, which I found very comforting now that I was really alone. One day, I got a shock when I lifted a bunch of grapes out of the metal colander where they had been draining. Staring me in the face was a bright copper penny! Seriously? How? I just had to shake my head and laugh. Spirits have such a great sense of humor.

I couldn't figure out what was going on with my iPod? I used it on my morning runs and was very careful to turn it off when I was done. Three days in a row, when I went to turn it on, it was already on. Huh? I got even more anal about making sure it was off, even checking in the middle of the day. Each time it was off but then… on again in the morning! After three days of this, "they" moved on to other tricks. Closing gates, I knew I had left open, stealing keys and something even more extraordinary.

One evening I noticed Libra, my 10-month-old Ridgeback, staring out the window. I followed her gaze to see a doe grazing outside the fence. Libra crept quietly out the dog door and walked slowly to the gate. I saw her put her face through the fence and to my surprise, she and the deer touched noses. About this time, the other dogs were alerted to something going on and bolted out the door barking like banshees. Instead of running away, like a normal deer, this one came towards the ravenous pack. Some were trying to pull the fence down with their teeth and others were about to jump over it. I thought it was all over for that doe as I tried to get the dogs in the house. I finally had to grab the most ferocious ones by the tail and drag them inside. Meanwhile, the deer just continued to calmly graze near the fence for another hour, before fading back into the forest.

The next morning, she was back which prevented me from taking the dogs for their morning hike. They weren't at all happy since feeding time came after the walk, but we had to wait for the deer to leave which took some time. Thankfully, we didn't run into her along the way but as the dogs were cleaning up their breakfast at the shop, there she was at the back of the building outlined against the plastic doors. Oh shit, I had just let two of the dogs out the front door! I quickly ran around and dragged them in before they spotted her. When I went back out to see where she was, I found her grazing near the greenhouse. When she saw me, she lifted her head and walked slowly towards me!

What? I figured she would run away as I moved in her direction but to my shock, she came right up to me! We were standing eye to eye as I reached out to stroke her neck and tell her how stupid she had been to challenge five Ridgebacks.

"You're lucky you weren't killed!" I told her. I was anxious to get her away from the dogs, so told her to follow me to the gate. Which she did! I opened it and without a backward glance, she disappeared into the willows by the creek. Never to appear again.

What the heck was that all about? She hadn't even looked like a normal deer. Her neck was long, and she had a short, thin, red coat unlike the thick gray coats of the mule deer. Was she a spirit sent to me for a reason? If so, why? My mother, who was very connected with the "other side" told me my father would come to her as a deer after he died. She would often find his deer spirit looking in the window at her. Was that him? Outside of the raccoon incident years ago, that was the strangest wild animal encounter I had ever had. It was all very weird!

All summer, I kept getting messages in the form of animals, birds and insects. All the signs and incidents helped pull me through those first few months after Herm left. He and I had always used signs in our life together. We were both aware the "Universe" is always showing us the way if we only pay attention.

CHAPTER 52

LOST

In July, the property had been on the market for a year. Even though there had been some visitors I hadn't had any offers. The divorce was final, and I wasn't sure what to do. Should I put it back on the market or just commit to staying there? I had no idea where I would go if I sold it, so I was very conflicted. I finally decided to change agents and give it another try.

Both my sister and Lexy lost their husbands to suicide and even though Herm hadn't died, I felt a similar grief. I spent a lot of time talking to them and as I thought about what we were each going through and how it had changed us, I felt a higher purpose to it all. It was time for the feminine healers to come into their power, to no longer give it away to men as we had been conditioned to do. What if we three couples had pre-birth contracts, which included the men leaving at a certain time, in order for us to grow and bring our gifts to the world? In that moment, I felt the enormity of the love those men had for us. They left us in love and continued to support us on another level. If I could only stay in that place of peace and acceptance for more than a few hours, it would be good!

I had Herm come pick up the rest of his belongings in the shop and tried not to feel guilty about it. I knew he would have to pay to put them in a storage unit, but it was too hard for me emotionally to keep looking at his stuff. I needed to make that space my own and clear out the energy. I told him it was his responsibility to take care of his things and to change his address, so I didn't have to keep forwarding his mail. That wasn't at all easy for me to do but I gritted my teeth and did it.

While he was there, he helped me do some work around the house. Since it was late when we finished, he stayed the night and loaded the rest of his things in the morning. I went out shopping early and when I returned, he was still packing. He was grumpy, tired and hungry, but for once, I didn't fall into the trap. I stayed loving, even offered him lunch, which he declined. When he got back to where he was staying, he texted he appreciated my kindness and not falling for his shit. Yay, one small victory!

A couple of days later I called him in a puddle of despair, hating life. As always, he was kind and supportive, saying he appreciated me sharing. I had fallen into the darkness the night before after talking with Lexy. She had a new beau and was moving on with her life. It felt like everyone was moving on but me!! I was confused and didn't know what to do about Herm. It seemed I did better when I didn't have contact but then I would miss him. I had so much I wanted to say but always got too emotional when I saw him. I decided to write him an email instead. I poured my heart out, talked about my regrets, how sorry I was I had hurt him. I told him how much I loved him and how both of our issues had gotten in the way.

Robert wrote a nice note back: *I have read your letter three times and feel a sadness each time. It is hard for me to believe we are done; I still love you. It is strange we communicate more openly when we are apart. Maybe someday we could have a grownup conversation. Do not beat yourself up, there is no right or wrong.*

CHAPTER 53

MELTDOWN

Another meltdown happened in October when I made the mistake of checking Herm's Facebook page. He had posted two pictures of himself hiking somewhere and I wondered if maybe his friend Margie had taken them. I went to her page and when I scrolled down, I saw she had gone to Alaska in August with a friend. My heart started racing and my stomach clenched, as I knew in my gut who that friend was. I held my breath as I scrolled through her pictures, not wanting to be right. Yup, there he stood, his arm around Margie with a big smile on his face! I totally fucking lost it!

Not only did he go to Alaska with her, he went in August and blew off his rock shows. Do you know how many times I had begged him to skip a show so we could do something together? THAT was devastating! He had also lied to me when I had spoken to him in August. I knew when I called, he would be at a rock show and wished him good luck with sales. He neglected to correct me to say where he REALLY was! The other gut-wrenching thing was, that he went traveling with someone else. WE were the traveling couple! WE had adventures together! To see him doing that with someone else plunged me into the pit of darkness.

I tried not to contact him about this, but it was eating me alive. After obsessing for about a week, I finally emailed him. I told him how hurt I was and asked what his relationship was with Margie. His response was she and her husband Sam, were good friends who had helped him through the transition. That Margie was committed to her marriage. At the last minute, Sam had been unable to go on the trip and suggested Herm go in his stead. I was in full ego mode and said snottily, "Well from what you have told me, and from the pictures, it sure doesn't seem it has been much of a transition. You seem to be living the life you wanted." He wrote back: "If you think the divorce and transition haven't been hard on me, you are very, very mistaken."

At 3:30 a.m. I couldn't sleep and wanted to know what had been hard for him? It seemed he had everything just like he wanted it. No commitments, no responsibilities, the freedom to do what he wanted. Traveling, doing shows, hiking, foot loose and fancy free. It sure didn't look like anything was hard! As I typed the email, I realized this was the same question I had asked him at that pizza parlor almost 30 years ago! We had come full circle.

With all these intense emotions came insights, but not ones that were easy to face. I realized I could be manipulative and controlling. I would pull him in, then push him away, a long-term pattern I had experienced in all my relationships. Certainly, something that had to be examined.

Prior to looking at that damn Facebook page, I had been experiencing such peace and oneness with the world, more than I had ever felt. Then whamo! The "Universe" says, "enough with the vacation already, get back to work!" As painful as all of this was, on one level, I was grateful for the opportunity to learn and grow. Herm had always been my greatest teacher and was still pushing me up that ladder to my higher self.

CHAPTER 54

SEARCHING

My first winter alone and single and I was still clinging to the hope Herm would realize his mistake and return. All the psychics and astrologers I consulted said we were perfect for each other, and he would be back. Whenever I told Herm what they said, he would just shake his head and say he had moved on and was happy with his freedom. That just cut my heart in two as I didn't feel that way at all. I missed my best friend, and everything reminded me of our life together. I would look out the front window and see him chopping wood or in the kitchen cooking dinner. I could see us dancing around each other in the small space as we fried veggies for our Friday night pizza. How was it possible we were no longer together? We are soulmates; we are meant to do our work in the world together. He is my support network, my cheerleader, the one who tells me I can be anything I want. How was I going to go on without him?

I think the "Universe" kept sending me strange animal occurrences to help me focus on things other than my despair. One day I walked into the laundry room at the shop and found a small wren perched on the windowsill. As I approached, it flew to the back of the room and ......

disappeared! Now, this room is fully sheet rocked, with no holes! Thinking it may have gotten by me and gone into the big room, I checked, but it was nowhere to be found! In fact, "how did it get in there in the first place?" I wondered. I finally gave up searching and went out the back door to the enclosed workshop. There it was sitting calmly on a rafter. Come on! Seriously? There was NO way the bird could have gotten there except by going THROUGH the wall! What the heck was going on, is this a riddle of some kind?

Yet another bird "spoke" to me one snowy day when I was sitting in the living room reading. I didn't think much about it when a little gray Junco kept fluttering at the picture window next to me. But it kept coming back, over and over. What the heck did it want? I filled the bird feeder earlier! Just in case that is what the bird was trying to tell me, I checked. Sure enough, it was empty! I filled it and never saw the bird again. That sure was one smart Junco!!!

To make it through those dark times, I needed all the help I could get. Books, podcasts, oracle cards, meditation, stayed aware of animal signs, anything that would throw me a lifeline. I wasn't always happy with what I read though. I wanted everything to say I was right, and Herm was wrong, but that wasn't the case. A blog post by Tenzin Palmo Jetsunma called "The Difference Between Genuine Love and Attachment" was one of those pieces. She wrote, *Grasping and clinging to a person/relationship is attachment, not love". "Attachment = make me happy. Love = I want you to be happy, with or without me." "Attachment is holding tight…. love is holding gently. The tighter we hold the more we suffer."* Well, she just described me in a nutshell! Grasping, clinging, fear, lack of self-love, wanting Herm to save me, make me happy. Crap! It was a struggle facing that side of myself and admitting he was the one taking the high road. He was the one showing love while I was just showing my woundedness.

CHAPTER 55

DEMON TRACTOR

I had a potentially disastrous incident one day which I'm sure was a reflection of all my negative thinking. It was a wake-up call to get my shit together.

The weather forecast was calling for snow, so I had to take the tractor up the hill. Our driveway was so steep it was next to impossible to plow UP the hill, so we left it on top, so we could plow down. Driving the tractor made me nervous but if I wanted to keep the roads open, I had to grit my teeth and just do it.

I switched on the orange monster, put it in low gear and started creeping slowly up the grade. Wanting this chore over with as quickly as possible, I shoved it into high. The tractor was not at all happy with that move. Just as we reached the steepest section, it demonstrated its displeasure by trying to kill me! It popped out of gear and off we went, flying backwards, engine screeching in outrage! Fuck!!!! I literally stood on the brakes which did nothing to slow our accelerated descent. What could I do? I couldn't get it into gear while it was moving! Oh shit, oh shit, oh shit!!!! I was in a panic, calling on my angels and guides to save me! Should I jump? If so, which side? I was frozen in fear as the tractor careened into the field.

I don't know how, but it came to a stop against the fence. I was shaking, heart pounding, clutching the steering wheel, trying not to slide off due to the 45-degree angle in which it was resting. I sat there for a bit trying to get my breath back and wondering what to do next. I just wanted to leave that fucker right there and forget about it. I couldn't do that though, I had to deal with it, I was the only one living there now. I thought of calling Kent at Mission Wolf but didn't want to be a wimp. I needed to put my big girl panties on and figure it out. I took myself by the scruff of the neck and said, "come on, you don't have to call anyone, don't be a crybaby, get it back on the driveway." Shaking like a leaf and praying up a storm, I turned the tractor back on. Verrrry slowly I crept at that sickening side angle to where the ground leveled out a bit. I then was able to get back onto the driveway. I paused, to gather my courage once again, not knowing if the tractor would pull the same stunt a second time. "Okay, here we go." I put it into low gear, and we SLOWLY crept up the hill with me barely breathing. I kept repeating to myself, "you can do this, you can do this" and I did! I got that sucker up there and would not drive it down again for the rest of the winter. I would rather snowshoe up and down to my vehicle than drive that creature up the hill even one more time!

The tractor wasn't done with me though. It got its revenge once again the day it stuck the road blade into the tire of my Suburban. It "bit" the heck out of both the tire and rim and I had to replace both! Stupid freakin' tractor!

CHAPTER 56

GROWTH

When Herm said things like, *"give from the heart without expectations"* it would trigger me, even though I knew it was true. He told me, not to rush things, to let things take their course without trying to control the outcome. I didn't want him to be so wise! I REALLY WANTED to control the situation and the outcome. I never realized how much of a control freak I was until he left. I knew I needed to surrender and trust but boy it was difficult!

The Oracle cards all pointed toward better days ahead. I just needed to have patience, open my heart, and have faith. The butterflies were telling me to lighten up. They "said" change and transformation are inevitable and doesn't have to be traumatic. Even the memes on Facebook were speaking to me: *"See if you can catch yourself complaining in either speech or thought, about a situation you find yourself in, what other people do or say. To complain is nonacceptance of what is. When you complain, you make yourself a victim. Leave the situation or accept it. All else is madness."* Yup! I was definitely caught in the madness. What was I going to do, "accept it or leave it?"

Every time I thought I had "accepted it" Herm would say something that made me want to "leave it!!" One such e-mail came in late April. He said we should support each other and be able to share what was going on in our lives, without the other being triggered. Of course, he was right, but I wasn't there yet. Every time I heard how great he was doing, it just gutted me. It was a tough decision, but I decided it would be better for me to break off communication and get on with my life.

I wrote a "goodbye" email but was scared shitless to send it. I was saying goodbye to my love of 30 years. It was like stepping off the edge of a cliff and I was praying I would grow wings! I sat looking at that send button for a long time before I got up the nerve to push it. To my shock, I got an immediate reply: *"I just sat down to write you an email, and I see yours, no surprise, the timing. Thanks for getting back. I just wanted to know you are ok. I can't imagine what you are going through, but knowing the strong person you really are, you will be ok. Always holding you in my heart."*

My romantic, idealistic-self had been hoping he would fight back. That he wouldn't want to lose me, since he had once said he "would be devastated if I weren't in his life anymore". It sounded more like he was glad to finally be rid of my drama. How could I blame him! I couldn't see that he was just being very loving and supportive.

As I sobbed, I consulted the Oracle cards for support, but they were on HIS side! *"See the other's point of view. You have strong emotions about this situation, and you may feel upset, misunderstood or used. You don't have to agree with these other individuals; you're simply asked to understand their motivations and to have compassion for their feelings. This process can positively shift the energy of power struggles, much like letting go of the rope during a tug of war. Forgive past hurts and begin anew."* ARGH! I don't WANT to see his point of view, I have VERY strong feelings, I feel misunderstood and USED! I don't understand his motivations and I certainly have NO compassion for him. I don't WANT to let go of the rope. Whoa! I was in FULL on tantrum mode!

To add insult to injury, the next card I turned read: *"You're too enmeshed in this situation so step back and see the bigger picture. You've lost perspective because you either believe there's something you absolutely need to have happen or else, you're simply being too stubborn to let go."* *"This all-too-familiar pattern stems from the guilty feeling that somehow you're not doing enough unless you completely immerse yourself into the problem or person, continually trying to fix the situation or rescue the person involved. While this may give you a temporary sense of satisfaction, doing so also creates unhealthy dependence – yours and others."* NO SHIT! WOW, the "Universe" was slapping me upside the head, I didn't want to hear any of that, even knowing it was true. Now the cards had even turned against me! Was I going to keep drowning in my sorrow or do something to dig myself out?

There were no new wild animal adventures, but the dogs were keeping me on my toes. One night I was in a total panic thinking I had lost Zoe. I had been annoyed with her earlier because she was begging for popcorn and had kicked her off the couch. I heard a noise outside and when I counted heads, she wasn't there. As soon as I opened the door, the other dogs streaked out barking like crazy and I had visions of a mountain lion carrying Zoe off. I got the flashlight and went through the woods, calling and calling, but no dog. A couple of times I thought I heard a faint whimper, but it didn't continue long enough for me to locate the sound. I was in a frenzy, I thought sure I had lost her. I kept saying, "don't do this to me", "this can't be happening", "this is a nightmare". On one of my rounds along the fence line, I noticed a bent over section with what looked like brown bear hair on it. I didn't remember that being bent previously. "Oh my God, had a bear gotten her?" but wait, a bear wouldn't carry off a dog!! I was losing it and shaking all over, heart pounding. I did one more circle along the fence line back to the gate and… there she was, with a look on her face that said, "geez it took you long enough, let me in already!" I was SO thankful and angry at the same time! When I got back inside, I just broke down crying, it was all too much!! If I hadn't yelled at her she would have been safely on the couch with me! Thank you again "Universe"!

Almost four weeks after no communication with Herm, I found a birthday card from him at the post office. I could tell he had put a lot of thought into choosing it and he included a sweet message. I found it interesting I had woken up that day with a feeling that something was about to happen. I sensed a breakthrough of some kind and then I found the card. I wasn't sure if I should write him back, so I consulted the cards and got: "You know what to do"; "Twin soul" and Gorilla, which was all about how important communication is to keep relationships healthy. With those in mind, I sent Herm a thank you for the sweet card and how much I appreciated it. He wrote back saying he hoped all was good with me. I felt a shift after being out of communication and was feeling more upbeat in the past weeks.

I think new growth was happening since I had been asking for help letting go, surrendering and trusting. I had been reading about how we push men away and saw myself in the words. I sent Herm an email telling him what I had learned: *"I have had lots of not-so-great observations and revelations about myself lately. I realize it is really all about ME when I blamed you for it being all about YOU, LOL! I know I have to surrender; I have SUCH an issue with control and holding on. I feel as if I let go of control I will die. I never knew how much control I use; it is insidious. I now know that is the root cause of all of our issues, how I made you feel small, unloved, unaccepted and unappreciated. That makes me feel terrible. I know there is nothing I can do about it now but just want you to know that I deeply apologize for your pain and take full responsibility for my actions. It is MY issue of being afraid of being vulnerable, being loved, being committed, being abandoned.* He thanked me for my apology and told me not to beat myself up over it.

I was glad I didn't have to beat myself up over losing another dog as I had yet another scare. As the five dogs and I were cresting a hill one morning, a large bull calf appeared and ran right towards us. It was such a shock; I had no time to grab the dogs. Off went my big male Saj, ignoring my yelling and zapping his shock collar at the highest setting. He grabbed the calf by the ear and it took off bawling and kicking with Saj hanging on. All that action was too much for the girls and off they went. I chased them all over the field zapping their shock collars and screaming. All four dogs were on the calf and I was in a total panic. This was the time of day the rancher usually came to check on the cows. If he saw what was going on he would shoot the dogs!

Momma cow was able to butt the dogs away a couple of times, but she finally quit and ran toward the road with the rest of the herd. Saj lost the ear, grabbed a leg which slowed them up enough for me to get to them. I grabbed Saj by the tail and he finally let go. The calf took off toward the road, with the three girls in pursuit. I was literally screaming at the top of my lungs!!! I was in despair, envisioning them running down the track with the herd and the rancher killing them. FINALLY, almost at the road, Jayda and Libra came back but not Zoe! I knew how determined she was and thought that was the end of her! Just as she was going out of site around a corner, she gave up and headed back. OMG, OMG OMG! Our angels were with us that morning as the rancher never came by. THANK YOU!

CHAPTER 57

REALIZATIONS

The winter had been dry, and the trend had continued throughout the year. The forests were like tinder, fires were cropping up all over the state and at the end of June it was our turn. A huge fire started not too far south of me and as it got closer, we were put on pre-evacuation notice. It was stressful, and I had been keeping Herm updated. He offered to come help do fire mitigation even though he had a rock show scheduled. I was very touched by the offer to give up his show, but I had other people helping, so told him to come the following week. I hadn't seen him in over 7 1/2 months and was so afraid I would mess things up. I later texted I didn't think I could do it. He said, "I'm coming anyway!"

"Okay," I said, "bring wine!"

I said lots of prayers leading up to the day of his arrival. I was an emotional wreck! The cards continued to tell me they were "working to open everyone's hearts" and "the period of darkness I had been in was now ending." I was holding on tight to those good omens and hoping for the best.

When he arrived, I didn't know how to act but we sat down and had a good conversation. He said we just wanted different things in life. He didn't know why we couldn't be friends. He still loved me but liked the life he had chosen and wanted no commitments. He had told me those things many times before but this time, I guess it finally hit home on a new level. He didn't want to be with me. I was no longer a part of his life. He wasn't coming back! That realization, just did me in. Instead of acting like an adult, I resorted to my usual childish actions, blaming him for my misery. I guess all the work I had done hadn't changed my behavior one iota. When push came to shove, I was the same old control freak just wanting everything my way. It was very discouraging.

The next morning, I apologized for my behavior and told him how grateful I was he had come to help out. We both cried when he left, but in a way, I was relieved he was gone. He probably felt the same way after how I acted.

Thinking about those three days, I came to yet another possible realization. Maybe I was using him to stay small and not realize my potential. What if I was holding onto the old with a death grip so I didn't have to be the brilliant person I could be? I had taken SO many courses in healing, vision quest guide, having your own business, personal growth and all had come to nothing. I never followed through. Herm was always telling me I had more experience and potential than most people he knew! I just didn't have the confidence in myself that he had in me. I always thought everyone else was better. Was this whole thing between Herm and me part of a soul plan? Was each incident just another nudge to keep me growing? Were our higher selves orchestrating all of it to help us evolve? When I asked those questions, my heart said yes, and I felt such profound love for Herm and the whole messy process.

I was listening to the audio book "The Big Leap" and the author asked if I was willing to have my life happy all the time? I was struck dumb when I thought about it and couldn't come up with a clear yes! That question brought up so much fear in my gut!! I realized I was attached to being a victim and always had been. All the times as a kid, acting miserable when we had to go somewhere. It was all to get attention, poor me, and control….ie fear!! If I was not a victim, a poor me, then would anyone pay attention to me or care about me?

After an unsatisfying conversation on the phone with Herm I was struggling to compose a text when I sent it by mistake! Oh NO! Why wasn't there a way to get those friggin' things back? I was afraid he wouldn't take what I wrote well. I guess the "Universe" must have been guiding that send finger as it turned into a good thing. He told me that our conversation had inspired him. That he wasn't quitting, that we would work things out because he cared too much to let it all go. Phew!! This was all such a slow and painstaking process to go from marriage to friends. It was a tumult of emotions, one day feeling, "no problem I can do this" to "there is no f—ing way I will ever get there!" We loved each other; we both felt a bond that couldn't be broken. No matter how many times I pushed him away or how crazy I acted. I wondered if we would ever reach equilibrium?

By the end of July, a year after our divorce was final, I was getting more and more signs of change and more insights into my issues. A dream about a Leopard highlighted my fear of embracing my potential and letting go of my misery. Leopard means: *"rebirth, a coming into one's own power after being lost through suffering"*. In the dream, *the Leopard was in a closet with only a piece of cloth for a door so could easily escape. I was alone and scared and thought the leopard was coming so I ran into another room.* It was clear no matter how much I wanted to hide, it was time to tell a new story about myself and life.

The energy around me seemed to be electric that August, it felt like something big was about to happen. Antelope told me: *to transmute negativity because change was on the horizon, to be ready to grab the opportunities that were coming my way because the angels and guides were with me.* Hawks, which are "messengers" were everywhere in my life those days, two flew so close to my windshield I thought I would hit them. Another swooped so low in front of me on a walk, the dogs almost caught it. It was obvious some message was trying to be delivered and I was soon to find out what it was.

CHAPTER 58

CHANGE

Two winters in the house by myself and heading toward a third. I wondered if the property would ever sell or was I meant to die there? I had so many lookers and two offers. One of those was too low and another which fell through at the last minute, came as a total shock. I was devastated that I had been SO close to being released, only to have it snatched away. I later came to realize it was a gift and a message from the "Universe".

My real estate agents had left me to do most of the showings since I knew the property best, and this particular day was no different. Glenn and Denise emerged from their car a bottle of organic wine in hand. This should have been the first indication these weren't my ordinary "lookers". How did they know I only drink organic wine? As I showed them the property we talked and found we had a great deal in common, from diet, animals, nature, world views, and so much more. We became instant friends and felt we had known each other forever. We agreed, it was a good possibility we were soul mates or of the same soul group. We hugged each other as they left, and Glenn told me he would be in touch soon.

In fact, it was the next day my agent called and said Glenn had put in a full price offer! WOW and .... oh shit! Where was I going to go? They asked if they could come spend time on the land and I was happy to say "yes" and "why don't you come for an overnight at the yurt?" They arrived on my birthday bearing gifts of food and more wine and also took me out to dinner. I brought them to meet Kent at Mission Wolf and they spent the afternoon lying on the grass by the house playing with my four-week-old puppies. We had a wonderful weekend together. I was so excited to have like-minded friends, I was even considering buying my neighbor's property and staying there!

A day after the property evaluation report, my agent called in a state of shock. Glenn had withdrawn his offer and there was no counter.

"What?" How could this be? I thought, totally confused. They had left that weekend overjoyed with the place and they couldn't wait to move in? I emailed Denise asking, "what the heck happened?" She said she wasn't sure but thought Glenn just got cold feet. I felt so defeated, would I be stuck here forever?

I later realized their "gift". They brought me great joy when I thought I would never feel that again and more importantly brought me a message about relationships. Denise and Glenn were obviously devoted to each other but weren't married. Years ago, they had been romantic partners, but Denise discovered Glenn tended to push people away. She tried being friends but couldn't handle his dating other women, so she moved out of state. Three years later he e-mailed and asked to see her. She had grown in the intervening years and by the time he asked her to come back, she was able to do the friend thing. They were sharing a house together, he lived upstairs and she down and each led their own lives. Their plan for my property was for Glenn to live in the house and Denise make an apartment at the shop.

I felt sure this was a message about Herm and me. That it was possible to be friends and still have a relationship. I had envisioned just their scenario many times, where Herm and I lived on the same property in different houses. Best friends, doing things together and sharing our lives without an obvious commitment. Was this a message from the future?

That aborted sale motivated me to start seriously thinking about where I wanted to move. Ideally, I would stay in Colorado and move closer to my friends. Unfortunately, with the cost of properties skyrocketing, that option wasn't looking feasible. My son and daughter-in-law wanted me to move back to New Hampshire, but I had a great deal of resistance to that. It felt like going backwards in life. I also didn't like the climate or the bugs. I was spoiled with blue sky, no humidity and absence of biting insects.

As the summer wore on, I started to prepare for yet another winter, even though there were signs pointing to a possible sale before years end. In July, my astrologer friend said if I continued to let go of the land energetically, it would sell soon.

In August things popped! A man from Vermont came to look. Even though he didn't put in an offer, I felt it was a sign something was going to happen. Only three days later a couple who were originally from South Africa, and grew up with Ridgebacks, wanted to see the property. They had even lived in New Hampshire for a few years and had friends in the town where my son lived! Those all looked like big "signs" to me! I wasn't surprised when, two days later, we were under contract! This time, I knew it would stick but where would I go?

It had been three weeks since I had heard from Herm but as often happened with us, we texted at the same time. I told him the house was under contract and he replied, "I am happy you are finally getting out of there!" He said he had been thinking of me, sending prayers and loving thoughts but said it took him a week to get up the nerve to write. "Why were you afraid to contact me?" I asked. "I wasn't sure if you wanted to hear from me," he replied. When I asked why he said, "deluded mind, full of fear." I just shook my head and told him I was happy he texted.

I had been thinking more and more about the fact that it made the most sense for me to move back East, as much as I didn't want to. I was getting older and was by myself, so I guess it was the practical thing to do. It made me sad Herm and I wouldn't be starting on a new adventure together. It wasn't much fun doing it alone.

I had my son look at a couple of places in New Hampshire, but they weren't what I was looking for. One day, my friend Diana, the woman I had gotten my first three Ridgebacks from, popped into my head. When I had visited her several years previously her mind was deteriorating. I had no idea what her condition was, or even if she was still alive. I wrote to a mutual friend who told me Diana had Alzheimers and was going to be put into long term care. I asked what was happening to her property and she put me in touch with Diana's brother. Now wasn't that interesting? Was I being guided?

Abe, Diana's brother, was onboard if I was interested in buying the house. He even offered to let me stay there, rent free, until all the legal matters were straightened out. The court had guardianship of the property so an assessment had to be done, an offer made, then approval of the offer by the courts, all of which could take months. The sticking point could be finding an opening at a long-term care facility for Diana before I had to move.

It was all very interesting how things were happening. Even though my closing was only three weeks away, I was confident everything would work out. It reminded me of when I decided to put my house on the market in New Durham and how all went so smoothly. When one was doing what was in alignment, the "Universe" seemed to remove all obstacles. Seriously, why did the thought of Diana's place even come to mind? I hadn't thought of her in years! That little voice again guiding me just like it did long ago. The timing of my sale, closing, her going into care, her brother needing someone to stay at the house, was beyond coincidence.

Aid from the "Universe" didn't stop there! There was a glitch in obtaining insurance which extended the closing date for my place. Then the buyers wanted me to stay an extra two weeks, rent free, until they could arrive for an orientation. Just in the nick of time a spot opened up for Diana. Even when her transfer was delayed by a flu outbreak, it all coincided beautifully with my proposed arrival date. All timing was neatly taken care of.

The next issue was how to get across the country with five dogs and a cat. There was no way I was going to attempt that trip by myself, I needed a driver. I asked friends, and friends of friends. Since the whole move was obviously being guided, I found a woman who loved to drive and have adventures. In fact, just the previous week she had bought a new road atlas and was trying to see how she could afford to get to New England! Brenda was thrilled to go, and we worked out I would pay for expenses and her flight back. It seemed my moving was benefiting more than just me!

Herm offered to help me pack for the move and it seemed like old times. It was all very strange. I felt emotionally strong and had no uneasiness and wondered how that shift had happened? As he was leaving, he gave me a long hug, said he loved me and asked if he could come stay with me that fall in NH and help out! I was thrilled, as I knew I had a lot of work ahead of me.

It was crunch time and I was starting to freak out! What was I doing buying a house that needed so much work? How could I ever afford to live there? Except for internet and phone, I hadn't had any bills in 30 years. Now I would have gas, oil, electric, house insurance and on and on! Then again, I wasn't even sure I wanted the property and didn't know if the court would sell it to me anyway! If I couldn't buy it or didn't want to stay, would I be able to find another place? Then there were the bugs, the humidity, little sun. I was so tired of making all the decisions myself, it was so stressful without a partner to talk things over with. It all felt SO overwhelming! It just felt wrong all of a sudden, why I was supposed to go to New Hampshire? What was waiting for me there, or was it a stepping-stone to something else? Everything was in motion, I had to trust there was a reason everything fell so neatly into place. As one of the hawk cards said: *"Let go and enjoy the ride, it is for the best."*

CHAPTER 59

THE TRIP

I had to laugh at that last quote, as I certainly had to "let go and enjoy the ride" on that trip to New Hampshire! It began with driving snow and ended with me buying a new vehicle. When Brenda started the Suburban, on the morning of our second day, it began shaking and the engine light was on. Hmmmm! With no garages open so early in the morning, we decided to keep going and see how things went. The shaking subsided and then even though the engine light stayed on, the car drove fine all the way from Ohio to the New York line. As soon as we passed through the toll booth into New York, the anti-skid light came on and the car could barely move. Thankfully, there was a small parking lot right there, so we pulled in and turned the engine off in order to clear the skid light. When Brenda tried to restart it, there was nothing, it was totally dead.

Oh crap! I was happy I had AAA! I called the number on my card, and they said they would send a tow truck as soon as possible. When the driver arrived, I insisted on riding with the dogs on top of the truck in case there were any issues but hadn't thought about the fact there would be no heat. By the time we arrived at our motel in Buffalo, one and half hours later, I was wishing I had ridden in the tow truck! We had to empty the Suburban, feed and walk the dogs, get the cat settled in the bathroom with her litter box, food and water, stuff our food into the refrigerator, get ice for the coolers containing the meat for the dogs and finally put some food in our own mouths at 11:30 p.m. It had been a very long day.

A call to AAA first thing the next morning brought a second tow truck to carry the Suburban to a garage down the street. They called me a few hours later saying it was the fuel pump, but I was skeptical. It hadn't acted like a fuel pump, and I had just had that replaced several months before, but what did I know? I told them to replace it and when they said I also had two bad tires, I agreed they should put new ones on as I didn't want a flat.

At end of the day, when I was expecting to hear the Suburban was being returned, they said it still wasn't running. They found some module needed replacing but had to wait until the next day to get the part and have it programmed. I wasn't very happy with this turn of events and was wondering if I was being taken for a ride by this garage. Apparently, I had just paid for a fuel pump I knew I didn't need! I was hoping to get on the road the next day as I was running low on dog food and the critters were going a bit bonkers.

Day 2 in the motel and the car still wasn't fixed! They finally admitted they had no idea what was wrong so they were towing it to the Chevy garage to see if they could fix it! Great! At that point, Brenda wouldn't make her flight back to Colorado that had been booked for the next day.

Day 3 in a motel with 5 dogs and a cat, running out of food, animals going crazy, people barely hanging in there and bills mounting. I was already into AAA for $3000, multiple nights in the motel and Brenda's return ticket! My planned fast, inexpensive trip to New Hampshire was turning into a very expensive one. I was wondering if I had made the right choice to move, the signs certainly seemed to be saying otherwise!

I got tired of calling the Chevy dealer and waiting for updates, so I had the motel shuttle take me to the garage so I could see what was going on. I met Dennis, the head mechanic, and he took me to the men who were working on the Suburban. It was up on the lift and three guys were standing around looking grim, scratching their chins, talking. I asked what was going on and they told me they didn't know and didn't think it could be fixed. I asked if I should buy a new vehicle and they said yes as it would cost thousands to fix the Suburban!! "Okay then", I said, "take me to a salesperson."

Buying vehicles is one of the things I like least in life, I find the whole routine of bargaining, asking managers and going back and forth totally annoying! I was thrilled to find this dealership didn't do that, it was left up to the salesperson and they pretty much had fixed prices. Before I left Colorado, I had looked into Minivans as the Suburban had almost 200,000 miles on it and I knew I would have to trade it in sooner or later. I asked James to find me a plain, used Honda Odyssey with less than 50,000 miles that was pretty cheap. He found a 2015 with 44,000 miles for just over $19,000. They would give me $3000 for the Suburban and when I pushed for a little more he took off another $300 and we called it a deal. Then came the issue of paying for it! They wouldn't take a check and my credit card wouldn't allow that much, but I had close to that amount in cash back in the motel room. The glitch came when James told me New York required 9 pieces of identification to purchase a vehicle. Seriously? I was two pieces short so I had to contact my bank to fax a bank statement and then we had to finagle a bit to get into my Verizon account online since I couldn't remember my password. Wow, that grueling process took most of the afternoon!

While they were getting the car from the other dealership, I was driven back to my motel to get the money and IDs. When I walked in the back door, I saw Libra running down the corridor toward the lobby with Brenda in hot pursuit! I quickly called Libra's name and was relieved she heard me and came right away. If the door to the lobby had been open, she could have escaped the motel! Brenda hadn't had an easy day with the dogs because they were nervous without me there. Besides Libra sneaking out the door to look for me, Zoe had liquid diarrhea. Poor Brenda had been cleaning all day and when I walked in the room, I found it filled with trash bags, cleaners and dirty laundry. I felt badly rushing in and right out again, but I had to get back to finish the paperwork.

The issues at the dealership continued when the bank gave me a problem with increasing the limit on my card and then I found my Colorado insurance company didn't cover me in the East. The money situation sorted, a new insurance company found, I now had to find a way to stuff everything from the car into the smaller van. I had jammed things into every nook and cranny of the Suburban, so it took a while to find and unpack it all. James very kindly helped me and by the time all was transferred to the van it was dark. I hate driving in the dark, plus I had forgotten to grab my glasses when I went back to the room AND this was a vehicle I knew nothing about! I was thankful the motel was only a few miles away, on this same highway but on the opposite side...somewhere!

I started up the van, headed for what appeared to be an exit and bottomed out with a big crunch! Oh crap! Did I just break another vehicle within a few feet of moving it? I had to remember I was no longer driving a high clearance Suburban; this thing was barely off the ground!! I was able to get off the obstruction and looked underneath to see if anything was leaking but it was dark, so wasn't sure if I had ruined anything. Even if the garage was still open, I wasn't sure I could have gotten up the nerve to have them look at it. I was embarrassed. Oh well! I got back in the car, found the proper exit and pulled onto the busy highway, still shaking from my blunder. When the windshield started fogging up, I began to frantically punch all the buttons trying to find the defroster while straining my body upward to see over the fog. Even with the window open it only allowed me a small patch to see through. Since I knew I would have to turn left across the highway to get into the motel parking lot, I stayed in the passing lane, pooping along, pissing off everyone behind me. My heart was pounding as I squinted in the dark and oncoming lights searching for the motel sign. At last, it came into sight, and I breathed a sigh of relief as I pulled into a parking space.

I barely slept that night and was up super early to pack the van, trying to figure out how to leave enough space for the dogs and cat carrier. By 6:00 a.m. with everyone stuffed in, ready to go, Brenda turned the key and .... nothing .... happened!

"You have GOT to be shitting me!" We looked at each other in disbelief! I immediately thought of when I bottomed out and figured I had killed it. I looked underneath and saw no puddles, so we popped the hood and discovered one of the covers on the battery poles was sticking up. Was that something? We stuck it down and tried again. Voila, we had lift off!

With all we had gone through there was no way I was going to leave without having it checked, so we drove to the Chevy garage and waited in line at the service entrance until they opened at 7:00 a.m. By that time, the whole garage knew me and my sad story and when I walked in everyone was in shock wondering what was going on. I told Dennis the issue and he had us pull right in and see the mechanic who had worked on the Suburban. He cleaned the battery poles, checked everything out and proclaimed us good to go. I sure hoped he was right!!

We had no more issues with the car, but poor Zoe had uncontrollable diarrhea and no matter how many times we stopped to let her out she still crapped all over the car. The other dogs were totally grossed out and were huddled in a corner trying to stay as far away from the mess as possible. When we arrived at the house at 5 p.m., the dogs piled out and ran and ran and ran after being cooped up for almost a week!

It was a full circle moment for Zoe as she was returning to her birthplace at age 12 1/2. I was sad Diana wasn't there to see her as she would have been delighted. It was also full circle for Herm and I as this was the state where we met 30 years before. I was sad he wasn't here to share this new adventure with me. I wasn't sure what I was doing here, or if I would stay or what the future held for us, but I held on to something he wrote to me not long before I left Colorado. I had posted this on my Facebook page one day, as it had made me think of "my Herm": *Sometimes we need someone to simply be there. Not to fix anything or do anything in particular, but just to let us feel we are cared for and supported.* In one of our ever-present synchronicities, Herm had actually seen that post and wrote: *"You are always cared for and supported."* Whatever the "Universe" had in store for me now, I would hold onto that.

EPILOGUE

2018 – 2021

The first year in New Hampshire was tough. Instead of feeling grateful for the property the "Universe" had provided, I was homesick for my sweet place by the creek in Colorado. I missed my peace and quiet, my greenhouse and being able to walk out my door and roam for miles through the mountains. After so many years of living with a deep connection to the natural world, being here felt like living in the city. People thought I was nuts when I complained since my new place comprised of a large log home on 60 acres, hidden 1/4 mile down a long driveway. What wasn't to love about that?

What was even more disturbing was the fact I didn't feel welcomed on this land. I wondered if some sort of negative presence was inhabiting this area or if there were portals like there had been on my Colorado property. I tried clearing the energy multiple times with offerings of sage and crystals, but nothing seemed to work, it still felt dark and intimidating. Every time I pushed myself to venture into the forest I would get turned around and walk in circles. That had never happened to me in all the years spent in the woods all over the US and Canada, after all, I had been named Pathfinder! I considered maybe my negative attitude was at fault until a forester came to do a survey and had the same experience of getting turned around. At least I then knew I wasn't imagining things!

Instead of being outside in nature, I spent all my time working on the house. This 2400sq foot project was a huge undertaking for an "old lady" but thankfully I always relished a challenge. Of course, I had to contract out the new roof and windows but everything else I did myself. For some reason many things had never been finished in the 30 years Diana and her husband lived here. Many windows and doors had no trim, the kitchen counters and floors were plywood and there were some rooms with only a subfloor. When I lifted the carpet in the living room one day, I discovered I could see directly into the basement! No wonder the oil furnace sounded like an 18-wheeler starting up!

One night, not long after moving in, I was to discover how important it is to have multiple layers of flooring. I was looking forward to my first night in a real bed after sleeping on a blow-up mattress for the past couple of weeks. I had spent the day cleaning and setting up my bedroom and as I settled into my clean sheets for the night, I looked around my new room with a smile and a sense of accomplishment.

It was 3 a.m. when I awoke to water splashing on my face. "What the hell?" I shouted as I threw on the light. I looked up to see liquid pouring through the ceiling, onto the nearby dresser where it bounced off and splashed onto the bed. Had a pipe burst? I thought. Up the stairs I dashed to check the bathroom, but all was dry. Where was the stream coming from, I wondered? There was no other water source up there!

Oh my God! In the space above my bedroom, there it was......a huge lake of dog pee! I scrambled to find towels to stem the flow pouring into the room below, then ran downstairs to mop up the puddles on the dresser and floor. Now I had water stains on the ceiling to add to the ones on the walls from the leaking roof! I quickly stripped the bed, threw the sheets and my new rug into the wash, found a blanket to put over me and crawled onto the bare mattress. So much for having one room all cleaned out and done!! I didn't know whether to laugh or cry!

Another time, I was in the kitchen making breakfast on my plywood counter tops when a gush of water poured onto the board where I was working. This time, I knew immediately what it was by the smell. Yup, the upstairs toilet overflowed! Another dash up the stairs where I grabbed the plunger to make the flood stop, then hauled towels out of the cupboard to mop up the mess. This time, the liquid even made it all the way to the basement! Oh well, I laughed as I got out the bleach, just another day in crazy land!

I never knew log houses were so dark. I was used to lots of light, so went on a tear, ripping down walls and reconfiguring rooms and hallways to get more light into them. I sanded and refinished the water-stained walls, trimmed the doors and windows, laid plywood and put down finished floors. I ripped up the whole dark kitchen, sanded the cabinets, made an additional door opening, tiled the countertops and turned it into a bright, fully functional happy space. Whenever I hit a snag or got frustrated, I would ask myself what Herm would do. I could clearly hear him telling me to calm down, take things slow and breathe. I probably listened to him better at those times then when we were together!

I was in my happy place doing the destruction/reconstruction work but when I wasn't working, my negative attitude about living in NH was getting me in trouble. That first winter and spring, I was shown very clearly how one's thoughts and states of mind can manifest outwardly. One morning I was stepping over the dog gate, fuming over some stupid thing when I smashed my toe and broke it. Talk about instant karma, but did I listen? Nope!

The "Universe" upped the ante when I tripped over a pile of flooring in the dark and bumped my head on the floor. But did that change my ways? Nope! OK, as usually happens when one doesn't listen to nudges, the "Universe" gets more serious.

One day I went to the basement in the semi-dark to put something away and clearly heard the "little voice" say "turn on the light". My ego-self scoffed and said, "that's silly, I don't need a light, I'm just putting this on the shelf over there." The next thing I knew I was seeing stars because I had forgotten the pile of boards in the middle of the floor.

My legs had been taken out from under me and I had plunged head-first into a big metal water pump. As I sat up and took stock, nothing appeared to be broken but once I dragged myself up the stairs, I discovered skinned and bruised legs and arms, a cut over my brow with my eye beginning to blacken and a jumbo sized "egg" on my forehead, swelling at an alarming rate. I was dizzy and disoriented and later found out I had a grade 2 concussion! I was basically bed ridden for two weeks and for months afterwards I suffered from brain fog, dizziness, nausea, weakness, and feeling totally disconnected from reality. I couldn't even be on the phone for any length of time as it would make me dizzy, and I had trouble finding words.

Yup, the "Universe" did finally get my attention. In those two weeks of doing nothing but lying in bed pondering what direction my life should take, I listened to a podcast which talked about people with big losses in their lives getting stuck in circling the story over and over and over keeping one from moving on. That is what I had been doing, just circling my same old "poor-me" story and it was getting boring. I needed a different version but had no idea what that would look like.

A year and a half after our divorce, Herm and I still didn't know what to do with each other. Everyone would tell me to just move on, he wasn't worth the trouble of holding onto, but I just couldn't do that. I had an overwhelming feeling I couldn't desert him. I felt strongly we still had work to do together, and he was still teaching me so much about myself. I could easily feel the beautiful love of his higher self which filled my soul like a warm loving embrace and from that higher perspective, I knew it was all a drama we were playing out in order to grow our souls. I could see our higher selves giggling together about the silly play we were caught up in.

It did seem the "Universe" agreed we needed to continue to be together on some level. Whenever we were out of contact for long periods, something would always come up for us to get in touch.

One time, Herm was at a rock show in Florida, talking with a dealer when the man pulled a flyer from beneath the table and handed it to him. On it was a picture of our friend Hawk, from Maine! It was advertising an event for the following weekend where Hawk would be playing his flute! Seriously, what were the odds of that? I just had to shake my head and smile at how those things happened over and over again. You just can't make this stuff up!

On another occasion I read a Twin Flame blog which said, *"the male twin has been thinking of and missing the other half lately, it is a good week for love and getting together."* Just after I read that, my friend Jane sent a text which weirdly went to both my phone and Herm's which prompted him to text back and say, "it must have been the "Universe". I have been thinking of contacting you and would love to talk on the phone!"

I was nervous about the phone call, as we hadn't talked in months, but a message from dragonfly reassured me all would be fine. I was seated on the porch when the insect landed on my shirt and looked me in the eye. I said, "hello, you are looking beautiful today," I heard in return a very distinct, "thank you". I then asked how the phone call with Herm would go and he said, "you will give each other hope." I called "thank you" as he took off on his daily hunting rounds.

The dragonfly was right, it was a great call. Herm's energy was calm, sweet and loving. He told me he had been thinking of me a lot lately and wanted to hear my voice! At the end he said he agreed we are almost one person, and he really does love me. I said, "I love you too!" It was the nicest conversation we had had since before the divorce. It sure did take a while to get here!

After that conversation, he started to contact me more and more and even began to share what he had been up to. One night he called out of the blue worried about a health problem and wanted my input! I was thrilled he would ask and told him it was nice to be needed. He replied: "you are needed more than you know but I am trying to do it on my own most of the time." I had no idea why he had to do it on his own, but I was grateful he was sharing. I told him we needed to find a solution to our never-ending communication issue. He said one of the problems was he worries I will be disappointed in him, that he won't be able to live up to my expectations. As always, he knew me too well. Yes, it is part of my nature to always want more but I had changed a lot and had become more realistic. We finally agreed to call each other any time we wanted and to stay in touch.

I also decided to change MY way of thinking about it all. Being upset about the fact I was the one to have to initiate conversations, certainly wasn't getting me anywhere. And what was that all about anyway, it was just an "idea", an ego thing. I mean, seriously, was it a "rule" he had to contact me first? Instead, I decided to flood him with love and not worry if I got anything in return.

I began to send him cute and funny good morning and goodnight GIFS every day and gave him updates on what was going on in my life. This strategy seemed to work, and we ended up being in touch most days. Without me issuing ultimatums and expecting him to behave in a certain way it seemed he was more comfortable communicating with me.

By 2021, the house was about done, and I started to think about another move. No matter how hard I tried to fit into this land and town, it just wasn't an energetic match. I needed to find a place that resonated with my soul and also had way shorter winters. I began to do some research and was putting SC on the maybe list when my psychic friend Lenny, who knew very well I lived in NH, texted one day and said, "you're in the Carolinas aren't you?" I laughed to myself and texted back, "No, but I will take that as a message I am on the right track, LOL." I called and asked where he saw me going and he affirmed somewhere on the SC/ NC line would be a good energy match and would be more supportive for my health and wellbeing. With that validation of my inner knowing, SC is where I will be focusing my energies in 2022.

Looking back over the last few years I find myself grateful for my dark night of the soul, my hero's journey. Without that initiation, I wouldn't be the strong powerful elder woman I am today. I am fine with being me, I enjoy living alone and I no longer need validation from others.

Of course, like all of us, I am still a work-in-progress with my moments of anger, frustration, sadness and wanting to be in control. Fortunately, those emotions pass quickly now, and I don't become attached to them like I did in the past.

I was recently looking over a psychic reading I had a few months after Herm first left. At the time I was in a dark place and all I wanted to hear was he would be back and couldn't accept what this woman was telling me. Reading it now, I can see she was totally correct in all she was sensing. She told me Herm and I were definitely soul mates, cut from the same cloth, that our spiritual similarities set us apart from others but there was a paradox in our relationship. Despite a deep love for each other, our purpose for being together wasn't for romance but for reinforcing each other's individuality. We needed to recognize our own soul energies as well as the soul energy of the other and then go our separate ways. She described us as a tree with the same root but with two trunks growing differently. That we are on track for our life purpose, that the bond we have can never be broken and at some point, that single root would pull us into a deeper connection.

Reading this was helpful in putting everything Herm and I had been through into perspective. It helped me understand why the "Universe" would always find a way to reconnect us no matter how hard we tried to let each other go. We were bound together by that root and that soul connection and yes, we had to individuate, we had become too enmeshed with each other. My heart filled with love as I thought about that tree with its two trunks, Daisy and Herm, growing towards the Light in their own separate but connected ways. Finding their places in the world, touching the lives of others, growing strong and sturdy. I did have to shake my head and laugh though as knowing these souls as I do, whatever they did and how ever they did it was sure to be unconventional.

ACKNOWLEDGMENTS

Whenever I told people about our travels, they would all say, "you have to write a book!" I wanted to and actually worked on organizing my travel diaries, but I just never went anywhere with it. Then time and life intervened with more adventures being added. It was my sister Cara who finally lit the fire under me. She had started writing her book, "Widow's Moon", about her dear husband's suicide and as I followed her progress, I got excited to put all my adventures together so we would have two authors in our family. She introduced me to her editor Rebecca Van Lear who I employed as a writing coach and when she stopped freelancing, Cara told me about Susan Nunn who became my editor. Having Cara to lead the way has been really helpful and it has been fun to support each other during the process. Thanks, little sis, I can't wait to see what we will do next!

My awesomely talented brother Bill took all the pictures that grace the covers of the book. Thank you, Bill, for always being there if I need you and for your kindness and compassion.

Susan Nunn has been a real gift, not only has she done a great job organizing and offering suggestions but has gotten me past my aversion of using Zoom! Thanks, Susan, for sharing your stories, loving my book and telling me I'm a good writer!

To all the awesome people we have met everywhere we've been, thank you for just being you and sharing your lives with us. You taught me so much about myself, about life, love, patience and compassion. I am forever grateful.

Finally, and most importantly, without my soulmate, best friend Herm there would be no book and I wouldn't have grown into the person I am today. Thank you from the bottom of my heart for always believing in me and telling me what a strong, talented person I am. You have backed this book from the start even though it exposes our private life, and I am ever grateful for your willingness to support that. You will always be my best teacher.

ABOUT THE AUTHOR

Never in my wildest dreams would I have imagined my life to take the direction it did. I grew up in a typical, boring 1950's neighborhood! I did all the things expected of me... college, marriage, baby and I even had my childhood dream of owning a farm!

In my late thirties I went back to college and got a BS in nursing and went on to a Master's Degree in Psychiatric Nursing. Once that was finished so was my marriage.

I regrouped, got a job at an agency which provided home-based family therapy to court referred families. Starting as a counselor, I quickly moved up to the supervisor of our Dover, NH office.

Life was good. I still had my farm and animals; I had a great job and I was enjoying being a single woman! Then....it all changed!

I met Robert/Herm and we embarked on a 30-year odyssey which led us to experiencing an unconventional life. What we learned and experienced in those years has never left me and to this day I am a pretty atypical 75-year-old.

As I write this in my NH home surrounded by my 4 Rhodesian Ridgebacks, I am getting ready for my next chapter. Moving south, to an area where I have never been, to a place where I know no one. Stay tuned to learn how this next stage of my life unfolds.

Go to my website, terralynjoy.com where you can read more about me, take a look at my blogs, see photos that relate to the chapters in the book, and more. I look forward to hearing from you. Enjoy.